PRESENTS

# ROCK IN PEACE

Published by Time Home Entertainment Inc.
135 West 50th Street • New York, NY 10020



ISBN 10: 1-60320-963-8
ISBN 13: 978-1-60320-963-2

We welcome your comments and suggestions about Time Home Entertainment Books. Please write to us at:
Time Home Entertainment Books, Attention: Book Editors, P.O. Box 11016, Des Moines, IA 50336-1016
If you would like to order any of our hardcover Collector's Edition books, please call us at 1-800-327-6388, Monday through Friday, 7 a.m. to 8 p.m., or Saturday, 7 a.m. to 6 p.m., Central Time.

PRESENTS

# ROCK IN PEACE

## Remembering the Guitar Legends Who Died Before Their Time

Published by Time Home Entertainment Inc.
135 West 50th Street • New York, NY 10020

# CONTENTS



## OBITUARIES

ROCK IN PEACE

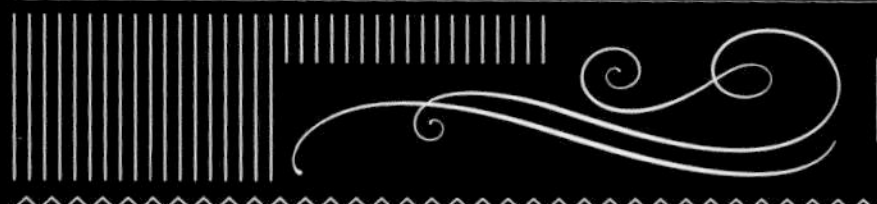

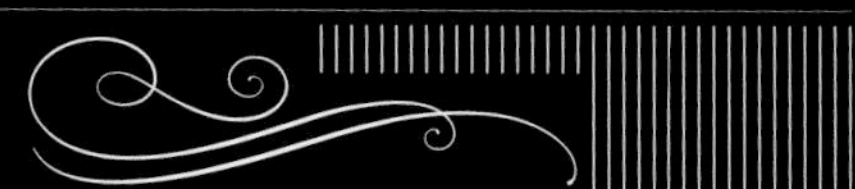

# AMERICAN BEAUTY

Guitar genius, hippie prince, King of the Dead.
Jerry Garcia was many things to many people. *Guitar World* pays tribute to one of the most influential musicians of our era.

BY BLAIR JACKSON

JERRY GARCIA 1942–1995

# FORGET FOR A MOMENT

the dilapidated VW vans plastered with colorful decals and bumper stickers. Forget the legions of long-haired, tie-dye-wearing, pot- and patchouli-scented fans lost in that formless, serpentine dance-trance. Forget the smiling pictures of "Captain Trips," resplendent in an American flag hat and paisley velour shirt. Instead, *listen*.

Listen to the crystalline notes as they ascend in a bright spiral, then blast into deep space, scattering like cosmic debris. Listen to the melancholy cry of six strings singing about life and death, love and loss, memory and regret. Listen to the joyous dance of life in a thousand buoyant strums and bright melodic filigrees. Ten years, 20 years, 50 years from now, it's going to be Jerry Garcia's music—and not the Day-Glo Deadhead sideshow—that most people will remember.

The clichés come so easily: "counter-culture guru," "rock legend," "Pied Piper of the Haight," "tragic outlaw figure," etc. There is truth in all of these. But when the day is done, Jerry Garcia was really just a working guy who loved to play music. Celebrity and deification were unfortunate by-products and distractions for this gentle, self-effacing man whose strongest addiction was music, not drugs, and whose legacy is a body of music that is breathtaking in its scope.

The Grateful Dead's music was a crazy-quilt of different styles and influences: They drew from folk, bluegrass, old-timey, blues, R&B, ragtime, rock and roll, modern classical, jazz, Indian, electronic and just about any other style you'd care to name. Their musical heroes were people like the Beatles, Bach, Bob Dylan, John Coltrane, Bill Monroe, Howlin' Wolf, Merle Haggard, Ornette Coleman, Stravinsky, Bill Monroe, Chuck Berry, Edgar Varese and Willie Dixon, and they wore their influences proudly—at the same time as they assimilated those influences, improvised around them, and magically blended them into their own thoroughly original amalgam. Where does a song like "Help on the Way" come from? "Tennessee Jed"? "China Doll"? "Days Between"? These are unique slices of the Dead's peculiar oeuvre, impossible to categorize precisely except to say that they are Grateful Dead Music, with all that implies.

Even outside of the Dead, Garcia's appetite for music was voracious and all-consuming. The Jerry Garcia Band's repertoire came from Motown and Trenchtown, Chicago blues and Southern gospel, Irving Berlin and Mick Jagger, Hoagy Carmichael and Van Morrison. Then there was the acoustic music he played with mandolinist David Grisman: old mountain tunes, sea shanties, ageless ballads, a few Dead tunes and cool jazz numbers like Miles Davis' "So What" and Milt Jackson's "Bags' Groove." In the last year of his life alone, Garcia's studio work included adding guitar to a song on fellow-traveler and occasional GD member Bruce Hornsby's album *Hot House*; cutting a version of the venerable pop standard "Smoke Gets in Your Eyes" with the Garcia Band for the superb film *Smoke* (directed by Wayne Wang, a one-time Garcia roadie); incomplete tracking on a new Dead album and, in what was his last session, laying down "Blue Yodel #9" for an upcoming Jimmie Rodgers tribute album. Who knows what other irons were in the fire at the time of Garcia's sad demise?

> **"NO MATTER WHAT GUITAR I PLAY, I WON'T HAVE ANY TROUBLE GETTING A SWEET SOUND, EVEN THOUGH THE MOST DIFFICULT THING TO PRODUCE IS A SWEET SOUND."**
>
> —*JERRY GARCIA*

Garcia grew up in San Francisco and lived his entire life in Northern California. He was named after composer Jerome Kern and was the son of a clarinetist and bandleader, Joe Garcia, who drowned while river fishing during a family vacation the summer before Jerry was going to start kindergarten. Around the same time, he lost part of the middle finger on his right hand when his older brother Clifford accidentally hit it with an ax. His mother, Ruth, remarried and tried to pick up the pieces for Jerry and Clifford, running a San Francisco bar frequented primarily by sailors and soldiers.

"I grew up in a musical household and took piano lessons as far back as I can remember," Garcia said in a 1993 interview. "The first time I decided that music was something I wanted to do, apart from just being surrounded by it, was when I was about 15. I developed this deep craving to play the electric guitar.

"I fell madly in love with rock and roll. Chuck Berry was happening big, Elvis Presley...I really liked Gene Vincent; the other rock guys, the guys that played guitar good: Eddie Cochran, Buddy Holly, Bo Diddley. At the same time, the R&B stations were playing stuff like Lightnin' Hopkins and Frankie Lee Sims, these funky blues guys. Jimmy McCracklin, the Chicago-style blues guys, the T-Bone Walker–influenced guys, that older style, pre–B.B. King. Jimmy Reed actually had hits back in those days. You listen to that and it's so funky. It's just a beautiful sound, but I had no idea how to go about learning it.

"When I first heard electric guitar, when I was 15, that's what I wanted to play. I petitioned my mom to get me one, so she finally did for my birthday. Actually, she got me an accordion and I went nuts—'Agggghh, no, no, no!' I railed and raved, and she finally turned it in, and I got a pawnshop [*Danelectro*] electric guitar and an amplifier. I was beside myself with joy.

"I started banging away on it without

MICHAEL OCHS ARCHIVES/GETTY IMAGES

Garcia circa 1970

Onstage at the Family Dog in San Francisco, February 1970: (from left) Garcia, Bill Kreutzmann, Phil Lesh and Bob Weir

ROBERT ALTMAN/GETTY IMAGES

having the slightest idea of anything. I didn't know how to tune it up; I had no idea. My stepfather tuned it in some weird way, like an open chord...I played it that way for about a year before I finally ran into a kid at school who could actually play a little. He showed me a few basic chords, and that was it. I never took any lessons. I don't even think there was anybody teaching around the Bay Area. The electric guitar was like from Mars, you know. You didn't see 'em even."

While still in high school, Garcia decided to pursue his interest in drawing and painting, and this indirectly led to a shift in his musical interests. "I was an art student at the California School of Fine Art, which is now the San Francisco Art Institute, and I was taking a Saturday class, and my teacher played a four-string banjo and a little guitar," Garcia said in 1991. "[*One day*] he was playing a Big Bill Broonzy record. I was 16 or 17...I knew what it was but I'd never heard anyone play blues on an acoustic guitar, and it knocked me out."

Garcia dropped out of high school and enlisted in the Army, hoping to perhaps see more of the world. Instead he was stationed at San Francisco's Presidio, where he quickly learned that heavy discipline and regimentation were not for him: he went AWOL several times, and felt more at home hanging out in San Francisco's North Beach area—then still the center for the once-thriving Beat culture—than in his barracks. About the only positive aspect of being in the Army for him was that he met a few people who turned him on to country guitar styles.

"After I got out of the Army," he said in 1990, "I fell in with [*future songwriting partner Robert*] Hunter, and we were influenced by the folk scare—the Kingston Trio and that kind of stuff. I didn't know how to find my way into that kind of music 'til I met some people who were more involved with it, like Marshall Leicester, who was a friend of mine from when I was 10 to 13. By now he was a college guy, and he turned me on to bluegrass music and old-time string band music. He played a little frailing banjo and introduced me to the [*blues fingerstylist*] Reverend Gary Davis. I heard that sound and I just had to be able to make it."

Garcia moved to the Peninsula (south of San Francisco) and lived hand-to-mouth for a few years, practicing the banjo and guitar night and day and playing in a succession of local string bands with fanciful names like the Thunder Mountain Tub Thumpers, the Sleepy Hollow Hog Stompers and the Black Mountain Boys. The endless hours of woodshedding in this wholly acoustic musical environment paid dividends that served Garcia for the rest of his career. His lifelong love of the clearly articulated note came in part from his passion for the banjo. And his devotion to improvisation was fueled by watching great country and bluegrass players.

"I get my improvisational approach from Scotty Stoneman, the fiddle player, who is the guy who first set me on fire—where I just stood there and don't remember breathing," Garcia recalled in 1991. "He was just an incredible fiddler. He grew up in bars and was a total alcoholic wreck by the time I heard him, in his early thirties, playing with the Kentucky Colonels [*featuring noted flatpicker Clarence White—later to play with the Byrds—and mandolinist Roland White*]. I went down to hear him the first time at the Ash Grove in L.A. They did a medium-tempo fiddle tune, and it's going along, and pretty soon Scotty starts taking these longer and longer

Garcia, circa 1970

phrases—10 bars, 14 bars, 17 bars—and the guys in the band are just watching him! They're barely playing—going ding, ding, ding—while he's burning. The place was transfixed. They played this tune for like 20 minutes, which is unheard of in bluegrass.

"I'd never heard anything like it. I asked him later, 'How do you do that?' and he said, 'Man, I just play lonesome.' He probably died of drinking hair tonic; he was another one of those guys... But his playing on the records he appears on—mostly anonymously—is this incredible blaze. He's like the bluegrass Charlie Parker."

Garcia was so deep into bluegrass that he spent a month in 1964 traveling through the South and Midwest with his Black Mountain Boys bandmate Sandy Rothman, recording various bluegrass bands. When Garcia returned to the Bay Area, however, he joined together with a bunch of his musical friends and formed what was actually a less serious group than many he'd been involved with: Mother McCree's Uptown Jug Champions, which included a scary-looking but soulful teenage blues singer and harmonica player named Ron McKernan—who'd already been dubbed "Pigpen" for his unkempt appearance—and a 16-year-old novice guitar player (actually a student of Garcia's at Dana Morgan Music in Palo Alto) named Bob Weir. Also playing with the group from time to time were future Grateful Dead soundman Bob Matthews and David Parker, who was to become the group's financial associate. This rag-tag bunch played a cool mixture of folk, blues and jug-band numbers in local clubs, but by 1965 the Beatles had shown what fun being in a rock and roll band could be, Dylan had plugged in, and Pigpen was looking to get down with some amplified Chicago-style blues. Garcia, Weir and Pigpen recruited a young drummer named Bill Kreutzmann to join their new electric band, dubbed the Warlocks, and when Dana Morgan, Jr., son of the music store owner, couldn't quite cut it on bass, they brought in a one-time jazz trumpeter and "serious" music composer named Phil Lesh—even though he'd never played bass before.

The band cut its teeth playing in small clubs, bars and even a pizza parlor down on the Peninsula, playing mainly R&B and blues covers, as well as a few amplified folk and jug tunes. They often played five sets a night and built their following slowly—first driving out the regular patrons with their skull-splitting volume and weirdly elongated tunes, then bringing in their own audience of misfits and thrill-seekers. Around the same time, the Warlocks hooked up with *One Flew Over the Cuckoo's Nest* author Ken Kesey and his fellow party animals, the Merry Pranksters, becoming the de facto house band at their LSD parties, the infamous Acid Tests. "It wasn't a gig, it was the Acid Test," Garcia once said. "Anything was okay. It was far-out, beautiful magic. We had no reputation and nobody was paying to see us or anything like that. We weren't the headliners, the event was. Anything that happened was part of it. There was always the option to not play... The freedom is what I loved about it. When you're high, you might want to play five hours, but sometimes you might want to stick your head in a bucket of water, or have some Jell-O or something."

The group had already been smoking pot for a while, but LSD, which was legal until October 1966, is what really blew the doors open and influenced the band to stretch out in weirder directions. Garcia, the guitarist, was being influenced by a number of different artists during this period, from Mike Bloomfield, whose incendiary blues playing fueled the music of Dylan and Paul Butterfield, to saxophonist John Coltrane: "I never copped his licks or sat down, listened to his records and tried to play his stuff," Garcia told an interviewer in 1981. "I [*was*] impressed with the idea of flow, of making statements that sound like paragraphs—[*Coltrane would*] play along stylistically with a certain kind of tone, in a certain kind of syntax, for X amount of time, then change the subject and play along with this other personality coming out. Perceptually, an idea that's been important to me in playing [*which also derives in part from Coltrane*] has been the whole odyssey idea—journeys, voyages, adventures along the way."

In December 1965, the Warlocks became the Grateful Dead and the group shifted its focus to San Francisco, where like-minded bohemians and psychedelic pioneers were quickly turning the Haight-Ashbury district into a hip mini-city with its own music, businesses and support services. The Dead were just one of a slew of bands that lived in the area, but from the beginning they were among the most popular—always guaranteed to get the crowds that drifted in and out of the various San Francisco ballrooms up and dancing, whether it was with a 10-minute version of Martha and the Vandellas' Motown smash "Dancing in the Street," a peppy rendition of Howlin' Wolf's "Sitting on Top of the World," or their half-hour workouts of Wilson Pickett's "Midnight Hour," with Pigpen leading the charge. During this period and through the recording of the Dead's Warner Bros. debut album in early '67, Garcia played a red Guild Starfire, with a single cutaway and two pickups, through a Fender Twin Reverb amp. From the outset, Garcia's guitar style was marked by active motion in his left-hand fret-work—bending and shaping notes and dancing around the song's melody.

The band started writing its own material in earnest in late '67 and '68: This is the era that produced the ambitious "That's It for the Other One" (from *Anthem of the Sun*) and Garcia's first few collaborations with lyricist Robert Hunter, including "China Cat Sunflower," "Dark Star" and "St. Stephen." In '68 Garcia switched from the Guild to a Les Paul; then in '69 he moved on to a Gibson SG, which he used to shape the classic Garcia sound heard on what remains the watermark of the Dead's most psychedelic period, 1969's *Live Dead.* This double album (now a single CD) showcases Garcia and the Dead at the height of their improvisational powers, as they boldly navigate through 21 minutes of intense instrumental exploration on "Dark Star"; build to one roiling, explosive climax after another on "The Eleven"; and rip through Bobby Bland's "Turn on Your Love Light" like some crazy, funky bar band on multiple hits of LSD-manufacturer (and occasional Grateful Dead sound man) Owsley Stanley's finest.

As the Sixties drew to a close, Garcia added to his already rich sonic palette by playing acoustic guitar with greater regularity (a number of 1970 Dead shows featured an acoustic set, as well as songs that blended acoustic and electric instruments), and tackling the pedal steel guitar (a ZB model) both with the Dead and the country-rock Dead offshoot the New Riders of the Purple Sage.

"What I'm doing with the steel is I'm going after a sound I hear in my head that the steel has come closest to," Garcia noted in 1971. "I'm really a novice at it, but I'm not really trying to become a steel player." Novice though he was, Garcia's sound on the instrument was quite distinctive, and he lent his steel talents to several excellent albums between '69 and '71, including the Jefferson Airplane's *Volunteers* ("The Farm"), Brewer & Shipley's *Tarkio Road*, Paul Kantner's *Blows Against the Empire*, David Crosby's *If I Could Only Remember My Name* and, most famous of all, Crosby, Stills, Nash & Young's *Déjà Vu* ("Teach Your Children").

The fall of '69 through 1972 represents the Golden Era of Garcia's songwriting partnership with Robert Hunter: Produced during this period were the studio albums *Workingman's Dead* and *American Beauty*, the solo *Garcia* (on which Garcia played all the instruments, except drums, himself), and the live *Grateful Dead* (better known as "Skull & Roses") and *Europe '72*. Between them, these albums cover a wide cross-section of American song styles, and contain many of the duo's best songs, including "Uncle John's Band," "New Speedway Boogie," "Black Peter," "Ripple," "Brokedown Palace," "Attics of My Life," "Wharf Rat," "Bertha," "Loser," "The Wheel," "Bird Song," "He's Gone" and "Tennessee Jed," to name just a handful. Garcia's guitar work in this era moved easily from twangy countrified picking—showing the influence of such masters of country's "Bakersfield Sound" like Don Rich and Roy Nichols—to completely dissonant wah-wah inflected flights into outer space. Though the early Seventies saw the Dead frequently dubbed a "country rock band," it was also a period when they played some of their spaciest, most "difficult" music. Garcia's main guitar of choice in this era was a heavily modified Fender Strat (with a '58 neck and a '63 body) given to him by Graham Nash. He moved away from Gibsons because "I got bored with them," he said in '81. "I felt I really didn't have any place else to go on them. [*The Strat*] was more of a challenge. It wasn't that I wanted to lose the SG part of my playing, but my reasoning was along the lines of, 'I think that no matter what guitar I play, I won't have any trouble getting a sweet sound,' even though the most difficult thing to produce is a sweet sound."

Onstage at the Polo Fields in Golden Gate Park, San Francisco, in November 1991

ED PERLSTEIN/GETTY IMAGES

**"WHEN YOU'RE HIGH, YOU MIGHT WANT TO PLAY FIVE HOURS, BUT SOMETIMES YOU MIGHT WANT TO STICK YOUR HEAD IN A BUCKET OF WATER."**

—*JERRY GARCIA*

As early as 1971 Garcia had been talking about having a guitar built for him, and by '73 this was a reality. A Northern California luthier named Doug Irwin built Garcia's first custom instrument, which he described as having the best features of both a Strat and an SG. "[*Irwin*] was working for a friend of mine, [*and*] I picked up a guitar that he had built the neck for at a guitar store and said, 'Wow, where did this come from? I gotta have this guitar!'" Garcia remembered a few years ago. "I bought the guitar and [*upon discovering that Irwin had built the neck*] I commissioned him to build me a guitar. He did, and I played this guitar [*nicknamed the Wolf because of its cartoonish hungry wolf inlay design*] for most of the Seventies. When he delivered it to me, I said, 'Now I want you to build me what you think would be the ultimate guitar. I don't care when you deliver it, I don't care how much it's gonna cost or anything else.' A couple of months later he told me it would cost about three grand, which at the time was a lot for a guitar, since it was the early Seventies. He delivered the guitar to me in '78, eight years later. I'd forgotten I'd paid for it. Whatever that guitar says to me, I play."

Since he first played the Wolf, Garcia played Irwin's guitars almost exclusively onstage, except from 1975-'77, when he favored a bone-white Travis Bean and late in his career when he briefly favored a custom model by luthier Steve Cripe. The mid-Seventies was another fertile period for Garcia and the Dead—it includes the albums *Blues for Allah* and *Terrapin Station*. Not many changes in his playing style crop up during this era, though the introduction of some new effects (like the envelope filter that's so distinctive on "Estimated Prophet") did color his sound in interesting ways. Garcia's involvement with the insidious and addictive drug known as Persian (a heroin-like opiate that is smoked) began in the late Seventies, and while it's hard to gauge its effects on his playing, his songwriting output nose-dived from '79 until the diabetic coma that nearly killed him in 1986. "For a long time there I sort of lost heart," Garcia told me in 1988. "I thought, I don't know if I want to do this. I don't know what I want. I felt like I wanted to get away from everything, somehow. But I didn't want to just stop playing, or have the Grateful Dead stop because that's what *I* wanted to do. I didn't even know consciously that's what I wanted."

For most of the Eighties, Garcia played an Irwin guitar nicknamed Tiger (again for its beautiful, distinctive inlay). When he became interested in incorporating a MIDI setup into his arsenal in the late Eighties, Irwin came up with "Rosebud," and Garcia used that guitar, along with two lighter, graphite-necked models, until his death.

Grateful Dead, circa 1970

It's not surprising that Garcia embraced MIDI so enthusiastically—he was always an explorer on the lookout for new sounds and new ways of thinking about his instrument. So, beginning in 1989, songs that he'd played a hundred times with a certain tonality suddenly opened up for him in exciting new ways—"Bird Song" might have a "flute" line, "Shakedown Street" a "soprano sax" break, "Standing on the Moon" a breathy, undefinable choral quality and "Let It Grow" a Mexican "horn" part. And he employed a hundred other textural variations, from a light, shimmering musical shadow to full-out MIDI "drums." The famous second-set "space" segment, in particular, became a MIDI playground for Garcia, Weir and Lesh.

Ask most hardcore Deadheads, and they'll probably admit that Garcia's playing during much of the last two years of his life wasn't as strong as it had been in the late Eighties, when he had recovered from the coma and was free of hard drugs. He produced his last great works—"Standing on the Moon" and "Days Between"—during this period. As his habit reasserted itself, from the middle of 1993 until his death, his onstage lapses and musical errors became more frequent, his playing often took on a listless quality for long stretches, and he seemed physically incapable of playing complex passages with any sort of precision. He had ongoing problems with carpal tunnel syndrome and just how much his slow but steady physical deterioration during this period affected his playing can only be guessed at. Still, even on his final tour in June 1995, he was able to rise to the occasion—particularly on his moody ballads, which were always perhaps his strongest suit—and rip into a solo with an unbridled passion and grace that was something to behold.

Jerry Garcia was never the type of player who topped guitar magazine readers polls. He was always an ensemble player: a brilliant and distinctive instrumental voice, to be sure, but still just one bright thread in the complex weave of the Grateful Dead's sound. He was the antithesis of the flashy guitar extrovert, choosing to stand stock-still most of the time, letting his fingers do all the dancing and fancy moves. He hit more clams than your average pro, but that's because he was fishing for pearls, always looking around the next corner, following his muse and his bandmates into uncharted realms. Constant improvisation involves higher risk, but the payoff is worth it: the musicians and the audience are witnesses to the birth of music that is completely fresh and new.

Looking around the musical landscape he left behind, we don't see many Garcia imitators per se, but there is now a generation of players who have been at the very least influenced by his and the Dead's way of doing things—staying true to themselves, their music and their fans, record biz be damned. And, of course, the counterculture the band literally helped create 45 years ago has evolved into a strong and vibrant community. Garcia may be gone—and, as the song says, "nothing's gonna bring him back"—but it's already clear that his sweet song will reverberate forever.

"People need celebration in their lives," Garcia said in 1989, trying to explain the Dead's appeal. "It's part of what it means to be human. I don't know why. We need magic. And bliss. [*We need*] power, myth and celebration in our lives, and music is a good way to encapsulate a lot of it." ◆

# CRAZY TRAIN

His career was meteoric—swift, brilliant and all-too brief. *Guitar World* pays tribute to Randy Rhoads, the groundbreaking guitarist who helped Ozzy Osbourne get his act back on track.

BY ALAN DI PERNA

RANDY RHOADS 1956–1982

## "THERE ARE SOME PEOPLE

who are like a shooting star. They come and hit the planet and explode into a beautiful rainbow of colors. Then they shoot off somewhere else. And that was the life of Randy Rhoads."

Ozzy Osbourne waxes uncharacteristically poetic on the subject of Randy Rhoads. The legendary guitarist was just 25 years old when he died in an airplane accident on March 19, 1982, while on tour with Ozzy's band. These days, Osbourne is a metal icon; a tattooed patriarch for a whole new generation of hard-music fans. But things were very different when the singer first met up with Rhoads in 1979. Ozzy had just been fired from his original band, Black Sabbath. For all intents and purposes, he was holding a one-way ticket to Palookaville.

"I was a drunken, drugged-out, fucked-up slob," Osbourne admits. "But Randy was patient with me."

Rhoads' composure benefited them both. Osbourne's solo career was launched by means of the two albums he recorded with Rhoads, 1980's *Blizzard of Ozz* and '81's *Diary of a Madman*, and those records form the basis for Rhoads' own formidable legend. More significantly, his stunning guitar technique, classical influences and admirable musical discipline on those albums helped launch the Eighties shred boom.

But Rhoads' appeal has long outlived the era of big hair and spandex leotards. While he doesn't have the status of dead rock stars like Jimi Hendrix, Jim Morrison or John Lennon, Rhoads nonetheless holds a special place in the rock guitar subculture. He is the all-American guitar hero, the golden-haired patron saint of every kid who ever labored long and hard to master metal licks in a suburban bedroom.

Rhoads was born December 6, 1956, in Santa Monica, California, and raised in the L.A. suburb of Burbank, which for many years was an enclave of conservatism and traditional family values amid the bizarre cultural circus that is greater Los Angeles. Rhoads' earliest musical instruction was given to him by his mother, Delores, a professional musician who ran a music school in Burbank and raised her three kids single-handedly.

By the time he was in his teens, Rhoads was teaching guitar at his mom's music school. He taught his junior high school friend Kelly Garni how to play bass, and together they worked their way through the usual assortment of garage bands, ultimately forming Quiet Riot with drummer Drew Forsyth and singer Kevin DuBrow. By the mid Seventies, Quiet Riot became the house band at the Starwood, Hollywood's archetypal rock dive. The Sunset Strip glam-metal scene was in its formative stages back then.

"The real hardcore music was going on at the Starwood," Garni recalls. "You had Van Halen down the street at Gazzarri's. They were doing a Top 40 thing."

Eddie Van Halen and Randy Rhoads were the two prime originators of the pyrotechnic guitar style that would come to dominate Eighties metal. Both brought a new level of technical expertise to rock guitar playing. But while Eddie's approach was intuitive and rooted in traditional rock aesthetics, Randy's arose from a classical foundation he acquired through his formal musical training. For the most part, he broke with rock's long tradition of spontaneously improvised solos, a custom that stemmed from African-American musical forms like jazz and blues. Instead, Rhoads brought the rock guitar solo closer to the spirit of the classical cadenza—a set piece specifically designed to showcase technical virtuosity.

> "RANDY CONFIDED IN ME THAT HE HAD ASPIRATIONS TO DO SOMETHING ELSE OTHER THAN PLAY WITH OZZY. JUST BEFORE HIS DEATH, I KNOW HE WASN'T THE HAPPIEST CAMPER OUT THERE."
>
> —TOMMY ALDRIDGE

Rhoads frequently shunned blues-based, African-American–derived pentatonics in favor of classical scales and modes, such as the natural minor (Aeolian) intervals heard in his solos for Ozzy's "Crazy Train" and "Believer." Rhoads was not the first axman to use these modes; earlier metal guitarists like Deep Purple's Ritchie Blackmore had also favored minor scales. What sets Rhoads' use of these modalities apart is the level of articulation he was able to bring to even the most difficult passages. His fluid legato feel was unique in all the world of rock.

Progressive rock bands such as Yes, Gentle Giant, Focus and Emerson, Lake and Palmer had also previously popularized the use of European classical modes and virtuosity in rock music. But Rhoads' appropriation of these elements is completely devoid of prog-rock's "high-brow," Euro leanings. Instead, while astoundingly precise and harmonically astute, his playing is unmistakably Caucasian American—and 100 percent heavy metal. His biggest heroes, after all, were people like Leslie West and Alice Cooper guitarist Glen Buxton, not Beethoven and Mozart.

In terms of his instrument and stage look, Rhoads took a major cue from the transgendered glam-icon image of David Bowie guitarist Mick Ronson and even began playing a white Les Paul, as Ronson did. Rhoads' stage outfits were designed by his longtime girlfriend Jody Raskin. They featured huge polka dots, which later became something of a Rhoads trademark, and big bow ties, generally worn over a bare torso. While DuBrow was Quiet Riot's

RON SOBOL/ATLASICONS.COM

Rhoads during his Quiet Riot years

extrovert onstage and off, it was Rhoads who "unquestionably stole the show," according to Garni.

"He was five feet seven inches, and he weighed only 105 pounds," says Garni. "His guitar was almost bigger than him. But he'd run around like a wild man with it and just be humongously loud. As shy as he was, Randy was the star."

The band recorded two albums, *Quiet Riot I* and *Quiet Riot II*, but was unable to secure U.S. releases for either disc; both records originally came out in Japan only. (Highlights from the albums were posthumously reissued in 1994 on the CD *Quiet Riot: The Randy Rhoads Years.*) Disillusioned with the band's inability to get any farther than Sunset Strip, Garni left in 1979, shortly after the recording of *Quiet Riot II*. He was replaced by Rudy Sarzo. The Cuban-born bassist, a former hairdresser, became Rhoads' new friend and took charge of his coiffure. The two would also go clothes shopping together. "The funniest thing," recalls Sarzo, "is that because Randy was so little—like, a size one—we used to go to girls' stores for his jeans and stuff like that. He couldn't find the right size in a men's store."

Despite his newfound friendship with Sarzo, Rhoads exited Quiet Riot a few months after Garni. "We were doing everything possible to get ourselves an American record deal," says Kevin DuBrow, "but the band was going nowhere fast, and Randy knew it. In October 1979, Randy—unbeknownst to me—heard that Ozzy Osbourne was auditioning guitar players, so he took his little practice amp and tried out."

Osbourne takes up the tale. "Even though I was fucked up on cocaine and booze, I remember when I first met Randy Rhoads. I was staying at a hotel called Le Parc on West Knoll off Santa Monica Boulevard [*in West Hollywood*]. I used to live like an animal then. And Dana Strum from Slaughter says to me, 'I've got this fucking amazing guitar player for you.' And I go, 'Yeah, sure.' 'Cause at the time, everybody was a fucking Hendrix clone. So it was one in the morning and I was fucking smashed. Off the wall. And this little guy comes in. I thought he was gay at first. He was very effeminate looking, and he wore little boots. He looked like a fucking doll. But even in my stupor, I realized he was great as soon as he started playing the guitar."

By this time, Ozzy had been ejected from Black Sabbath in a manner less than friendly. His excessive drinking and drug use had estranged him from his first wife, Thelma Riley. His management had been undertaken by Sharon Arden, daughter of former Sabbath manager Don Arden. Sharon and Ozzy's business relationship grew into a love affair, a frequently explosive romance that, nonetheless, would eventually result in marriage. Along with Rhoads, they recruited two British rock vets: former Rainbow bassist Bob Daisley and ex–Uriah Heep drummer Lee Kerslake. This would be the group to launch Ozzy's solo career.

Singer, manager and band decamped for England, where they began preparations for Ozzy's solo debut album. Despite differences in age, nationality, personal discipline, professional experience and capacity for alcohol and drug consumption, Ozzy and Rhoads soon became fast friends. "Sharon, Randy and I and a couple of roadies, we'd go out and be goofy," Ozzy recalls. "We loved that. I remember Randy liked to drink Kahlúa and milk. We'd get drunk and start fights. And Randy was a hundred and fucking five pounds wet, you know."

Rhoads' legend tends to paint the guitarist as something of a choirboy, an innocent adrift in the decadent world of rock and roll. But the human being behind

NEIL ZLOZOWER/ATLASICONS.COM

Quiet Riot in the late Seventies: (from left) Drew Forsyth, Kelly Garni, Kevin DuBrow and Rhoads

the legend wasn't quite so angelic. "Randy's consumption of drink was nowhere near Ozzy's," says Sharon. "But when Randy did drink, he had a wicked little sense of humor. He would love to wind people up. Like we were once in a hotel bar somewhere. Randy went and pissed in his drink, then he gave it to the waitress and said, 'You know, this scotch doesn't taste right. You wanna taste it?' And she was tasting it and, like, dying."

Women in particular seemed to be Rhoads' chosen prey when it came to practical jokes. "He used to fuck around with girls—not sexually, but mentally," says Sharon. "He used to like to play games with them. He was a gorgeous-looking guy, but he was terrible with women! He would really make fun of them."

Perhaps it was a defense mechanism, or a way of venting frustration as he struggled to remain faithful to Jody, his girlfriend back home, amid the temptations of his new surroundings.

"Jody was Randy's real girlfriend," said Ozzy. "But he'd go out on dates. Whether it was physical or not, I don't know."

For a while Ozzy and Rhoads shared an apartment in Kensington, one of London's tonier neighborhoods. By all accounts the household was like a heavy metal reenactment of *The Odd Couple*, with Rhoads playing Felix Unger to Ozzy's Oscar Madison. "I was always fucked-up stoned and drunk, like a big, bloated, beer-drinking pig on the floor," Ozzy recalls. "And Randy used to clean the pots and pans, clear away the empty beer bottles and fuck knows what else."

Shortly afterward, Ozzy, Sharon and Randy took up residence together in the nearby, but more working-class, London environs of Shepherd's Bush. "Above the Townhouse recording studios they had apartments that they rented," Sharon recalls. "We all lived together there. And it was just fucking mad. Shepherd's Bush is a very Irish area, and on every corner is a pub. On a Sunday in England, the pubs would close at three o'clock, and the streets would be full of drunken Irishmen. So the three of us would make this 'special mixture' and throw it out of the window on all the Irishmen walking down the street. The guys used to piss in a great big bowl. We used to put soup in it, and stale old food. There was crap in it; we used to shit in it. Then we'd warm it up on the stove until it smelled. And then as people would walk past, we'd pour it on them. It was funny for a while, but eventually it became a big-time problem. Irishmen would gang up and wait on the corner for us!"

> "AFTER SPENDING AN HOUR ONSTAGE PLAYING SONGS THAT HE CO-WROTE WITH OZZY, **RANDY JUST FELT UNCOMFORTABLE DOING BLACK SABBATH SONGS,** WHICH WERE NOT REALLY HIS STYLE."
> —RUDY SARZO

Somewhere amid the boozing and excremental pranks, the band buckled down to write and rehearse material for Ozzy's solo debut album. "It was a writing team," says Ozzy. "Randy wrote the riffs, Bob Daisley wrote the lyrics and I came up with the vocal melodies." The material that became the *Blizzard of Ozz* album marked a move away from the sludgy sound and satanic overtones of Black Sabbath. The album is relatively devoid of demonic imagery, apart from the goat horns and skull in the sleeve art and a song about British occult author Aleister Crowley. Tracks like the classic rock radio staple "Crazy Train" seem to owe more to the pop metal style Rhoads cultivated back when Quiet Riot were vying with Van Halen for control of the Sunset Strip. Rhoads turned out to be an ideal musical partner for Ozzy. While Ozzy possessed the veteran rock perspective Rhoads lacked, Rhoads had the discipline Ozzy had never cultivated.

"I remember when we started to work on 'Goodbye to Romance,'" says Ozzy. "Randy said, 'Maybe if you tried it in this key…' He worked with me. He had the patience because he was a guitar teacher. And he gave me a lot of confidence. He wouldn't intimidate me. Because, believe it or not, I'm quite easily intimidated."

Once writing for the album was completed, Ozzy, Sharon and the band repaired to Ridge Farm, a residential recording studio in rural Sussex. Ozzy was still without a record deal; the sessions were financed from his own private funds, so the project was on a tight budget. The sessions were initially engineered by Chris Tsangarides, who'd helmed the console on Judas Priest's *Sad Wings of Destiny*. But the band was reportedly dissatisfied with the initial sonic results, and Max Norman, who would later produce Megadeth and Grim Reaper, took over as engineer.

"The sessions went pretty fast," Norman recalls. "Everyone played together, and the stuff was already written, except for the vocals and guitar solos." Norman reports that Rhoads would always record scratch guitar solos as part of the basic track. "Randy would recut the main solo as an overdub, and then he'd recut the [*outro*] solo as well. And Ozzy would tell me, 'No, turn that off and put on the original one.' And then Randy would go, 'Oh, all right, but at least let me double it.' So he'd get in there and double or triple it, and whip some other stuff on there as well."

According to Norman, Rhoads mainly used a polka-dot Gibson Flying V and his white Gibson Les Paul for the sessions. These were played through a 100-watt Marshall head with two cabinets. "Randy had read somewhere about using the Variac [*variable voltage regulator*]," says Norman. "So we dragged it in and dropped the Marshall down to 90 or 92 volts. You get a creamier edge to the distortion that way."

Rhoads' cabinets were pointed at a flight of stone steps leading up from the basement area at Ridge Farm and close-miked using two Shure SM57s per cab. In addition, a Neumann U87 mic was placed six to eight feet from the cabinet and a second U87 was situated 12 feet to 20 feet away to pick up room ambience. His effects consisted of a pedal board containing some MXR effects and a Vox wah. Norman treated the guitar with control-room effects as well. "The main thing we had in the studio back then was the AMS 1580 digital delay, which was the first good, long digital delay," he says. "It went to 408 milliseconds, which was a big deal in those days. A lot of the echoes on Randy's guitar on that album are 408 milliseconds."

The actual recording of guitar solos was a lengthy process, according to Norman. "Randy would say, 'I'm going to need to listen to this a lot of times. You can just go to the pub for a couple of hours.' I'd make him a 1/4 stereo mix of the backing track: I'd record maybe 15 or 20 passes of the section where he'd be soloing, starting about 15 seconds before the solo and ending about 20 seconds after. I'd play that back and send it through Randy's headphones or through the two big 15-inch Tannoys that we had out on the studio floor. Randy would stand at the top of the steps [*leading to the basement where the amps were*] and try out ideas for solos. I'd go to the pub for a couple of hours. And when I got back, he usually still wasn't ready. But once he knew what to do, he'd slam down a good one, and then we'd get it doubled and tripled up."

The *Blizzard* album also contains Rhoads' solo acoustic composition "Dee." The title comes from a nickname for his mother, Delores. "Randy absolutely adored his mother," says Ozzy. "And one day Randy came to me and said, 'Do you mind if I do this classical guitar piece for my mum?' And I said, 'Fuck, what yer askin' me for? Go ahead.'"

Max Norman remembers Rhoads as a confident, focused studio musician. "I think everybody was in awe of his composing. His chord changes were great. He was the sort of guy you didn't argue with; you just tried to keep up. At some point, Ozzy would say, 'This is taking forever. We don't need

**"RANDY AND I HAD A CHAT ONE DAY AND HE SAID, 'THE BAND IS JUST A LOT OF GEEKS. YOU DRINK TOO MUCH.'"**

*—OZZY OSBOURNE*

Onstage in 1982: (from left) Rudy Sarzo, Tommy Aldridge, Ozzy Osbourne and Rhoads

NEIL ZLOZOWER/ATLASICONS.COM

all these tracks.' Remember, the first album was being done on Ozzy's money and it was all the money he had in the world, I think, for four weeks in the studio. So we didn't have a lot of time to hang around trying different ideas. But if Randy really wanted to do something, he could usually bring Ozzy around."

Actually, quite a bit of time was spent "pulling vocals out of Ozzy," as Norman phrases it. "It would take about six or seven hours. And it was always a question of getting it out of him before he collapsed, because he'd be drinking scotch or doing blow. One time, toward the end of those sessions, I was recording Ozzy and I couldn't hear anything. I soloed out the track and I could hear this dribbling sound. And it was Ozzy pissing on the studio carpet. He didn't even bother to sing. Another time I listened in and he was throwing up."

Like everyone else, Norman remembers Randy's consumption of intoxicants as being very moderate. "He'd never take a drink in the studio. Maybe after the session, but that was it. One of his little fingers had a very long fingernail on it, and maybe he'd have a tiny bit of cocaine on there, maybe at the end of the week. He was a very straight guy; he was into playing. I saw him do coke maybe three times I can think of. And in those days, that was like being a Christian. Everybody else was crazy."

Shortly after *Blizzard of Ozz* was completed, Ozzy signed a deal with Don Arden's CBS-distributed Jet Records, and the band started to tour behind the album's September 1980 release. At first, the going wasn't easy. The general perception was that Ozzy's best days were behind him and that he'd become just another booze-and-dope casualty. And at the dawn of the Eighties, heavy metal was far less popular than it is today. Seventies metal, the music's first wave, had long since peaked. A significant portion of the rock audience had moved on to newer styles such as punk, post-punk, hardcore, industrial, Two-Tone ska, new wave, no wave, synth pop and the rockabilly revival, among other genres. Ozzy Osbourne and his new band had to scramble to gain a toehold.

"We had nothing in the beginning," says Sharon. "We weren't earning a lot of money from the dates, and it was really, really rough. When we were first starting out, the hotels we stayed in were shit holes. I mean, Motel 6 was a luxury for us. And the first thing Randy would do when he got into one of those rooms was jump up and down on the bed and put the light under the fire alarm. We wrecked a few hotel rooms together."

According to Sharon, however, Rhoads was not discouraged by the spartan touring conditions. "Randy wasn't a limo kind of guy. That wasn't his thing. All he wanted was to play."

The band's bassist and drummer, apparently, were somewhat less tractable. "Bob Daisley and Lee Kerslake did nothing but complain from day one," says Ozzy. "I remember one occasion where Sharon comes to us and says, 'Good news, guys: our show at the New York Palladium sold out in half an hour and they want to add another show.' So Daisley and fucking Kerslake go and have a little chinwag, and they come back and say, 'Okay, we'll do the second show if we can have double per diem.' Randy looked at me and said, 'What the fuck are they on about?' He didn't even know what per diem meant."

Rhoads, of course, was considerably less seasoned than Daisley and Kerslake. To be seeing the world while touring with Ozzy Osbourne was plenty for him. "Every country we went to, Randy would love it," says Sharon. "He was a real little tourist. When we got to a town, he'd find out what the local tourist attraction was and go visit it. He loved to collect model trains, so he'd go find some local toyshop that specialized in that. You would never have Randy stuck in the hotel room. He'd be out exploring. I mean, he did find the food in Europe a bit difficult. He loved his American food. But he ate a lot of McDonald's and candy, so it was fine."

In a sense Ozzy and Sharon became surrogate, if somewhat dysfunctional, parents for Rhoads in his strange new surroundings. "I remember, we were somewhere on the road and Randy had a toothache," Ozzy recounts. "The problem was a wisdom tooth. Have you ever had a wisdom tooth pulled? It's like having your fuckin' head ripped off. So Randy goes to this dentist that rips his face out. By the time we got him back to the hotel, there was about six big Kleenex boxes soaked in blood. And I go, 'What the fuck have they done to him, Sharon?' And Sharon's going crazy, like a mom."

The band's hard work paid off and *Blizzard of Ozz* became a substantial success, with two singles—"Crazy Train" and "Mr. Crowley"—making the charts. Eager to capitalize on their good fortune, Osbourne, Rhoads, Daisley and Kerslake returned to Ridge Farm studios to cut a follow-up to *Blizzard of Ozz*, with Max Norman once again at the controls. Pleased with the way *Blizzard* turned out, they went about things much the same way, even down to the placement and miking of Randy's amp.

"The main difference was that Randy wanted to be in the control room when we recorded the second album," Norman recalls. "So we set him up using D.I.s [*direct injection*]. What we ended up doing was preamping the guitar through the board, which was cool because we could actually change the amount of drive into the front end of the amp without killing it. This was before people started making separate preamps and power amps for guitar."

While preamping the signal to the board, Norman also took the opportunity to add a wider variety of control room effects to the signal. This was partially because more gear had become available since the making of *Blizzard*. "On the second album, we had a Lexicon 240 [*reverb unit*] with new chips in it. We used it for some of the spacey clean-guitar stuff. The Lexicon had a long, 30-second delay, and we doubled those guitar figures into it. That made them sound kind of spooky."

The guitar sounds are generally bigger and warmer on *Diary of a Madman*, the second Ozzy Osbourne album. Octave-divider and envelop filter–style effects from an Eventide Harmonizer and AMS Flanger impart a sense of depth. In addition, Randy played a wider range of guitars on the album than he had on *Blizzard*. In the time since making the first album, he'd supplemented his Gibson Les Paul and Flying V with several custom-made V-shaped Jacksons. Compared with *Blizzard*, the music on *Diary of a Madman* has more of the stagey, dark melodrama one might reasonably expect from Ozzy Osbourne. The guitar tones have more depth, and much of the soloing possesses a kind of hellbent urgency.

ROSS HAFLIN

"I remember Randy wasn't really happy with the guitar solo on 'Diary of a Madman,'" Ozzy recalls. "I said, 'You know what, Randy? The studio is yours. You can spend as much time on that solo as you want. It's my record deal, and as far as I'm concerned, you can stay a fuckin' month in there.' I remember him coming out of the studio a few days later with this big shit-eating grin on his face. And when I heard the solo, it blew my fuckin' mind, man."

But all was not well in the Osbourne camp. Toward the end of the sessions for *Diary of a Madman*, Ozzy and Sharon fell into a dispute with Bob Daisley and Lee Kerslake. "There was a bit of contention about the publishing," Norman says. "I remember Daisley and Lee getting pretty pissed off about it at the end. I remember Ozzy talking to Sharon and saying, 'They're fucking gone.' And Ozzy fired them, basically. Ozzy fires everybody. He's fired me more than once!"

**"SHARON WAS SCREAMING, 'HOW COULD YOU LET THAT BABY GET ON THAT AIRPLANE?'"**
*—TOMMY ALDRIDGE*

Ozzy claims that Randy also had a role in his decision to fire the bassist and drummer. "Randy never liked Lee Kerslake," Ozzy states. "And Bob was always intimidating him. And I can remember that Randy's mum came to him and said, 'What the fuck are you playing with those fucking idiots for?' I was sitting next to Randy's mum at the time. And she said, 'What's wrong with you, Randy?' Then Randy said, 'I think I'm gonna leave the band.' I asked him why. We had a chat apart one day and he said, 'The band is just a lot of geeks. You drink too much.' I said, 'Well, that's just me. But what do you mean "a band of geeks"?' And he said, 'Look, how are we gonna conquer America with that fucking lot?'"

Rhoads suggested his old Quiet Riot pal Rudy Sarzo as a replacement for Daisley. And Tommy Aldridge was a drummer that Ozzy had known and admired for years. A veteran of Black Oak Arkansas, as well as Pat Travers' and Gary Moore's bands, Aldridge had first met Ozzy back in the Seventies, when Black Oak Arkansas opened for Black Sabbath.

The appearance of Sarzo and Aldridge meant that Randy was no longer the rookie of the team. "I depended on Randy just to get a feel for surviving the sometimes chaotic world of Ozzy," says Sarzo. "It was my first experience playing in an arena band, so I was as green as they come. Randy had already been with Ozzy and Sharon for about two years. There were basic questions I had, like, 'Why are they doing this or that?' And he'd say, 'That's just the way they are.'"

"There was a lot of upheaval going on between Ozzy and Sharon at times," says Tommy Aldridge. "That's inevitable when you hook up two people as volatile as them. So there was a lot of drama going on."

Perhaps too much drama for Randy Rhoads. The guitarist's childhood friend Kelly Garni would sometimes get calls from Randy out on the road. "It's no secret that he was trying to get out of Ozzy's band," says Garni. "After struggling so much for success, I think it was a big letdown for Randy when he finally got there with Ozzy. I don't think he enjoyed being famous. He didn't say too much about it, just that it was really grueling and that there's a lot of weird people out there—which is what Ozzy attracted. Things like a guy coming backstage with a dead goat and saying, 'Here, I brought you this as a sacrifice.' That kind of thing really put the sap on Randy's head. He didn't understand that."

But Sharon didn't see it that way. "Was Randy disturbed by all that? No way. We all used to laugh about it. Randy had such a great sense of humor. He would find humor in everything."

While the Sarzo-Aldridge lineup never made a studio recording with Ozzy, a live show from '81 was captured on tape and released in '87, five years after Rhoads' death, as the *Tribute* album. And while Ozzy's intentions in releasing the disc may have been sincere, Tommy Aldridge feels that Randy would not have been pleased to have people hear that particular tape. "Randy and I both hated the recording," says the drummer. "It's sloppy. It's all over the ranch. I have boxes of board cassettes that are better than that."

Another thing that Rhoads wasn't particularly crazy about was having to play Black Sabbath material every night as part of Ozzy's live set. "Randy understood that there is a legacy to Ozzy prior to his solo career," says Sarzo. "He knew the importance of doing those songs. But I wouldn't go so far as to say that was his favorite part of the show. After spending an hour onstage playing the *Blizzard* and *Diary of a Madman* songs that he cowrote with Ozzy, Randy just felt uncomfortable doing Black Sabbath songs, which were not really his style."

"Randy was most disheartened to have to play 'Iron Man' and all those Black Sabbath tunes," Aldridge confirms. "Neither he nor I were big Sabbath fans. Sometimes there were train wrecks on those songs, only because we were not that diligent about putting them together, to be painfully honest."

While Rhoads may or may not have been freaked out by Ozzy's morbid Sabbath followers, it's certain that, toward the end of his life, he was certainly looking to a musical existence beyond touring around with heavy metal's number-one madman. His interest in classical guitar had grown obsessive over the years, as Rudy Sarzo witnessed. "From the start of the *Diary of a Madman* tour on December 30, 1981, up until the time Randy died, every time we arrived in a new town he would take out the yellow pages, look for a music school and line up a classical guitar lesson. I would say 99 percent of the time he knew more than the teacher. Sometimes he would wind up paying for a lesson that he would give rather than receive."

"Not long after I joined the band," says Aldridge, "Randy confided in me that he had aspirations to do something else other than play with Ozzy. Just before his death, I know he wasn't the happiest camper out there."

According to Ozzy, Rhoads confessed as

Osbourne and Rhoads onstage in the U.K., in 1980

much to him on the final night of his life, as the band traveled from a gig in Knoxville, Tennessee, en route to a show in Orlando, Florida. "We'd just got *Diary* going," says Ozzy. "*Blizzard* was happening. We were filling up arenas. And Randy turns to me on the bus and says, 'I want to quit rock and roll.' I said, 'What?' I asked him, 'Are you fucking serious?' He said, 'Yeah, I want to go to UCLA to get a degree in classical music.' I said, 'Randy, put your head on right. Make your money in rock and roll and then when you get enough dough you can fuckin' *buy* UCLA.' But that wasn't Randy."

As it turned out, Rhoads never had to decide between Ozzy and UCLA. The 600-mile bus ride from Knoxville to central Florida was to be his last. The horrific events that took place on the morning of March 19, 1982, are still vivid in the minds of those who survived them. The band had been traveling all night in order to make a gig in Orlando: the Rock Superbowl XIV festival with Foreigner and UFO. The bus driver, 36-year-old Andrew Aycock, had persuaded Sharon that it was necessary to make a stop at the Flying Baron Estates in Leesburg, Florida, to obtain spare parts for the vehicle. Aycock lived there, and the stop would enable him to drop off his ex-wife, who had been traveling with him.

The Flying Baron Estates, according to Sharon, belonged to Jerry Calhoun, who owned the bus company, Florida Coach. "It was a huge piece of property—private property—and there were two houses on it [*one owned by Calhoun, the other by Aycock*]. There was also a little landing strip with helicopters and small planes."

The bus arrived at the compound in the early hours of the morning. Aycock, also a licensed pilot, talked the band's keyboardist, Don Airey, into going up for a spin in one of the aircraft on the site: a small, single-engine 1955 Beechcraft Bonanza F-35. In some accounts of the incident, tour manager Jake Duncan is also said to have been on this flight. At this point, most of the band and crew members onboard the bus, including Rhoads, were still asleep. But Tommy Aldridge remembers being awakened by the sound of the airplane in flight. "I kept hearing the plane fly overhead. That's when Don Airey had gone up with our bus driver. I was trying to go to sleep, but the plane was so loud it was irritating."

After a brief joyride, the plane landed. Airey got back on the bus and apparently persuaded Rhoads to go up on a second flight, despite the fact that the guitarist had a well-known fear of flying. Fifty-eight-year-old Rachel Youngblood also agreed to board the plane. The band's seamstress and cook, Youngblood was an old friend of Sharon's, having worked as a domestic in Don Arden's home when Sharon was growing up. Rhoads also invited Sarzo and Aldridge to join him and Youngblood on the plane. Neither one accepted.

"Randy woke me up and tried to get me to come on the plane," Sarzo recalls. "That was the last time I saw him. Rachel was with him. She was a wonderful woman. I can still remember the smell of the chili she used to cook for us on the bus. She thought it would be a special occasion for her to go up on a small plane, so she got all dressed up and everything. The pilot knew that Rachel had a heart condition. So the pilot told Jake that it would be just going up and down. Nothing fancy. Nothing crazy, right? And that's why Randy had said, 'Well, in that case, I'll join you guys. I want to take some photos.' Randy loved taking photos, and he really enjoyed being in Florida. So he went up there, basically, just to take a photo."

"Randy actually stuck his head in my bunk when he was going off the bus to get on the plane," Aldridge remembers. "If I recall correctly, I said to Randy, 'That guy's been driving a bus all night. I don't think he has any business flying a plane.'"

Apparently no attempt was made to

awaken Ozzy or Sharon to invite them onto the plane, a detail that haunts Ozzy to this day. "Without a shadow of a doubt in my mind," he says, "I know that, had I been awake at that time, I would have been on that plane with Randy."

Aycock, Rhoads and Youngblood left the bus, boarded the plane and took off. Sarzo went back to sleep, but Aldridge remained awake. "I tried to get back to sleep," says the drummer, "but the plane just kept getting louder and louder. I got up to fix a cup of tea, since I couldn't sleep because of all the racket. I was leaning against the microwave, mixing my tea and—*ba-da-boom-bam!*—all of a sudden there was an impact. It didn't seem that big, but there was a strong smell of fiberglass. The top section of those Greyhound Eagles at the time was essentially made of fiberglass. The wing tip had hit the side of the bus, and I remember the bus driver's [*ex-wife*] was standing in the doorway of the bus, screaming, 'Oh my God, they've hit the bus, they've hit the bus!' "

The impact jolted Sarzo awake. "I jumped out of my bunk and went into the lounge," the bassist remembers. "There was glass all over the place. I looked to my right and saw Jake Duncan, our tour manager, down on his knees pulling his hair out, crying, 'They're gone, they're gone!' "

The left wing of the plane had clipped the back of the bus at about five feet two inches above ground level, by the estimation of Sarzo, who later stood beside the bus and measured the gash against his own five-foot-seven height. After striking the bus, the plane flipped over, severed the top of a large pine tree and crashed into the garage of a large house near where the bus was parked.

"I go running out of the bus and the [*driver's ex-wife*] is screaming," Aldridge resumes. "I yelled, 'Who's on the plane?' And she said, 'Randy and Rachel.' I think at that point I started kinda numbing out. At 7:30 in the morning it was really muggy and hot. It all seemed surreal. We were in the middle of nowhere. I looked to the left and we had parked the bus in the cul-de-sac drive of this big antebellum-looking southern home. I don't see another house anywhere. I'm trying to figure out where the heck we are and what the heck we're doing here. And then I see smoke coming out of the house. So I go running around the side of the house and the garage door was open. I stuck my head in the house and there was a man sitting there in his underwear reading the paper. I ran in and said, 'Your house is on fire!' And he just kind of looked at me wide-eyed and sat there. I don't know if he was deaf or he was just shocked to see a guy like me running into his house in the middle of the morning. I went out and ran back around to the side of the house and by that time the whole garage was in flames. When I had first looked at the garage, you could still see the outline of the plane. But it wasn't that way for long."

"The last thing we remember was being on the fucking freeway," says Ozzy, "and the next thing we know we're in this fucking field. And I didn't know where the fuck we were. I thought we'd just rolled off the fucking freeway. And I couldn't find the freeway, you know? And everyone's pointing at this fucking big colonial house on fire. I'm going, 'Where is everybody?' I'd just been asleep on the bus. Sharon was out of her mind."

"Sharon was visibly very upset with Jake Duncan," Aldridge recalls. " 'How could you let that baby get on that airplane?' she was screaming. But it wasn't Jake's responsibility. It was a day off and people were doing what they wanted to do."

"Everyone was in total shock," Sharon recalls. "You have to realize it was Randy and Rachel, who was my best friend in my life. They were both missing, and I kept screaming and screaming, and everybody was terrified. Nobody could talk. Most of them were in a seated position on the grass, just crying."

Three bodies, burned beyond recognition, were later recovered from the area in and around the razed garage. Rhoads' remains were identified by the jewelry he was wearing, Aycock's via dental records. Toxicology reports later revealed that Aycock had cocaine in his system. Nothing stronger than nicotine was discovered in Rhoads.

"There were some theories that [*Aycock*] was trying to kill his ex-wife and commit suicide at the same time," says Aldridge. "But I don't believe that. What I believe is that he got too close to the friggin' bus. I think that his flying skills had been somewhat compromised by the fact that he was up driving the bus all night. And I know for a fact that he wasn't unassisted in being able to stay awake all night. I never told anyone this before, but I found a big freezer bag filled with cocaine stashed on the bus, beside the driver's seat. I knew there was something up there 'cause [*Aycock*] was always tweaked, you know? So I pulled the top off the instrument panel to the left of the driver's seat, where all the knobs and switches are. And there was a huge bag in there. I'd never seen that much before. The last thing I wanted to happen would be for some redneck Florida cop to come out and find drugs on a rock band's tour bus. So I took the bag and threw it in the woods. I don't know if that was the right thing to do or not, but I thought it was the best thing under the circumstances."

Numb with grief, Ozzy and Sharon decided to continue the tour, albeit reluctantly. "I said to Sharon, 'It's over,' " Ozzy recalls. " 'This is a warning, a sign that my career is over.' And Sharon yelled at me. She goes, 'No, we do not stop now. Because Randy would not have liked it that way.' "

Guitarist Bernie Torme filled in for Rhoads on a gig at Madison Square Garden in New York. Then Brad Gillis finished out the tour on guitar. "That Madison Square Garden show was the toughest I'd ever done," says Sarzo. " 'Cause Randy had really looked forward to playing the Garden for the first time. It became very hard to get up onstage every night. Everything was the same—the staging, the set list—but Randy was missing. I never got rid of that feeling."

"Sharon took it real, real bad for a long time," says Ozzy. "She couldn't listen to the set. She'd have to leave when we started playing the old songs. Or we'd be moving house and she'd find a piece of Randy's clothing. It's fuckin' weird, man."

Some four months after Rhoads' death, Ozzy's divorce with his first wife was finalized. He and Sharon were married. "But it was a bittersweet occasion," says Sharon. "Yes, it was one of the best things that's ever happened to me in my life. Yet Randy and Rachel weren't there. And I so wanted them there when we were married. Because they had gone through so much with me and Ozzy and our crazy relationship. I wished they could see that we ended up together."

But Tommy Aldridge delivers perhaps the best eulogy for his fallen bandmate. "They say no one is irreplaceable. That's bullshit. Randy Rhoads is irreplaceable." ◆

SONY MUSIC ARCHIVES/DON HUNSTEIN

# LIFE WITHOUT YOU

Thirty years ago, Stevie Ray Vaughan took the world by storm with *Texas Flood*. As Sony releases the ultimate anniversary edition of that album, we celebrate the phenomenal rise of the last great blues guitar hero of the 20th century.

BY CHRIS GILL

STEVIE RAY VAUGHAN 1954–1990

# IN MAY 1983 ONLY DAYS

before Stevie Ray Vaughan was scheduled to play his first concert with David Bowie on the Serious Moonlight tour, his career had reached a fork in the road. Bowie's album *Let's Dance*, on which Stevie performed, had just been released to rave reviews. At the same time, Vaughan's own debut album, *Texas Flood*, made with his band Double Trouble, was in the can and set for release the following month.

Unfortunately, the Bowie tour was scheduled to last until the end of the year and thus threatened to postpone Stevie's ability to effectively promote the album until 1984. Facing a choice between increasing his exposure as a supporting member of Bowie's band or supporting his solo career on his own while the album was still fresh, Vaughan chose the latter.

The choice was not as difficult as it might have seemed initially. According to Chesley Millikin, who was Vaughan's manager at the time, Bowie's management reneged on an agreement to allow Double Trouble to open select dates on the tour, and even prohibited Vaughan from doing interviews without prior permission, which made it difficult for Vaughan to even talk about *Texas Flood*.

Then there was the issue of Vaughan's pay. While the $300-per-show rate was the same as what other members of Bowie's band were being paid, and was certainly not out of line for a supporting touring musician in the early Eighties, Millikin thought that Stevie deserved more. It seemed arrogant and reckless for Millikin to demand higher pay for a relatively unknown musician than the seasoned pros in Bowie's band, but when Millikin pointed out that Bowie was being paid $1.5 million for a headlining appearance at the US Festival, it made Bowie look unreasonable and cheap.

In the end, Vaughan wasn't actually given a choice between staying with Bowie or bowing out. Millikin made the decision for him moments before Bowie's band boarded a bus headed to the airport to catch a flight to Brussels, Belgium, where the tour's first show was scheduled. Bowie's tour manager was instructed to remove Vaughan's bags from the bus, leaving a confused Vaughan on the sidewalk, wondering what he was going to do next. Millikin's decision turned out to be the right one, however, as Vaughan earned instant notoriety for allegedly telling Bowie to take a hike while gaining the freedom to concentrate fully on promoting *Texas Flood* and giving his burgeoning career the full attention it needed.

While it would have been fascinating to hear Vaughan jamming on Bowie classics like "Station to Station," "Rebel Rebel," and "Fashion," had he remained with Bowie the world would have been deprived of his now-legendary show at the El Mocambo Tavern in Toronto, his pairing with Albert King for the Canadian *In Session* broadcast, and his first appearance on the *Austin City Limits* television program. We also would have missed his fiery performance at Ripley's Music Hall in Philadelphia, originally broadcast on WMMR radio and officially released for the first time on Sony's new 30th Anniversary Legacy Edition of *Texas Flood*.

**RECORDED IN JUST TWO DAYS, *TEXAS FLOOD* ESSENTIALLY CAPTURED VAUGHAN AND DOUBLE TROUBLE PERFORMING A LIVE SET AT A MAGICAL MOMENT IN VAUGHAN'S CAREER.**

It's likely that, even if he had remained with Bowie, Vaughan would have risen to premier guitar-hero status upon the release of *Texas Flood*. The album was about as perfect a showcase for his immense talents as he could deliver. Recorded in just two days, *Texas Flood* essentially captured Vaughan and Double Trouble performing a live set at a magical moment in Vaughan's career, where his seasoned performing experience, fresh excitement over new opportunities and desire to make a definitive statement coalesced.

"Stevie said that we waited all of our lives to make that first record," Double Trouble bassist Tommy Shannon says. "After that, making records was work."

"We didn't know we were making a record," adds Double Trouble drummer Chris Layton. "We basically played all the songs we had been playing at the gigs. We'd record something, listen to it, and if it sounded good we'd go on to the next song."

If Vaughan's playing on *Let's Dance* provided only a fleeting glimpse of his talent, *Texas Flood* laid it all on the line. The depth and diversity of his talent were perfectly presented in the rollicking rockabilly boogie of "Love Struck Baby," the swinging blues of "Pride and Joy," the burning instrumentals "Testify" and "Rude Mood," and the ethereal jazz-inflected closing track, "Lenny." Although blues and roots music were far from pop music staples at the time (the only exceptions being a handful of artists like George Thorogood and the Stray Cats), Vaughan and Double Trouble gained exposure on MTV via an honest, low-key performance video of "Love Struck Baby," shot on the band's Austin, Texas, home turf at the Rome Inn bar. Looking like a gunslinger in a Clint Eastwood spaghetti western, Vaughan cut a commanding figure that was in strong contrast to the girlie-man glam-metal musicians and prissy new-wave guitarists then dominating MTV's playlist.

For the first few months after *Texas Flood* was released, Vaughan and Double Trouble booked shows at clubs and

PHOTO BY CLAYTON CALL/REDFERNS/GETTY IMAGES

Onstage at the Keystone Berkeley in Berkeley, California, on August 19, 1983

theaters, playing to sold-out audiences numbering from 400 to 2,000 fans. When their booking manager landed them the opening slot for the Moody Blues' U.S. tour, they suddenly found themselves in front of audiences of 10,000 to 20,000, greatly increasing their exposure.

"Our first gig with the Moody Blues was at the Meadowlands in New Jersey in front of 21,000 people!" Shannon recalls. "Our record hadn't become that successful yet, but we were playing in front of coliseums full of people. We just went out and played, and it fit like a glove. The sound rang through those big coliseums like a monster. People were going crazy, and they had no idea who we were. We started drawing bigger crowds and playing bigger places. That validation by so many people gave us more strength to really take off."

By the end of 1983, *Texas Flood* was certified Gold in the United States, with sales exceeding 500,000 units. To keep the momentum going, Vaughan and Double Trouble entered the studio in January 1984 to record their second album, *Couldn't Stand the Weather*. The band spent 19 days at the Power Station recording the album, and this time around executive producer John Hammond (who also co-produced *Texas Flood*) was present during the tracking sessions. "We had this big budget," Layton recalls. "We were camped out in New York City, and we felt like we could do whatever we wanted."

Vaughan wrote four of the album's eight songs, including "Scuttle Buttin'" and the title track. Compared to *Texas Flood*, the cover songs that he chose for *Couldn't Stand the Weather* were a better reflection of the band's live sets, particularly the Jimi Hendrix song "Voodoo Child (Slight Return)," which had been a highlight of Vaughan's performances for a long time. "Cold Shot," a hit on MTV and rock radio, was written by members of Vaughan's previous band, Triple Threat, and "The Things That I Used to Do" and "Tin Pan Alley" were blues standards that dated back to the Fifties.

" 'Tin Pan Alley' was the first tune we cut for the record," Layton recalls. "We had been doing that song for quite a while, and when we were in the studio getting sounds, Stevie said, 'Why don't we just go ahead and play something?' So we played 'Tin Pan Alley,' sort of as a warm-up. When we were done, John Hammond said, 'You'll never get it better than that,' and he was right."

Double Trouble immediately hit the road in February 1984 after completing the album, booking a world tour that took them to Europe, Australia, New Zealand, and Japan, in addition to North America. Thanks in part to their relentless touring schedule, *Couldn't Stand the Weather* enjoyed instant success, selling more than 250,000 copies within its first month of release and reaching a peak position of Number 31 on the *Billboard* 200 chart. Later that year, on October 4, 1984, Vaughan and Double Trouble performed a historic concert at Carnegie Hall, joined by Dr. John on keyboards, the Roomful of Blues horn section, Stevie's brother Jimmie, who played rhythm guitar, and vocalist Angela Strehli.

"It was a dream for Stevie to play Carnegie Hall," Shannon says. "He went to all lengths to make that show happen. We had special mariachi suits made just for the gig. We brought all of the special guests to a soundstage in Austin called Third Coast, rehearsed for three days, and had everyone fitted for their clothes. The record [Live at Carnegie Hall] tells the whole story of that gig. That's some of my favorite playing from Stevie, ever."

Unfortunately, as the gigs got bigger, so did the group's problems with drug and alcohol abuse. The band members had picked up the habits from years of playing in clubs, and the effects began to wear heavily on Vaughan. It showed on his next studio

# THE POWER OF TEN

## *GW*'S GUIDE TO THE CATALOG OF **STEVIE RAY VAUGHAN**

### TEXAS FLOOD
1983

As Stevie Ray Vaughan's proper introduction to the world beyond Austin, *Texas Flood* is the best starting place for anyone curious to discover his music. Recorded live in the studio over three days, the album captured a hungry and aggressive Vaughan, who was in peak form throughout. Sony's newly released 30th anniversary Legacy Edition adds a stunning live performance recorded at Philadelphia's Ripley's Music Hall on October 20, 1983.

### COULDN'T STAND THE WEATHER
1984

This sophomore effort followed a similar formula as *Texas Flood*, but he displayed greater range beyond the blues with the funky title track, a hard-rocking cover of Hendrix's "Voodoo Child (Slight Return)" and the bebop swing of "Stang's Swang." The 2010 Legacy Edition release includes alternate tracks, a live concert at Montreal's Spectrum recorded on August 17, 1984.

### SOUL TO SOUL
1985

Of Vaughan's four studio albums, *Soul to Soul* is generally considered the weakest of the bunch, but it would have been considered a masterpiece if a lesser guitarist had released it. On it, Vaughan focused on the big picture of each song's arrangement, playing down his guitar-hero theatrics and giving more room for his Double Trouble bandmates and newly added keyboardist Reese Wynans to shine.

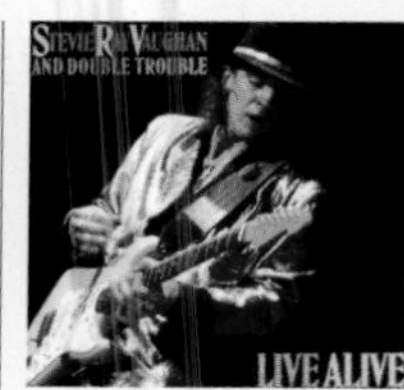


### LIVE ALIVE
1986

Recorded during the most tumultuous period of Vaughan's career, *Live Alive* does not offer the best representation of Vaughan's performance prowess, but it's still an impressive effort. His covers of Stevie Wonder's "Superstition" and Hendrix's "Voodoo Child (Slight Return)" reveal that, even in his darkest moments, Vaughan was capable of delivering the goods with intensity and fire.

album, *Soul to Soul*, released in September 1985. After a failed attempt to add a rhythm guitarist and second vocalist to Double Trouble, Vaughan hired keyboardist Reese Wynans to give himself more freedom to concentrate on his singing and solos. But even with the additional support, Vaughan seemed distracted, and both the original songs that he wrote and his selection of cover material wasn't as strong as it had been in the past. *Soul to Soul* failed to light a spark with his audience, and it remains the only one of his studio efforts that failed to achieve Gold certification.

After finishing the recording of *Soul to Soul* in May 1985, Vaughan and Double Trouble toured almost nonstop for more than a year. While on tour in Ludwigshafen, Germany, on September 28, 1986, Vaughan's alcohol and cocaine addiction finally took its toll on him, and he passed out from dehydration. Layton recalls that when doctors revived Vaughan, Stevie told him, "I need help." When the tour arrived in London a few days later, Vaughan sought the care of Dr. Victor Bloom, who had helped Eric Clapton and Pete Townshend recover from their addiction problems. After Vaughan returned to the U.S., he checked into a rehabilitation program at Peachford Hospital in Atlanta, Georgia.

During this time, Epic released the live album *Live Alive*, compiled from four concert performances recorded during 1985 and 1986. Vaughan admitted that the performances were not among his best and noted that numerous overdubs were recorded later to fix mistakes. While on tour to promote *Live Alive*, the newly sober Vaughan started writing songs for *In Step*, and he remained on the road for most of 1987 and 1988. On January 25, 1989, he entered the studio to start recording that album and completed it two months later. When *In Step* was released in June 1989, critics hailed it as his best album to date, praising both the maturity of his playing and his honest treatment of his addiction problems in the songs "Wall of Denial" and "Tightrope." The album also featured fewer cover songs than his previous efforts and benefited from several collaborations with Austin singer-songwriter Doyle Bramhall. *In Step* was also Vaughan's most commercially successful release and his first to achieve double-Platinum status.

With his destructive habits behind him, Vaughan's creative muse was renewed. In late 1989, he went on a coheadlining tour with Jeff Beck, and in January 1990 he filmed a live acoustic performance for *MTV Unplugged*. That March he entered the studio to record a long-overdue collaboration with his brother, Jimmie, appropriately titled *Family Style*. Vaughan and Double Trouble spent the summer of 1990 touring extensively, including a pair of shows on August 25 and 26 opening for Eric Clapton at the Alpine Valley Music Theatre in East Troy, Wisconsin. During the early hours of August 27, after joining Clapton, Jimmie, Buddy Guy, and Robert Cray to perform a rousing version of "Sweet Home Chicago" for the second show's encore, Vaughan boarded a helicopter to fly to Chicago. However, the pilot's vision was impaired by fog and the helicopter slammed into a nearby ski hill, killing the pilot, Vaughan and other passengers.

Vaughan was buried next to his father at Laurel Land Cemetery in Dallas, Texas, on August 30, 1990. His spirit still lives on today among countless blues guitarists who steal his licks and futilely attempt to duplicate his powerful tone and touch. While many guitarists have kept the blues alive over the years, there's no doubt that the blues would not be as popular and vital as it is today if Vaughan had not come along and changed the public's perception of the genre. ◆

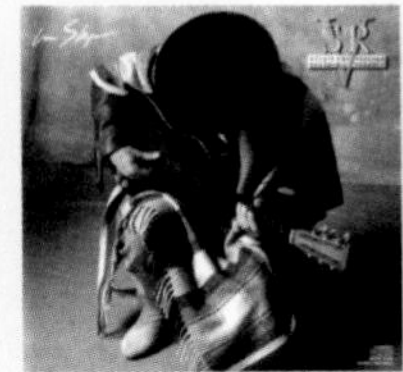

**IN STEP**
1989

Recorded after he kicked his alcohol and cocaine dependencies, *In Step* is rightfully heralded as Vaughan's most fully realized effort, showcasing his growth beyond blues guitar-hero status into a new role as a superstar performer, rivaled only by peers like Eric Clapton. The songs that honestly dealt with his addictions—"Crossfire," "Tightrope" and "Wall of Denial"—remain some of his greatest achievements.

**FAMILY STYLE**
(WITH JIMMIE VAUGHAN)
1990

Despite pairing two superstar guitarists (who also happened to be brothers), *Family Style* isn't quite the guitar extravaganza one would expect but rather a finely crafted album of roots-oriented blues boogie and funky Memphis soul. The instrumental track "D/FW" and the rousing "Long Way from Home" feature the album's best guitar performances.

**THE SKY IS CRYING**
1991

Although this album is a compilation of alternate tracks left over from prior sessions, it's as strong as any of Vaughan's studio efforts. The covers of Jimi Hendrix's "Little Wing," Lonnie Mack's "Wham" and Elmore James' "The Sky Is Crying" encapsulate his most significant guitar influences, while Vaughan's solo performance of "Life by the Drop," accompanied only by a Guild 12-string, is a rare glimpse at his acoustic prowess.

**IN THE BEGINNING**
1992

Vaughan and Double Trouble had been playing in a trio format for less than a year when this performance at Austin's Steamboat was recorded for broadcast over radio station KLBJ-FM. Even so, Vaughan's talents as a frontman and showcase guitarist are in full force. Although his playing is a little rough around the edges, his abilities are definitely world class.

**LIVE AT CARNEGIE HALL**
1997

Many incredible live concert recordings of Vaughan have surfaced since his death, but few rival the electric energy of this historic performance at Carnegie Hall, where he is accompanied by an all-star band. However, his finest moments are those where he plays completely solo on "Lenny" and "Rude Mood," delivering a virtuoso performance.

**IN SESSION**
(WITH ALBERT KING)
1999

Vaughan sits in on a performance of King's standard set list (with the exception of Vaughan's "Pride and Joy"). King gives him plenty of space to flex his muscles on songs like "Stormy Monday" and "Blues at Sunrise." While the respect that King and Vaughan had for each other is evident, the competitive environment of a master confronted by a talented protégé results in some dazzling guitar duels.

ROCK IN PEACE

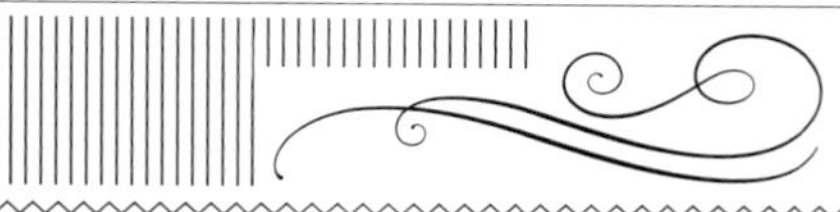

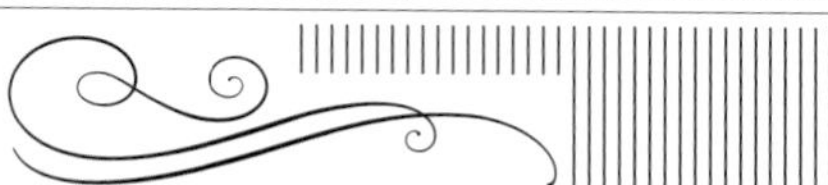

# KING SIZE

Freddie King was a giant among blues men, who lived life and played guitar with outsize passion. In this *Guitar World* tribute, his daughter Wanda shares first-hand stories about the man whose music shaped electric blues and rock and roll.

BY TED DROZDOWSKI

FREDDIE KING 1934–1976

# BLUES INNOVATOR FREDDIE KING

sang like a lion and struck his guitar's strings with the intensity of a rattlesnake. Those talents, paired with his compositional brilliance, took King to the pinnacle of success in the blues world of the Sixties and Seventies, and even made him a rock star.

Thanks to his ingenious gift for hooks and melodies, King's 1961 instrumental hits "Hide Away" and "San-Ho-Zay" broke the race music barrier and landed on the pop charts. King's songs carry an emotional charge that still showers sparks across the decades.

Eric Clapton, Duane Allman, Jeff Beck, Keith Richards, Stevie Ray Vaughan and many other guitar heroes have been influenced by King's burning style, which twined the roots of Texas and Chicago blues to create a swinging hybrid that also tapped the molten energy of rock and roll. King's signature picking technique—terse, biting, almost belligerent phrases torn from his gold-top Les Paul and various Gibson ES-345s and ES-355s by a plastic fingerpick on his thumb and a metal fingerpick on his index finger—added to the juggernaut performances that, along with his six-and-a-half-foot-tall 250-pound frame, won him the nickname the Texas Cannonball.

The only thing that could stop King was death. At age 42, in 1976, he was claimed by complications from the acute ulcers and pancreatitis that came with his hardcore, road-bound lifestyle. Nonetheless, the momentum of King's legacy has continued, and in 2012 he was inducted into the Rock and Roll Hall of Fame by Billy Gibbons and Dusty Hill of ZZ Top, dedicated fans who also shared the stage with King during their own musical apprenticeship in Texas.

King was born on September 3, 1934, in the small East Texas town of Gilmer to Ella May King and J.T. Christian. Ella May and her brother Leon began teaching Freddie guitar when he was six, in a country blues style similar to Sam "Lightnin'" Hopkins, who King would later credit for his own approach to picking. The youngster also fell under the spell of rock and roll forefather Louis Jordan. King played along to the recordings of Jordan and his Tympany Five jump blues band, learning the pleasures of swinging rhythms and modeling his blunt, supremely confident six-string phrasing on Jordan's saxophone.

In 1949, King's family moved to Chicago in pursuit of the better opportunities the North had for African-Americans. Soon he began sneaking into the Windy City's blues clubs, which stayed open around the clock and offered the spectacle of Howlin' Wolf, Muddy Waters, Elmore James, harmonica virtuoso Little Walter and other giants at the height of their powers. Wolf took King under his wing after hearing the 16-year-old sit in with a local band, and soon the brawny youngster was being tutored onstage—and on the streets of the South Side—by Waters, Little Walter and guitarists Eddie Taylor, Jimmy Rogers and Robert Lockwood.

As he got schooled in the club scene, King toiled in the city's steel mills. "My daddy lied about his age so he could get a job in a mill at 16," says Wanda King, the legend's eldest daughter and a blues performer who leads her own band. "He was a hard worker from an early age, and he never slowed down."

At 18, King married another Texas expatriate, Jessie Burnett. He spent his days rolling steel and his nights playing blues. He'd often play with Rogers, who'd already played a key role in defining the Chicago electric blues ensemble sound with Waters' band, and with Taylor, who helped Jimmy Reed perfect the *chunking* rhythm that was essential to Reed's crossover hits like "Big Boss Man." King found his own opportunities in the small taverns of Chicago's West Side and formed his first band, the Every Hour Blues Boys, with guitarist Jimmy Lee Robinson and drummer Frank "Sonny" Scott in 1952.

> **"I NEVER SAW FREDDIE PASS UP A MEAL IN FAVOR OF A DRINK."**
> — *LEWIS STEPHENS*

It took most of the Fifties for King to stake his claim as a recording artist. Several sides he cut for Chicago DJ Al Benson's Parrot Records in 1953 went unreleased. His late-Fifties sessions with Willie Dixon at Cobra Records were similarly ill fated, and Leonard Chess refused to sign King to his label despite multiple auditions, complaining that Freddie sang too much like B.B. King. His only luck was with the obscure local label El-Bee, which released King's debut single in 1956. Side A, "Country Boy," was a duet with singer-songwriter Margaret Whitfield, backed by King's own up-tempo shuffle "That's What You Think." Both songs failed to chart, but King caught the attention of Alfonso "Sonny" Thompson, a jazz and R&B bandleader who doubled as an A&R man for Cincinnati's King and Federal labels.

Freddie signed with Federal in 1960 and began cutting a string of influential records produced by the label's owner Syd Nathan. His first single on Federal was "Have You Ever Loved a Woman" backed with "You've Got to Love Her with a Feeling." The latter reached only Number 92 on the pop chart, but both performances have become part of the fabric of blues and rock history. "Have You Ever Loved a Woman," in particular, has been reinterpreted by a slew of King's torchbearers, most notably Eric Clapton, who first cut the song in 1970 with fellow guitar virtuoso Duane Allman for Derek and the Dominos' *Layla and Other Assorted Love Songs* and has since included the tune on five live recordings.

The next Federal single, 1961's "Hide Away," defined King's early Sixties career. "Hide Away" hit Number Five on the R&B chart and cracked pop's Top 40 at Number 29. The instrumental was inspired by fellow Chicagoan Hound Dog Taylor's "Taylor's Boogie," a slide guitar romp. King couldn't

DAVID WARNER ELLIS/GETTY IMAGES

Onstage at the Montreux Jazz Festival in Switzerland, June 29, 1973

Onstage in Denmark, November 23, 1971

JORGEN ANGEL/REDFERNS/GETTY IMAGES

play slide, so he created a passage in the tune that featured sliding chords. The title was a nod to a West Side dive called Mel's Hide Away Lounge, and King's own innate sense of swing was reinforced by the jazz-honed Federal house band, which featured Sonny Thompson on piano, bassist Bill Wills and drummer Phillip Paul.

Smelling green, Nathan encouraged King and Thompson to co-write more instrumentals. They recorded 30 in Federal's Cincinnati studios over the next three years including "San-Ho-Zay," "The Stumble," "The Sad Nite Owl," "Sen-Sa-Shun" and "Side Tracked." Titles like "Low Tide," "Wash Out" and the 1963 album *Freddy King Goes Surfin'*—reflecting the spelling he used for his first name until 1965—aimed to cash in on the burgeoning surf-rock instrumental craze, and they did. Although King never placed another single on the Top 40 pop chart, he was a fixture in Sixties R&B and garnered enough white teenaged fans to sell more albums than any other blues artist from 1961 to 1963.

Federal's Nathan, in a move typical of the era's white record label owners who recorded African-American artists, bought King an Oldsmobile for touring as a "gift," using King's own royalty money. "It was a big old four-door station wagon that had my dad's name and the titles of his hits written all over it," Wanda King recounts. " 'Hide Away,' 'San-Ho-Zay,' 'The Stumble'..."

King's instrumentals crossed over more effectively than those of his blues contemporaries because of his compositional intellect. He wove a sophisticated sonic tale into the 12-bar form, employing arrangements—rather than jams—with hooks, melodies, bridges and distinct movements. And as blues crossed the color line to reach an emerging generation of white players, negotiating the turns of King's deftly performed instrumentals was a rite of passage for the likes of Clapton, Jeff Beck and Mick Taylor. "Hide Away," in particular, became a litmus test for would-be guitar slingers after Clapton cut the tune with John Mayall's Bluesbreakers in 1966.

Today, Wanda King is the guardian of her father's legacy, but as a child in the early Sixties she didn't even know he was a bluesman. "One Saturday afternoon when I was six my mother took us kids to the Regal Theater in Chicago," she explains. "I thought we were going to see a movie or cartoons, not a concert. This guy came out onstage and said, 'My name is Redd Foxx,' and he proceeded to tell us the lineup: 'We got the Shirelles and Chuck Jackson. We got Freddie King. We got Jackie Wilson.' Now, when he said 'Jackie Wilson' my mama jumped up with our youngest baby in her arms and screamed, 'Jackie, Jackie!' She was a big fan and had his signed pictures and everything, so I knew about Jackie Wilson. But I didn't put it together that the Freddie King he was talking about was my daddy until he came out onstage with this beautiful red guitar in his hands. It looked like a big cherry, and he was layin' the blues down and *wailin'*. And my uncle Benny [*Turner*] was beside him playing bass.

"I was so excited! *'That's my daddy!'* Then all I could think of was how mad as hell he was two weeks earlier when me, my sister and my brother were running around the apartment and knocked over his goldtop Les Paul and the headstock broke off. My mama had warned him not to leave it propped in the corner, but he'd say, 'Aw, Jessie, it'll be fine.' I guess that night or in a couple days he had a gig, so he went down to the pawnshop. They didn't have any Les Pauls, but they had that big ES-345, and after he played it a few times, he never wanted to play anything else."

By the time King's contract with Federal lapsed in 1966, he'd relocated to Dallas with Jessie and their six children, although not by choice. "My dad loved the night life in Chicago, but my mom didn't," Wanda says. "He was making unbelievable money. But Dad began to spend too much time gambling and staying out late, and my mom got upset and said, 'I'm taking the kids and going back to Dallas.' He didn't believe her, but she moved us all back to Texas to live with her sister and her brother-in-law.

"My dad was the talented one, but my mama had the brains in the family," she continues. "Dad had never gotten any of his royalty money from Syd Nathan, so my mom called Syd up and told him she needed some money to buy a house and take care of us kids. He said he'd see what he could do, and he sent a check for $3,000 to get us going."

After that, King returned to Jessie. In the absence of new recordings he needed to tour the chitlin circuit relentlessly to keep his family fed, but a series of appearances on the Nashville-based syndicated R&B TV show *The !!! Beat*, which featured a house band fronted by Clarence "Gatemouth" Brown, led to his next record deal. The great King Curtis, who had recorded a version of "Hide Away" in 1962, saw King's visceral performances on *The !!! Beat* and signed him to Atlantic Records' Cotillion subsidiary. The two resulting albums, 1969's *Freddie King Is a Blues Master* and 1970's *My Feeling for the Blues*, began a renaissance that would make King a living nexus of blues and rock.

Jack Calmes became King's first professional manager in 1969 and immediately booked him for the Texas Pop Festival, where King shared the bill with Led Zeppelin, Sly & the Family Stone, Ten Years After and others. His incendiary performance resonated throughout rock's counterculture and ultimately led to his signing with Leon Russell's Shelter Records.

*Getting Ready*, released in 1971, would define the rest of King's musical life much as "Hide Away" had cast his early career. In a delicious twist of fate, the disc was recorded in Chicago at the former Chess studio with a team of crack session players, including Stax bassist Donald "Duck" Dunn and Russell on piano and guitar. King's muscular take on Memphis songwriter Don Nix's "Going Down" became a blues-rock anthem that would be faithfully recorded by the Jeff Beck Group a year later and remains a staple of the genre today. Billy Gibbons, Derek Trucks and Joe Bonamassa played an incendiary version of "Going Down" in tribute to King at the 2012 Rock and Roll Hall of Fame induction ceremony in Cleveland's Public Hall, along with a galloping "Hide Away." But during the *Getting Ready* sessions, King also recut a definitive version of his 1961 Federal single "I'm Tore Down" and a rendition of Big Bill Broonzy's "Key to the Highway." Both became cornerstones of his subsequent live performances.

King made two more albums for Shelter as he became a fixture of the American and European rock concert circuit. He shared stages with Clapton and Grand Funk Railroad—who name-checked him in "We're An American Band"—and was a regular at the Fillmores East and West. By 1974, when King signed with RSO Records, an affiliation shared with his friend and acolyte Clapton, his days on the chitlin circuit were unquestionably in the past. King's 1974 RSO debut, *Burglar*, named for the Jerry Ragovoy–penned song "She's a Burglar," even featured Clapton and his touring band on the Tom Dowd–produced track "Sugar Sweet." It was followed in 1975 by *Larger Than Life*, which featured a new version of his hit song "Have You Ever Loved a Woman."

Circa 1970

**"ALL I COULD THINK OF WAS HOW MAD AS HELL HE WAS WHEN ME, MY SISTER AND MY BROTHER WERE RUNNING AROUND THE APARTMENT AND KNOCKED OVER HIS GOLD-TOP LES PAUL AND THE HEADSTOCK BROKE OFF."**
—*WANDA KING*

As King entered the ranks of rock stardom, he kept his family a priority. "Whenever there was a break of a couple days in touring, he would hop a plane and fly home," says Lewis Stephens, who played piano in King's band from September 1973 to October 1976.

"When he was home he'd take all of us kids fishing," Wanda adds. "He had 10 fishing rods and reels, so we'd all have our own line. Before he bought a boat, we'd go to a fishing barge that had a restroom in it, and he'd keep us out all night. It was so much fun."

Wanda says her father used to talk about Clapton, Led Zeppelin, Peter Green and the other young white players who were his blues acolytes with pleasure and respect. "He enjoyed that they understood what he did and embraced him, and that they were taking the blues and his music forward. He was proud of them."

On the road, King took great delight in beating almost everyone at poker. "He used to love taking money off of people, like Clapton and the guys in the band," Stephens says. "A couple times I saw band members sign the pay book and then turn around and give the money back to Freddie. He was a good poker player, and I watched him play for about a year before I would join the games. He played all kinds of crazy Chicago games with 13 wild cards. Sometimes you'd need six aces to win."

But onstage, King was all business. "I was playing with the Texas rock band Nitzinger, and they'd broken up," Stephens says. "Our manger also worked with Freddie and he asked me if I wanted to be in his band. He gave me the three Shelter Records and told me to learn them in a week. My first gig was an outdoor show for 20,000 in Atlanta. I met Freddie at the top of the stairs just as we were about to go onstage, and it was, 'One, two, three, go!' I was just 18, so I got my education from Freddie.

When King and his group weren't jetting to concerts and festivals in Europe, they traveled in the used GM bus that had replaced the Oldsmobile station wagon years earlier. "When I first joined, it just had seats," Stephens says. "Then Freddie had some work done on it so there was a big bed in the middle, and later he had it redesigned again for bunks. Freddie always put retread tires on it. Those retreads would always let go driving through the heat of the South. I have many pictures of the bus on the side of the road and the band loading all the gear into U-Hauls to get to the gigs."

Although stories of cocaine-and-alcohol-fueled days and nights are part of King's mythology, Stephens notes, "I never saw Freddie pass up a meal in favor of a drink."

Indeed, King cut a full and imposing figure until the end. The performances he continued to deliver for 300 nights a year as he reached the zenith of his popularity gave no indication that his health was failing. Yet nearly two decades of relentless touring and hard living had taken a toll. On December 28, 1976, he died in Dallas, Texas, leaving behind a catalog of recordings that continues to enshrine his legend and inspire new generations with his nearly incomparable energy, originality and artistry. ◆

# GODDAMN ELECTRIC

*Guitar World* looks back on the life and times of Dimebag Darrell, the original cowboy from hell whose explosive style and live-wire personality forever changed the face of heavy metal guitar.

BY CHRIS GILL

DIMEBAG DARRELL 1966–2004

# AS A GUITARIST, DIMEBAG

Darrell was larger than life. Onstage and in the studio with his bands Pantera and Damageplan, Darrell played precision riffs and dazzling solos that earned him a reputation as one of hard rock and metal's greatest guitarists.

He consistently earned multiple honors in *Guitar World*'s annual readers poll, and the magazine's editors regularly placed him on their lists of honorees, including the Top 10 Metal Guitarists of All Time, the 100 Most Important People in Guitar and the 100 Greatest Guitarists of All Time. It's possible his name or photo has appeared in every issue of *Guitar World* since 1992.

Yet, despite the accolades, Dimebag Darrell remained the genuine, down-to-earth person he'd always been. He made himself accessible to his fans at every opportunity, never leaving an in-store appearance, autograph session or backstage meet-and-greet until every person got to say hello, shake his hand and maybe share a drink or two. Perhaps that's because Darrell was himself still a fan at heart. He could often be seen in the audience at shows by his favorite performers, which included Metallica, Kiss and Ozzy Osbourne, rocking out and banging his head like anyone else. He knew that a little of his time meant everything to those who loved the music he made.

So it is for the man, as well as his music, that we mourn his passing. Dimebag Darrell Abbott's murder on December 8, 2004, robs us all not only of the music he played and would have gone on to play; it also deprives us of the joy and pleasure we took in the company of his spirit. Dimebag Darrell was a rare figure in rock music, a star with a big heart and a dose of humility. It's no wonder he left an indelible impression on everyone who spent time with him. Mention Dimebag to a group of metal fans and someone will inevitably have an outrageous story to share. His joy of life, playful sense of humor and enthusiastic love of music made him a person everyone wanted to be around, a friend to all. Which is why, wherever Dimebag went, the party was certain to follow.

Born Darrell Lance Abbott on August 20, 1966, Dimebag grew up surrounded by music. His father, Jerry Abbott, is a professional country musician who owns a recording studio and played piano on numerous sessions, including 1998's *Prince of Egypt* soundtrack. He also composed songs that were recorded by Buck Owens, Freddy Fender, Moe Bandy and Bobby Vinton. Although Dimebag's father didn't push Darrell into music, neither did he discourage him from learning how to play.

"The opportunity to become a musician was always there," the guitarist told Brad Tolinski in the April 1994 issue of *Guitar World*, which featured Darrell's first cover interview. "I can remember one birthday where he said, 'Son, you can either have a BMX bike or you can have *this*,' and he pointed to a guitar. I ended up taking the bike, but he did plant a seed in my mind."

The lure of rock and roll proved too tough for Darrell to resist, however; once he discovered the music of Kiss and Black Sabbath, there was no turning back. "I went back to my old man and asked if I could trade my bike back for the guitar. [*But*] I didn't get my first guitar until my next birthday. I was about 11, and he gave me a Les Paul copy and a Pignose amp."

> **"DARRELL WAS BANNED FROM EVERY GUITAR COMPETITION BY THE TIME HE WAS 18 BECAUSE HE ALREADY WON 'EM ALL."**
>
> —BUDDY BLAZE, FRIEND AND GUITARIST

Darrell initially taught himself to play Deep Purple's "Smoke on the Water." Then his dad showed him how to play barre chords. "That's when things really started getting heavy," he recalled. "The turning point came when I discovered an Electro-Harmonix Big Muff fuzz. *Feedback! Distortion!* Dude, that was *all* she wrote."

Darrell progressed quickly as a player, and in 1980, at the age of 14, he entered his first guitar competition. Ricky Lynn Gregg, who worked with Darrell's dad in the studio and performed with numerous groups before he became an acclaimed country-rock solo artist in the Nineties, recalls judging that contest: "Darrell was destined to become a superstar. Kim Davis of [*southern rock band*] Point Blank, Dean Guitars' [*founder*] Dean Zelinsky and I were judges at this contest that was held at the Agora, which was the top rock club in Dallas at the time. There were 10 other contestants, who ranged in age from 19 to 35 years old. Then this 14-year-old kid who called himself Diamond Darrell went on last. He started off with some licks of his own and then played 'Eruption' in its entirety, note for note. Dean looked at me and said, 'It's a shoe-in. He's the winner.' Darrell wasn't even finished yet; he went into his own thing that blew us all away. He was a maniac virtuoso, even way back then."

Darrell's prize was a Dean ML guitar, which became his signature ax from that day on. Two years later, when he was 16, he sold the guitar to raise money to buy a car. The Dean wound up in the hands of guitarist Buddy Blaze, who had the instrument custom painted with a blue finish and white lightning bolts. "Later, I got to know Buddy, and I used to beg him to sell me back my guitar," Darrell recalled for *Guitar World*. "He would always refuse. He was going to put together another guitar for me in exchange for a Flying V that I had. I gave him the V, and a month went by, and Buddy just couldn't seem to find the time to put the ax together for me. One day he showed up on my doorstep with a box. I opened it up and inside was the Dean. He said, 'Dude, it was your prize to begin with. Here you go.'"

Blaze and Darrell's friendship contin-

Young Darrell onstage in Dallas, in 1983

STUART TAYLOR/FRANK WHITE

ued. When Darrell was interviewed for his first guitar magazine interview, published in *Guitar World*'s December 1990 issue, Blaze testified to the guitarist's previous glories. "Darrell was banned from every guitar competition by the time he was 18 because he already won 'em all," Blaze told *GW*'s Joe Lalaina. "Every hard rock band in the state was compared to Pantera and every guitarist compared to Darrell."

Even in their early incarnation, Pantera were setting the bar high. Darrell and his brother "Vinnie Paul" Abbott formed the group in 1981, when Darrell was only 15. Recruiting bassist Rex Brown and singer Terry Glaze, they recorded their first album, *Metal Magic*, in 1983, and released it on their own independent label. The group recorded two more albums, *Projects in the Jungle* (1984) and *I Am the Night* (1985), before Glaze exited and formed the glam-metal group Lord Tracy. Darrell, Vinnie and Rex replaced him with singer Phil Anselmo and adopted a harder sound. While the first three Pantera albums sounded like a heavier version of early Eighties glam rock, Pantera's first album with Anselmo, 1988's *Power Metal*, bore a closer resemblance to late-Seventies Judas Priest.

On the strength of that album, Atlantic Records' East West subsidiary signed Pantera to a record deal, which resulted in the band's major-label debut, *Cowboys from Hell*. Released in July 1990, the album displayed a tougher sound that bore the influence of Eighties thrash metal bands like Metallica, Slayer and Megadeth. (Significantly, Darrell had been offered the lead guitar spot in Megadeth but lost the gig when he insisted they hire Vinnie Paul to be the band's drummer.) Thanks to airplay on Los Angeles' legendary hard rock station KNAC, metal fans throughout the country soon learned about these newcomers from Texas and their fresh new sound, which effectively bridged the gaps between hair metal, thrash, hardcore and industrial.

In the early Nineties, when the bands that influenced Pantera's new direction began softening their sounds, Darrell and company made theirs heavier than ever. "We look at our music as ball-busting, gut-wrenching heavy *whatever*," Darrell said in 1990. "We're a superaggressive band and all our songs are meant to be played live. We play a new groove—we call it 'power groove.' We're like fine-tuned, clean-cutting machinery. After listening to *Cowboys from Hell*, you'll view the world with a bigger pair of balls. The album makes you another foot taller and gives you crushing, go-for-it power."

Always willing to share his techniques and tips with other guitarists, Darrell, still going by the moniker of Diamond Darrell, agreed to be interviewed by *Guitar World* for an exclusive lesson—his first—in the September 1991 issue. Shortly after it appeared, Darrell sat down for his first Q&A interview with *Guitar World*, which appeared in the April 1992 issue. In it, he discussed Pantera's *A Vulgar Display of Power* album, which featured the Pantera favorites "Walk" and "Fucking Hostile." He also revealed a wide range of influences that included Ace Frehley, Randy Rhoads and Eddie Van Halen.

Most notably, though, he used the opportunity to discuss players he admired, whose impact might not have been felt by the readers but whom he nevertheless wanted to acknowledge. "I'm from Texas, dude," said Darrell. "There are so many people who, overnight, claim they play bluesy, but I grew up down here watchin' dudes play with my dad. I used to come home from school and watch all these incredible players goin' through their chops—Jimmy Wallace, Bugs Henderson, Ricky Lynn Gregg. They're not known very much outside of Dallas, but they're all incredible—and seeing them play had a hell of an influence on me. And, of course,

STUART TAYLOR/FRANK WHITE PHOTO AGENCY

Pantera in the late Eighties

there's the Reverend G—Billy Gibbons. We've seen him more than once at clubs and stuff."

The interview also marked the first time Darrell let the public know that, henceforth, he preferred to be called Dimebag. "People have been calling me *Diamond* Darrell for too long," he said. "It's a mistake. I've always been called Dimebag Darrell by my friends. That's my real name. Dimebag Darrell—got it?"

Although Dimebag received a fifth-place Best New Talent nod in *Guitar World*'s 1991 Readers Poll, the following year he took third for Best Heavy Metal Guitarist and fourth in the Best New Talent category. Pantera, meanwhile, took second for Best Heavy Metal Album with *A Vulgar Display of Power*. The results appeared in the March 1993 Future Shock issue, the first of many *Guitar World* issues to feature Dimebag's photo on the cover.

His 1991 *GW* lesson marked the beginning of a beautiful friendship that eventually led to Dime's long-running monthly instructional column, Riffer Madness. Debuting in the April 1993 issue, the column was a favorite with readers, who were shown how to play everything from the main riff to "Cowboys from Hell" to the harmonic squeals in "Cemetery Gates." From his first column, Dimebag was an enthusiastic contributor. "When the guys at *Guitar World* asked me to do a column for 'em, my immediate reaction was two four-letter words: HELL YEAH!!" he wrote in his debut column. Dime's sense of humor and generosity made Riffer Madness a must-read. Among the many highlights was his offer to buy a six-pack of beer for each of the first 50 readers to master his lesson in natural harmonics.

Throughout this time, Pantera's rise continued. Their third album, *Far Beyond Driven*, stunned the music world by debuting at No. 1 on the *Billboard* magazine Top 200 album chart upon the record's release in 1994. By then, Dimebag had earned enough acclaim to appear by himself on *Guitar World*'s April 1994 cover, which rightly billed him as the World's Most Dangerous Guitarist. "At the epicenter of Pantera's musical mosh pit is the band's larger-than-life guitarist, Dimebag Darrell," Tolinski wrote in the cover story. "His trademark crimson goatee, custom guitar and colorful command of good-ol'-boy slang has made him a hero among hard rock fans. But his bone-rattling rhythm work, inventive soloing and distinctive razor-sharp 'Darrell tone' is what has made him a legend among a whole generation of guitarists searching for a new Edward Van Halen. And like Van Halen, the key to the Texan's large talent is his healthy disregard for rules and regulations."

> "THIS 14-YEAR-OLD KID WHO CALLED HIMSELF DIAMOND DARRELL WENT ON LAST. **HE STARTED OFF WITH SOME LICKS OF HIS OWN AND THEN PLAYED 'ERUPTION' IN ITS ENTIRETY**, NOTE FOR NOTE."
>
> *—RICKY LYNN GREGG, MUSICIAN AND FAMILY FRIEND*

"The story of Vinnie and me is almost identical to the Van Halen story," Dime said in the accompanying interview. "Both Eddie and Alex played drums at first, but Alex killed, so Eddie decided to pick up the guitar. The same thing happened with Vinnie and me. I grew up a heavy metal kid, and we are a heavy metal band. I know it's not fashionable, but I'm proud to say that's what we are and what we do. We'll remain true to our roots while shit keeps twisting around us."

Even so, the band had begun making a few subtle changes to its sound. Dimebag played fewer solos on *Far Beyond Driven*, as Pantera preferred to concentrate on skull-crushing grooves. "We're into topping ourselves," Darrell revealed to me in

Pantera in 1994

an interview at the time. "Most bands come out with a heavy record, then they get lighter and lighter. You're stuck listening to the first record, wishing and dreaming. That ain't what we're about, though. We wanted these songs to have the most impact, period. Everything we do is for the band as a whole. It's not like you've got a spotlight lead guitar player in the band. You're going to hear me, Rex, Vinnie, Phil, everybody."

Despite Dimebag's modesty, plenty of people still enjoyed hearing him play blazing leads and searing riffs. "Dimebag Darrell's tone is my favorite of any guitarist I've worked with," once said producer Terry Date, who, in addition to producing and engineering Pantera's first four major-label albums, worked with Soundgarden, White Zombie and Prong. "The thing that's so special about Darrell is he's the only guitarist I've worked with who has played the same guitar since he was like 14 years old. He won't take it off. It's become an appendage. His tone is as familiar as his voice."

When the next Readers Poll appeared in the March 1995 issue, Dimebag took top honors in the categories of Best Heavy Metal Guitarist, Best Solo ("Planet Caravan") and Best Heavy Metal Album (*Far Beyond Driven*). He also took second place in the Most Valuable Player and fourth in the Best Live Band spots. Now at the height of their popularity, Pantera had become a significant influence on modern metal bands such as Deftones, Korn and Godsmack, who were beginning to make rumblings of their own. Dimebag's razor-sharp

tone and machine-like riffing appealed to fans of death metal and industrial music alike, and new bands imitated Pantera's postmodern angst and brutal assault.

But changes were taking place in the mainstream. By 1996, grunge had faded like a worn-out flannel shirt, replaced by a new breed of alternative rock bands, including Smashing Pumpkins, Bush and 311. When Pantera released *The Great Southern Trendkill* that year, the album didn't slay its competitors on the charts. Still, when the group joined a reunited Black Sabbath for 1997's Ozzfest premiere, they stunned audiences with their aggressive, energized performance, proving that Pantera and metal were still forces to be reckoned with.

"Dimebag was such a nice, genuine bloke and a great player," Tony Iommi recalls. "He was always very respectful toward me, and it was lovely to have him on tour with us."

Once again, *Guitar World* readers awarded Dimebag with numerous accolades in the 1996 Readers Poll, the results of which appeared in the March 1997 issue. In addition to being named Most Valuable Player for the second time, Dime was voted the Best Hard Rock/Metal Guitarist and took third place for Best Rock Guitarist and Best Solo ("Floods"). The poll also gave Pantera second-place honors for Best Album (*Trendkill*). Upon receiving the news, Dime responded in his characteristic fashion: "Please tell your readers I'm real flattered and would obviously like to say a big-assed 'thank you' to all of 'em that voted for me."

Readers continued to heap praise on Dimebag the following year when they chose the 100 Greatest Solos of All Time for *GW*'s September 1998 issue, voting for "Floods" (#15), "Cemetery Gates" (#35) and "Walk" (#57). While Dimebag continued to downplay his lead playing, it was obvious that his fans still loved it whenever he broke out some choice solos.

During the four years between *The Great Southern Trendkill* and Pantera's 2000 album *Reinventing the Steel*, the band toured and issued a live album, *Official Live: 101 Proof*. Though Dimebag remarked that the band needed a break, he made it more than obvious in his May 2000 cover interview that he was thrilled to be recording and touring again with Pantera.

"We looked back on all of the good times we had, all the hell raising we've done, and all the kick-ass music we've made," he said. "We fuckin' love what we do. We're happy how we are. We've watched what's gone on around us, and we've been like a steel rod in the center of it all. I'm still the same cat I always was. I don't get all caught up in that rock star shit. I don't sit at home. I go out. I'll hang out with whoever, wherever and whenever, and probably drink them under the table, if I can. If I can't, then I'll have them drive *me* home."

Unfortunately, Pantera's subsequent Ozzfest tour appearance in support of *Reinventing the Steel* turned out to be the band's last. Relations between Anselmo and Dimebag and Vinnie had quickly gone south once the band returned home, and the singer expressed his intent to work with his numerous side projects, like Superjoint Ritual and Down. Dimebag and Vinnie

NEIL ZLOZOWER; STUART TAYLOR/FRANK WHITE

had no choice but to let Anselmo pursue his muse, but by 2003, they were tired of putting their own creative urges on infinite hold. In the March 2003 issue of *Guitar World*, the cover of which featured Dimebag and close friend Zakk Wylde, Darrell made the announcement that Pantera had broken up. (Rex Brown decided to follow Anselmo and work with Down.)

In the following March issue, in a *GW* cover story interview conducted by longtime friend Nick Bowcott, Dimebag introduced his and Vinnie's new band, Damageplan. He also opened up about the problems that led to Pantera's demise. "I don't like to have to go into this at all, but I'm gonna step up to the plate and tell the truth," Dimebag confessed. "I firmly believe that Pantera fans deserve an honest answer about what went down and broke this thing apart. They've been awesome to us, and I want to let them know first and foremost that me and my brother *never* let them down. We're embarrassed about what happened, but we had no control over it. We tried every goddamned angle we could to make things right, but we couldn't. It crushed the shit out of us and took two prime years out of our careers, but at this point it's totally out of our hands—so we've accepted it and moved on.

"The main reason Vinnie and me waited around for so long and tried so hard to make it work was because we wanted to do Pantera forever. We were the heart and soul of that band, and it meant everything to us. We honestly thought we were going to be the Rolling Stones of heavy metal. Then I got the time to sit back, look at the band, reflect on it and go 'Damn, look what it's headed for!' Sometimes, when you're driving 150 miles an hour, you don't have time to see the wall you're about to smash into."

**"SOMETIMES, WHEN YOU'RE DRIVING 150 MILES AN HOUR, YOU DON'T HAVE TIME TO SEE THE WALL YOU'RE ABOUT TO SMASH INTO."**
—DIMEBAG DARELL, 2003

Damageplan's debut album, *New Found Power*, didn't sell as well as Pantera releases, but Dimebag enjoyed his new creative outlet. He was enthusiastic and excited about the numerous opportunities that seemed to reach out to him from around every corner. He renewed his relationship with Dean guitars, which he originally endorsed up until 1994, and was at work on new guitar designs with Dean's. "Seeing Dime onstage with a Dean in his hands again brought back feelings I thought were gone forever," says Zelinsky.

Dimebag also started using Krank amplifiers, and his new rig made him anxious to get back in the studio to record the second Damageplan album. "I plug straight into the Krank and let it blaze," he said. "This amp puts the fun back into playing for me."

In early December 2004, having finished a coheadlining tour with Shadows Fall, Damageplan were making their way back to Texas, where they planned to start recording new tracks. A handful of shows had been booked for the route home, including a December 8 date at the Alrosa Villa, a nightclub in a seedy area of Columbus, Ohio. On the night of the gig, as Damageplan launched into the first song of their performance, 25-year-old Nathan Gale climbed onto the stage brandishing a 9mm handgun and murdered Dimebag Darrell before hundreds of fans and his stunned bandmates.

Immersed in his performance, Dimebag perhaps never saw the fate about to befall him. As sad and senseless as his murder was, Dimebag left this earth doing the one thing that gave him the most joy: playing his guitar to a crowd of people who appreciated his remarkable gift and loved him for the unique, loving and giving individual he was. He died with his boots on, as did so many other hell-raising cowboys who plied their art in the untamed wild. Dimebag Darrell was the original cowboy from hell. There will never be another like him.

*"All of us hit a point in life where we need resurrecting, and it's up to you to make it happen, straighten things out and let go of the things that are fucked up. Where I sit, man, I'll never quit—I love music and I love the fans too much. So I put on my badass shoes and started kicking ass with this band. It's been a lot of hard work to crawl out of the hole, and it hasn't been easy, but at this point I've got my family, my brotherhood, my music and a crushing new band. I've got everything back that was taken from me, and I'm in a good fucking place. What was once a miserable nightmare has bloomed into a very sweet, comfortable place. Amen!" —Dimebag Darrell,* Guitar World, *March 2004* ◆

Frank Zappa at Utility Muffin Research Kitchen, his home studio in Laurel Canyon, 1982

# PERFECTLY FRANK

The life and times of Frank Zappa—composer, satirist and towering giant of the electric guitar.

BY ALAN DI PERNA

FRANK ZAPPA 1940–1993

## "THERE'S NO SINGLE IDEAL listener out there who likes my orchestral music, my guitar albums and songs like 'Dyna-Moe-Hum,' " Frank Zappa told me in 1988. "That's why sometimes I'll do an orchestral album, and the people who like guitar stuff can't stand it. And then a guitar album comes out, and the people who liked the orchestral album can't stand *that*. But you know, they're all my friends in their own way. So why not accommodate them all?"

Now that Frank is gone, it's somehow comforting to reread those words. Frank Vincent Zappa was notoriously intolerant of the imperfections in human nature. With a few curt remarks, he could decimate an audience member foolish enough to shout out a song request, or a journalist presumptuous enough to concoct a half-assed theory about him. Yet he was willing to consider all of us who love his music as "friends."

There are rabid Zappa fanatics out there who would insist that it *is* possible for one person to admire Zappa's knotty, inventive orchestral compositions, his honking, brilliant guitar work *and* the prickly combination of sociology, satire and schoolboy scatological that went into his song lyrics. But it's no small undertaking. Frank Zappa's 60-album oeuvre is an imposing body of work. Some of the records are better than others, but the overall quality level is astonishingly high. Unlike many of his contemporaries, Zappa was still in top creative form at age 52, when he succumbed to prostate cancer—on December 4, 1993—after battling the disease for several years.

We'll never know what he would have achieved had he lived another 20 or 30 years. But we can console ourselves with the fact that, in the brief time allotted to him, he accomplished far more than most humans. Beyond his having been a superb composer and musician, Frank Zappa was also a committed and capable political activist, an innovative filmmaker, able businessman and one of our century's all-around *bona fide* smart guys. He raised rock's IQ more than a few notches.

### FRANK'S FIRST STEPS

"SCIENTISTS BELIEVE THAT the universe is made of hydrogen, because they claim it's the most plentiful ingredient. I claim that the most plentiful ingredient is stupidity." That's what Zappa said in an interview, just a few months before his death, with *Pulse!* magazine's Dan Ouellette. The "hydrogen" quote was one of Frank's favorites; it cropped up a lot in interviews down through the years. And in many ways, Zappa's whole life was a battle against stupidity—the stupidity of mass media conformity, the stupidity of greedy, inept, ignoble government, the stupidity of thinking it's *cool* to be stupid.

Frank liked facts, so here are a few now: He was born on December 21, 1940, in Baltimore, Maryland. When he was around 10 his family moved to the dismal suburban environs of Lancaster, California. There, he became interested in two strangely dissimilar forms of music: the black R&B and blues sounds of the day, and the early 20th century avant garde compositions of Edgard Varese, Anton Webern and Igor Stravinsky. Both influences can be heard throughout his music. But his blues inspiration is most strongly felt in his guitar work. In 1988, he told me about one of the key experiences of his youth:

"It was when I first heard the guitar solo in 'Three Hours Past Midnight,' by Johnny 'Guitar' Watson. That's probably one of the most important musical statements I ever heard in my life. And also the guitar solos on 'I Got Something for You' and 'The Story of My Blues,' by Guitar Slim. And 'Lover Man' by Wes Montgomery."

Another blues artist influenced Zappa in a way that is often overlooked. In a 1980 interview for *Trouser Press*, Frank told Michael Bloom that he first grew his trademark goatee and mustache because he "thought it looked good on bluesman Johnny Otis."

As a teenager, Zappa played drums and guitar in a variety of local R&B hands. By the time he reached his early twenties, he'd owned and operated his own recording studio (Studio Z), composed B-movie scores, tried his own hand at filmmaking and co-authored a doo-wop tune called "Memories of El Monte," which was recorded by the Penguins. Around 1964, Zappa took control of the R&B bar band he was then playing with—the Soul Giants—persuading them to try some songs he'd written. He also changed the name of the band to the Mothers, an event of incalculable sociological importance.

The Mothers came into their own on the mid Sixties Los Angeles freak scene. It is generally accepted that hippiedom began in San Francisco. "But the scene in Los Angeles was far more bizarre," Frank wrote in his autobiography, *The Real Frank Zappa Book* (1989). It was the L.A. underground that gave birth to the Doors, the Byrds, the Seeds and several other fine bands whose names have not become part of Official Rock History. Needless to say, the Mothers were far weirder than any of these acts.

In an era when even the "dangerous" rock bands were still pretty clean and cute, the Mothers were unkempt and ugly, and some of them would very obviously never see 25 again. The wild melange of sounds they generated included some decidedly

**_FREAK OUT!_ IS GENERALLY CONSIDERED THE FIRST "CONCEPT ALBUM" AND ALSO THE FIRST DOUBLE ALBUM IN ROCK. IT CONTAINS THE SEEDS OF ALL ZAPPA'S LATER WORK.**

JAN PERSSON/REDFERNS/GETTY IMAGES

Zappa and The Mothers of Invention in Copenhagen, Denmark, 1968

IAN PERSSON/REDFERNS/GETTY IMAGES

unfashionable musical styles like doo-wop and lounge jazz. But at this particular juncture in cultural history, the weirder something was, the better it was generally esteemed to be. This was one of those times when record companies couldn't figure out what the hell was going on with "those crazy kids" and their music, so they were signing all kinds of interesting acts with "no commercial potential." This included the Mothers, who were offered a contract with MGM's Verve label.

## FREAKING OUT THE WORLD

**NINETEEN SIXTY-SIX** saw the release of *Freak Out!*, the debut album by the Mothers of Invention. (The record company suggested adding "of Invention" to the band's name, since the word "Mothers" by itself sounded too close to the popular shortened form of "motherfucker," which—for reasons too complex to detail here—was a very potent word in the hippie counterculture of the mid to late Sixties.) By any reckoning, *Freak Out!* is one of the most influential rock albums of all time. It is generally considered the first "concept album" and also the first double album in rock. It contains the seeds of all Zappa's later work. The first two sides are devoted to songs—satirical, humorous, angry, topical, carefully and resourcefully arranged songs, played with exacting precision. On the second disc, the presentation grows increasingly free-form, culminating in "The Return of the Son of Monster Magnet." This piece takes up all of side four (pretty revolutionary in '66) and offers an aural glimpse of "what freaks sound like when you turn them loose in a recording studio at one o'clock in the morning on $500 worth of rented percussion equipment," to quote Zappa's liner notes.

*Freak Out!* and the Mothers' subsequent Verve albums did much to establish the Zappa mythology. Frank's log cabin home at 2401 Laurel Canyon Blvd., in an L.A. neighborhood heavily populated by rock stars, assumed Olympian proportions in the minds of his fans. John Mayall even wrote a song about his stay there. Frank's friends and associates—who bore names like Suzy Creamcheese, Dakota and Motorhead—acquired the larger-than-life stature of Zeus, Hera, Pan and Aphrodite to a generation of suburban teenage misfits. These youths felt tremendously empowered by *Freak Out!*, and its implication that not only was it okay to be a bit strange, frizzy-haired, unpopular and a little too intelligent, it was positively *cool*. But not everything about the Zappa myth was pleasing to the man at its center. *Freak Out!* almost instantly acquired a reputation as the Number One Album to Take Drugs To, much to the chagrin of its composer, who was resolutely straight all his life.

> **EVEN TODAY, TRACKS LIKE "MAGIC FINGERS" AND "MYSTERY ROACH" STAND UP AS STERLING EXAMPLES OF MASTODON UNISON RIFFOLOGY AND EXTENDED FRETBOARD EXPLORATION.**

By 1967, Zappa and the Mothers had migrated to New York, where they began their now-legendary six-month residence at the Garrick Theatre in Greenwich Village. The Mothers basically moved into this decaying old 300-seater, doing two shows a night. Nobody could be certain in advance what was going to occur on any given evening. Jimi Hendrix was one of the notable musicians who came down to jam. But in many ways, it was the audience who often provided the real entertainment. Here, during the height of the Vietnam War, Zappa one night convinced three drunken Marines to attack a baby doll with a bayonet onstage.

According to eyewitnesses, the ensuing spectacle made a more powerful anti-war statement than any protest song or political speech ever could.

These "audience participation" segments were to become a popular element of Zappa concerts throughout his career. There's something completely emblematic of his work in the contrast between the perfectionist discipline of his music and his willingness to entrust a portion of his con-

certs to some inebriated schmoes randomly selected from the crowd. It's as though he wanted, not to *impose* order on chaos, but to *incorporate* chaos into the ordered perfection of his art. If the universe was gonna insist on being inherently stupid, Zappa was determined to find some positive, creative use for all that stupidity.

His entrepreneurial energies were boundless. 1967 also saw the release of his first solo album, *Lumpy Gravy*. The following year, after his relationship with Verve ended, he started two record labels of his own: Bizarre and Straight, both distributed by Warner/Reprise. Straight was Zappa's label for presenting new talents he had discovered. It was Frank Zappa who brought the world the first recordings by Captain Beefheart and Alice Cooper, as well as less-well-remembered artists like folksinger Tim Buckley, the aptly named Wild Man Fischer and the GTOs. The last was a vocal ensemble comprised of Hollywood scenemakers—including kiss-and-tell rock diarist Pamela Des Barres—who apparently had enough "pull" to entice talents like Jeff Beck and Rod Stewart to perform on their disc.

Bizarre was the label for the Mothers' own records. The first to appear on the new imprint was 1968's *Uncle Meat*. This double-album set is another landmark Zappa work, exhibiting a compositional flair and a gift for woodwind arrangement that far exceeded anything that had come before. The liner notes describe this record as "an album of music from a movie you will probably never get to see." Which was almost true. It took the invention of the VCR and the formation of Zappa's own Honker Video company in the Eighties for the world to see this bizarre cinematic document of the Mothers' first incarnation.

## MY GUITAR WANTS TO KILL YOUR MAMA: ZAPPA IN THE SEVENTIES

**ZAPPA HAD NEVER** abandoned the interest in moviemaking that he developed back in his pre-Mothers Studio Z days. But it wasn't until 1971 that he was able to get a film into commercial release. This was *200 Motels*, a surrealistic inquest into the proposition that "touring can make you crazy." *200 Motels* deserves a place in film history because of the video editing and effects techniques that Zappa pioneered in making it. Also, it has become a perennial favorite among zonked-out midnight-movie patrons everywhere.

The accompanying soundtrack album is an essential Zappa work for several reasons. For one, it fully exploited the considerable capabilities of the new Mothers of Invention lineup that Zappa had debuted on the previous year's album, *Chunga's Revenge*. Zappa disbanded the original Mothers in 1969, largely for economic reasons. (By this point, by the way, he was firmly ensconced back in Los Angeles.) The newly formed Mothers were fronted by humorists/vocalists Howard Kaylan and Mark Volman, formerly of the mid Sixties teen pop group, the Turtles. The lineup also included jazz piano ace George Duke and British drummer Aynsley Dunbar, fresh from a stint with John Mayall's Bluesbreakers. True to form, Zappa had surrounded himself with a fantastically diverse assortment of musical personalities.

*200 Motels* was also the first recording on which Zappa fans got the opportunity to hear his music played by a real symphony orchestra, Britain's Royal Philharmonic, under the baton of Elgar Howarth. In stark Zappa-esque contrast, *200 Motels* was also one of the first albums where Frank played really heavy guitar. Even today, tracks like "Magic Fingers" and "Mystery Roach" stand up as sterling examples of mastodon unison riffology and extended fretboard exploration.

Zappa regarded his guitar solos as a form of "instant composition. It's basically the same intellectual process that I would go through writing music on a piece of paper, except that I don't have to write it down; it gets done right away. But it's really no different. You have a certain amount of time that you're going to fill up by making a piece of music. And you hope that the people who are working with you onstage are also interested in inventing music on the spot. When it works, which is not very often, I'm glad I have a recording truck. I can snag it. Because it's gone after that. That's the only time it exists."

Zappa was incontestably one of the most interesting guitar soloists of all time. His blues grounding gave him an insistent earthiness, while his sense of avant garde, dadaist absurdity pushed him in directions that confounded all expectation. But more than anything else, it was his tone that made him a fiercely distinctive player. His guitar sounded like a gander with a bad sinus condition. He made brilliant use of a wah wah pedal, and was one of the few guitarists of the Seventies and Eighties to exploit the lower strings and fret positions to their full potential. He laughed when I complimented him on this.

"Well, I think most guitarists have a tendency to play in some way like they talk," he said. "And since I'm not much of a squealer—I happen to be a baritone kind of guy—to play on the low strings is a little more in phase with my reality."

Zappa really came into his own as a gonzo guitarist in the Seventies. The decade's inaugural year saw the release of his exquisite, heavily guitar-driven solo album, *Hot Rats*. The same year also brought the Mothers' aforementioned *Chunga's Revenge* and *Weasels Ripped My Flesh*. Both feature some flaming beauties of guitar solos. The latter album includes the original recording of Zappa's ax anthem, "My Guitar Wants to Kill Your Mama."

The lineup in Zappa's bands changed regularly throughout the Seventies and early Eighties. His groups became increasingly polished from a technical standpoint as he found himself more and more able to draw on top session talent and noted players from every field of music. Zappa was a formidable, notoriously demanding bandleader. His band was generally recognized as a hothouse for extremely proficient players; it's alumni include the guitarists Lowell George, Adrian Belew and Steve Vai.

Some fans of the original Mothers felt that Zappa's work had become a little slick at this point. The truth is, however, that he'd always used session players. Examine the liner notes to *Freak Out!* and you'll find studio aces like Carol Kaye—and even Lawrence Welk's guitarist, Neil Le Vang—clearly credited. Frank never paid much attention to his musicians' underground credibility. Original Mothers fans also tended to find Kaylan and Volman's brand of humor a little too broad, obvious and infantile. A new legion of fans, however, liked it just fine.

What *did* happen during the Seventies is that Zappa's albums began growing more "unidirectional." He began sorting out the different strands in his work. His early albums combined satire, serious composition, gross-out jokes and jazzy improvisation, all in one gloriously multifaceted package. Later on, he would focus on just one of these elements for any given album.

A record like 1973's *Overnite Sensation* is heavy on humor, whereas *The Grand Wazoo* (1972) is mostly about composition and jazz-based soloing.

## THE HIGHLY SPECIALIZED EIGHTIES

**IN THE EIGHTIES,** Zappa took this trend toward specialization to a new level with the release of the *Shut Up 'N Play Yer Guitar* series, an orgy of guitar solos and nothing else, directed straight at the coterie of Zappa ax junkies. By this point, he had started a new label, *Barking Pumpkin*, and his own marketing/mail order operation, Barfko-Swill, after his deal with Warner/Reprise and a subsequent arrangement with Mercury Records had gone sour. Zappa maintained close ties with his fans. Unlike many rock stars he was highly accessible.

"When we're on the road there are kids who follow us from town to town," he explained in 1988. "If we see the same faces when we arrive at the venue for an afternoon soundcheck, we let them in and they sit through the soundcheck. And you know, I talk to these people. They tell me interesting things. For example, a fan in Germany was the first to point out that there were incorrect dates and locations in the liner notes for *You Can't Do That on Stage Anymore*."

Frank deemed this kind of networking essential in the face of what he regarded as an increasingly incompetent, crooked and imbecilic music industry. Marketing his own music was "the only way I can exist," he told me. "There's no way that what I do can fit within a corporate format. In the United States, radio is a cultural embarrassment. Most of the music that's broadcast is harmful to your mental health."

Onstage in Copenhagen, Denmark, October 1967

JAN PERSSON/REDFERNS/GETTY IMAGES

The early Eighties brought many opportunities for Frank's orchestral and chamber compositions to be recorded and performed. 1983 saw the release of the first *London Symphony Orchestra* disc, which was followed a year later by *The Perfect Stranger: Boulez Conducts Zappa*. During this period, there were also performances of Zappa's music by ensembles such as the Kronos String Quartet and Aspen Wind Quintet. These developments were very gratifying to the composer, who had long sought an outlet for his more serious work. But he entertained no illusions about the classical music power structure. He found it every bit as frustrating and foolish as the pop music industry. Zappa was no snob.

"I have no following or any pretensions to a following in the normal classical consumer environment," he told me in a 1984 interview. "The normal audience for an orchestral piece wouldn't be caught anywhere in the vicinity of what I write. It's just not relevant to their lifestyle, nor is it written for their tastes. Basically, the material is written to amuse me and anybody else who has a similar musical outlook."

Zappa may have found his ideal musical collaborator in the Synclavier computer music system (a high-end music workstation), which also entered his life in the mid Eighties. "What I've been waiting for since I started writing music was a chance to hear what I write played without mistakes and without a bad attitude," he said in 1984. "The Synclavier solves that problem for me."

**"IN THE UNITED STATES, RADIO IS A CULTURAL EMBARRASSMENT. MOST OF THE MUSIC THAT'S BROADCAST IS HARMFUL TO YOUR MENTAL HEALTH."**

—*FRANK ZAPPA*

The Synclavier-based *Jazz from Hell* album won Zappa a Grammy in 1988. He was somewhat obsessed with the device. When I spoke to him in 1988 he estimated that he had some 500 new compositions stored on computer disc: "I work every night on that. My Synclavier hours are usually from about 11:00 at night until 7:00 in the morning." Nocturnal in his work habits, Zappa preferred to be asleep while the rest of the world went about its dubious business.

Frank embraced the digital revolution wholeheartedly. As soon as the Compact Disc format established itself, he threw himself into the monumental task of remastering his entire back catalog for CD release through Rykodisk. Later he embarked on the equally ambitious "Beat the Boots" series for Rhino Records, offering quality masterings of his live concerts as an alternative to the unauthorized bootleg Zappa product that has been flooding the market ever since the Sixties.

The pristine digital perfection of the Synclavier took Zappa entirely away from guitar playing from 1984–'88; he said he didn't touch the instrument once during that period. But in 1988, he assembled a band, its members culled from the cream of the players he'd worked with during the Eighties—including guitarists Ike Willis and "stunt" axman Mike Keneally—for a world tour. The results, which are among Zappa's last public performances on guitar, can be heard on two discs: *Broadway the Hard Way* and *The Greatest Band You Never Heard in Your Life*.

Amid all these projects, Zappa also found time to become a vigorous political activist. In 1985, he testified at the U.S. Senate's "porn rock" hearings. He became one of the most outspoken and eloquent campaigners against the censorship of rock music, a tireless free speech activist and protector of constitutional rights. In 1989, after the collapse of communism in Eastern Europe, Zappa was invited to Czechoslovakia by the country's new president, Vaclav Havel, as an economic advisor. For several months, he acted as the country's economic representative to the West. Zappa was increasingly drawn to politics. It's reported that he was planning a serious presidential campaign.

This was one of many plans that were canceled when he was diagnosed as having prostate cancer in 1990. According to an article in *Pulse!*, the condition had been developing for some eight to 10 years before it was detected. Rumors of Frank's illness began to spread in the music industry shortly after the diagnosis. At first, they were widely disbelieved; it just seemed like another stupid, obviously untrue Frank Zappa story. But when the family confirmed the rumors, there was no more denying the grim fact.

Zappa continued working right up until the end. As a result he was able to see the release of one last recording of his music, *The Yellow Shark*, performed by Frankfurt's Ensemble Modern. This lavish and beautifully realized album reaches all the way back to compositions from *Uncle Meat*—a fitting end to a wondrously rich career.

"I am a realistic kind of guy," Frank told *Guitar World*'s John Swenson in 1982. "I just try and look at things the way they are, take them for what they are, deal with them, and go on to the next case. But Americans thrive on hype and bloated images and bloated everything. They turn away from anything that's realistic. They want the candy gloss version of whatever it is."

And that's the one version that Frank never played. ◆

# THE QUIET STORM

He was the soft-spoken lead guitarist for the Beatles, the world's greatest rock group. But George Harrison's playing shook up the world and helped create guitar rock and roll.

BY ALAN DI PERNA

GEORGE HARRISON 1943–2001

Harrison with the Beatles performing on the *Ed Sullivan Show*, August 14, 1965

# TO THE MILLIONS WHO GREW

up on his music, he was the Quiet Beatle. To the Hamburg teens that in the early Sixties witnessed the Beatles' evolution from crude protopunks to polished professional rock stars, he was the Beautiful One.

But as far as George Harrison was concerned, he could be best described by the name he chose for his record label in the late Seventies: the Dark Horse—the straggler who vaults from behind to win the race.

The choice of title was ironic for Harrison, the Beatles' former lead guitarist, who died of cancer on November 29, 2001. Of the group's four members, he was the one most disinterested in the spoils of stardom, the loner less concerned with winning the race than running it on his own terms. For those who watched as he abandoned the spotlight for a more domestic lifestyle in the Eighties and Nineties, it was hard to know what to make of Harrison; normality, after all, was not what we'd come to expect from a member of the Fab Four, the group that rose out of Liverpool, England, to conquer our senses. Beatles were supposed to be larger than life, yet iconic enough to be describable within a space the size of a postage stamp: guitarist John Lennon was the outspoken radical, bassist Paul McCartney the eager-to-please prodigy and drummer Ringo Starr the happy-go-lucky luminary. Harrison, on the other hand, defied easy definition.

As he noted in 1989, long after his career had passed its zenith, "I don't have to prove anything. I don't want to be in the business full-time, because I'm a gardener: I plant flowers and watch them grow."

He was a lead guitarist first, of course, an ace practitioner of R&B and rockabilly riffs who became the master of his own singularly fluid guitar tone. In this alone he was essential to the Fab Four's success, since neither Lennon nor McCartney possessed his talent on the instrument. More consequential, Harrison's skills as a lead guitarist are what elevated the Beatles from a rhythm-based pop act to a guitar rock group, and it was in this form that they changed popular music permanently: Before the Beatles, few pop groups wrote and performed their own material. After them, no self-respecting band would not.

It was easy to overlook Harrison's significance, for he made no show of it. The youngest of the Beatles, he was, in the group's early days, its most humble member, a young man unguardedly insecure of his talents, who would greet reporters' questions with self-mockery and a large dose of laconic Liverpudlian charisma. When in 1964 he and his shaggy bandmates were asked at their first U.S. press conference when they planned to get haircuts, it was Harrison who impishly replied, "I had one yesterday."

Some six years later, when the Beatles broke up, how those charms seemed to fade. As ex-Fabs go, Harrison seemed the loneliest, a hermit lodged in his mock-Gothic English mansion and hiding behind a mane of hair and squire's beard. No longer required to beguile and amuse, Harrison seemed eager to be taken seriously, and he gave the world good reason to do so. As a solo artist he released what many regard as the best solo Beatles album, 1970's *All Things Must Pass*, and launched a benefit show the following year to help war-ravaged Bangladesh, thus laying the foundation for Live Aid, Farm Aid, Concert for New York City and every other music-oriented charity event since.

**“ GEORGE HIMSELF IS NO MYSTERY. BUT THE MYSTERY OF GEORGE INSIDE IS IMMENSE. ”**

*—JOHN LENNON*

In more recent years, when Harrison's albums came more slowly and his life appeared more monkish, it was hard to remember he was there at all. Having renounced the fame that bloomed from his diligence and talent, Harrison followed a path of solitude few celebrated artists dare to tread. No wonder he remained an enigma to so many, not least his former bandmate John Lennon, who once remarked, "George himself is no mystery. But the mystery of George inside is immense."

To George Harrison, however, those who questioned the complexity of his choices were simply missing the point. "It's good to boogie once in a while," he remarked a few years into his post-Beatles career. "But when you boogie all your life away, it's just a waste of a life and of what we've been given."

George Harrison was born on February 25, 1943, at 12 Arnold Grove, in Liverpool, to Harold and Louise Harrison. The youngest of four children, he was a favorite, doted on by both his mother and siblings, and a source of constant concern to his practical-minded father. Even at a young age, Harrison demonstrated the self-reliant disposition for which he would later become famously known. "George was always very independent," his mother recalled. "He never wanted any assistance of any kind."

Early on, his independence turned to outright rebellion. In 1954, at age 11, he began attending the Liverpool Institute, and although he was a good student, he resisted the school's attempts to mold him and his mates into model citizens. "I hated being dictated to," he said. "That's when things go wrong, when you're quietly growing up and they start trying to force being part of society down your throat. I was just trying to be myself. They were trying to turn everybody into rows of little toffees."

Harrison rebelled not only by shirking on his schoolwork; he also began to dress outlandishly and to grow his hair out. "George used to go to school with his school cap sitting high on top of his hair," his mother recalled. "And very tight trousers."

"Going in for flash clothes was part of the rebelling," he explained. "I don't know what made me do it, but it worked. They didn't get me."

It was a good time to be a rebel. Rock and

Harrison in Hamburg,
Germany, 1962

roll was on the horizon, and Harrison was already beginning to develop an interest in music through his father's record collection, where he discovered American country artists like Jimmie Rodgers and Hank Williams. "Waiting for a Train" was one of his favorites. "That led me to the guitar," he said.

Harrison received his first instrument—an Egmond acoustic purchased from a fellow student—at the age of 13. As he recalled, "It was a real cheapo horrible little guitar, but it was okay at the time." Harrison received lessons from one of his father's friends for a few hours every Thursday night. Though his skill on the instrument came slowly and with difficulty, he kept at it, sometimes practicing "till his fingers were bleeding," according to his mother.

He eventually got a proper guitar, a Hofner President, with *f*-holes, that was based on the big Super Gibson guitars. "I would sit around for hours, playing and trying to figure things out. I used to sit up late at night. I didn't look on it as practicing, more learning. It was the only thing I really liked."

By 1957, rock music had arrived in England through the records of Elvis Presley, Fats Domino, Little Richard and Buddy Holly. Simultaneously, Great Britain's teens were under the spell of skiffle, a British form of fast country-western folk music played on acoustic guitar, washboard and string bass. The undisputed king of the genre was Lonnie Donegan, a Scottish guitarist whose version of "Rock Island Line" was known to every teenager from Brighton to Aberdeen. "I loved him," recalled Harrison. "He was a big hero of mine. Everyone got guitars and formed skiffle bands because of him."

Among those caught up in the craze was a boy on Harrison's school bus. Paul McCartney was a grade ahead of Harrison, but the two had known each other casually since Harrison's arrival at the Institute. When skiffle hit, their shared interest in the guitar brought them closer together. "Paul came round to my house one evening to look at the guitar manual I had, which I could never work out," said Harrison. "We learned a couple of chords from it and managed to play 'Don't You Rock Me Daddy O' with two chords."

By now, Harrison was good enough to sit in occasionally with local bands. McCartney, however, had actually joined a group. The previous summer, in 1956, he'd attended a fair at Woolton Parish Church, where he saw a skiffle act called the Quarry Men. The band wasn't so good, but the group's leader impressed McCartney enough that he decided to make his acquaintance. "It was John," McCartney recalled. "He was 16 and I was only 14, so he was a big man. I showed him a few more chords he didn't know. Then I left. I felt I'd made an impression, shown them how good I was."

Figuring that McCartney was as good a guitarist as he was, Lennon invited him to join the Quarry Men. Though McCartney showed talent on the instrument, his skills were limited. During one early performance, while attempting a solo on "Twenty Flight Rock," he froze. It was his first and, for many years, last attempt to play lead guitar.

Harrison had no such difficulties. Though only 14 years old, he'd begun to develop lead guitar skills by copying the guitar riffs from records of the day. At McCartney's invitation, he attended a Quarry Men performance in 1958.

"There was this other guitarist in another group that night," Harrison recalled. "He was great. John said if I could play like that, I could join them. I played 'Raunchy' [*a 1957 instrumental hit*] for them, and John said I could join. I was always playing 'Raunchy' for them. We'd be going somewhere on the top of a bus with our guitars and John would shout out, 'Give us 'Raunchy,' George.' "

Lennon, nearly three years Harrison's senior, was slow to accept him into the group. "George was just too young," he recalled. "I didn't want to know him at first." But Lennon was impressed by his talent and saw the potential for the Quarry Men to develop into a stronger group. It probably helped that Harrison taught Lennon some guitar rudiments he severely lacked. "His guitar was cheap, with a little round sound hole," Harrison recalled. "It only had four strings. John didn't even know that guitars should have six strings. He was playing banjo chords, big extended finger chords. I said, 'What are you doing?' He thought that that was how it should be. So we showed him some proper chords—E and A, and all those—and got him to put six strings on his guitar."

Said Lennon, "George wanted to join us because he knew more chords, a lot more than we knew. So we got a lot from him."

But all of Harrison's hours of practice could not compare with the experience he and his bandmates would get playing in the German seaport of Hamburg. By 1960, the skiffle boom had given way to the beat music of American rock groups, and the Beatles—as Harrison, Lennon and McCartney were now known—were among Liverpool's top rock and roll acts. With Lennon's Liverpool Art College friend Stu Sutcliffe on bass and Harrison's friend Pete Best on drums, the group was holding down regular gigs at the Cavern, a Liverpool jazz club that had begun opening its doors to rock acts as beat music grew in popularity. Through a local nightclub owner named Alan Williams, they were invited to play in Hamburg, a town infamous for its rowdy nightlife.

"Before we played Hamburg in 1960 we were very ropy—just keen young kids," Harrison told *Guitar World* in 1997. "As a band, we weren't a unit; we didn't have a clue." Hamburg changed everything for the group. Shoved onto a stage at the Indra and, later, the Kaiserkeller—two of the strip's lower-tier clubs—the five innocents from Liverpool played grueling 10-hour sets. The hard work not only fused the group's sound; it also honed Harrison's guitar-playing skills.

By now playing a solidbody Czech-made Futurama, the youngest Beatle was beginning to develop his own style based on the double-stop leads of Chuck Berry and the countrified licks he'd learned from his favorite guitarist, Carl Perkins. As one of the main artists on the legendary Sun Records label, Perkins had made an impression on Harrison, as well as Lennon and McCartney, with his rapid-fire leads. What's more, Perkins wrote and performed his own material—songs like "Honey Don't" and "Everybody's Trying to be My Baby," and, not least, the rockabilly anthem popularized by fellow Sun artist Elvis Presley, "Blue Suede Shoes."

"Carl Perkins and 'Blue Suede Shoes'—they don't come more perfect than that," said Harrison.

Perkins' guitar work influenced Harrison's playing on many of the Beatles' early recordings. By the time the group—now a four-piece with McCartney on bass and Ringo Starr on drums—had become international celebrities, his clean and sinuous lead guitar work was helping to forge the sound of guitar rock and roll.

But while Harrison was celebrated for his playing, songwriting was—and for years remained—his weak suit. Lennon and McCartney had been writing songs practically from the day they met, but Harrison didn't begin to develop his songwriting talent until after the Beatles' first album, *Please Please Me*. His first effort produced "Don't Bother Me," the minor-key song that appeared on the group's second album, *With the Beatles*, in 1963. "I decided to write a song, just for a laugh," he explained. "I got out my guitar and just played around till a

**"PEOPLE SAY: 'YOU'VE ONLY ONE LIFE.' BUT YOU'VE GOT AS MANY AS YOU LIKE, AND MORE, EVEN ONES YOU DON'T WANT."**

—GEORGE HARRISON

The Beatles leaving Heathrow Airport in 1966 for their final tour of Germany

CUMMINGS ARCHIVES/REDFERNS/GETTY IMAGES

song came. It was a fairly crappy song."

Though his assessment was unduly harsh, it may explain why nearly two years passed before Harrison attempted to write again. When he did, the results were more often than not refreshingly original. "Think for Yourself" and "If I Needed Someone," both from 1965's *Rubber Soul*, have a melodic angularity that's missing from McCartney's lilting melodies and Lennon's harmonically dissonant vocal style. Likewise, "Taxman," the lead track on 1966's *Revolver*, is written with a stingingly personal malevolence previously absent from the Beatles' catalog.

Harrison could also demonstrate striking melodic invention, as he did in the *Revolver* track "I Want to Tell You." The song's disturbing sentiment is neatly underscored by a jarring chord that appears near the end of each verse. Though dissonance is common in today's rock and metal music, it was practically unheard of in popular music prior to "I Want to Tell You."

"That's an E7th with an F on the top, played on the piano," Harrison explained to *Guitar World* in 2001. "I'm really proud of that, because I literally invented that chord. The song was about the frustration we all feel about trying to communicate certain things with just words. I realized the chords I knew at the time just didn't capture that feeling. So after I got the guitar riff, I experimented until I came up with this dissonant chord that really echoed that frustration."

It's not coincidental that Harrison's growing musical expression occurred in the same period that he began taking drugs. Pot and LSD had a profound effect on him, as it did on the other Beatles, drawing him deeper into his psyche and away from the pervasive glare of stardom.

"Around the time of *Rubber Soul* and *Revolver*, I became more...conscious," Harrison recalled in 1997. "Everything we were doing became deeper and more meaningful. All the music started happening for me when I started smoking reefers. I've come out the other end of that now and I don't do it. Instead, you learn to get your own cosmic lightning conductor, and nature supports you. You begin to realize that you are very small, and yet everyone and every grain of sand is very important. You listen deeper, somehow."

It was in this frame of mind that Harrison, in 1965, found himself drawn to Indian music and the spiritual philosophy behind it, a fascination that culminated in 1968 with the Beatles trip to India, where they studied for several weeks under Maharishi Mahesh Yogi, the spiritual leader behind Transcendental Meditation. Harrison's interest in Indian music grew after Lennon asked him to add some sitar to his 1965 song "Norwegian Wood."

"'Norwegian Wood' was the first use of sitar on one of our records," said Harrison, who recalled that "during the filming of *Help!* there were some Indian musicians in a restaurant scene and I first messed around with one then."

The impact on pop music was seismic. Before long, bands like the Rolling Stones, the Byrds and the Hollies were working the instrument into their songs. By 1967, the instrument was so ingrained into psychedelic music that Danelectro was manufacturing several electric sitar models that could be played like a standard guitar.

But while the sitar was a fad for some, it was part of a larger spiritual journey for Harrison. "When I first consciously heard Indian music, it was as if I already knew it. When I was a child we had a crystal radio with long- and shortwave bands and so it's possible I might have already heard some Indian classical music. There was something about it that was very familiar, but at the same time, intellectually, I didn't know what was happening."

Toward the end of 1965, at a friend's suggestion, Harrison purchased an album of

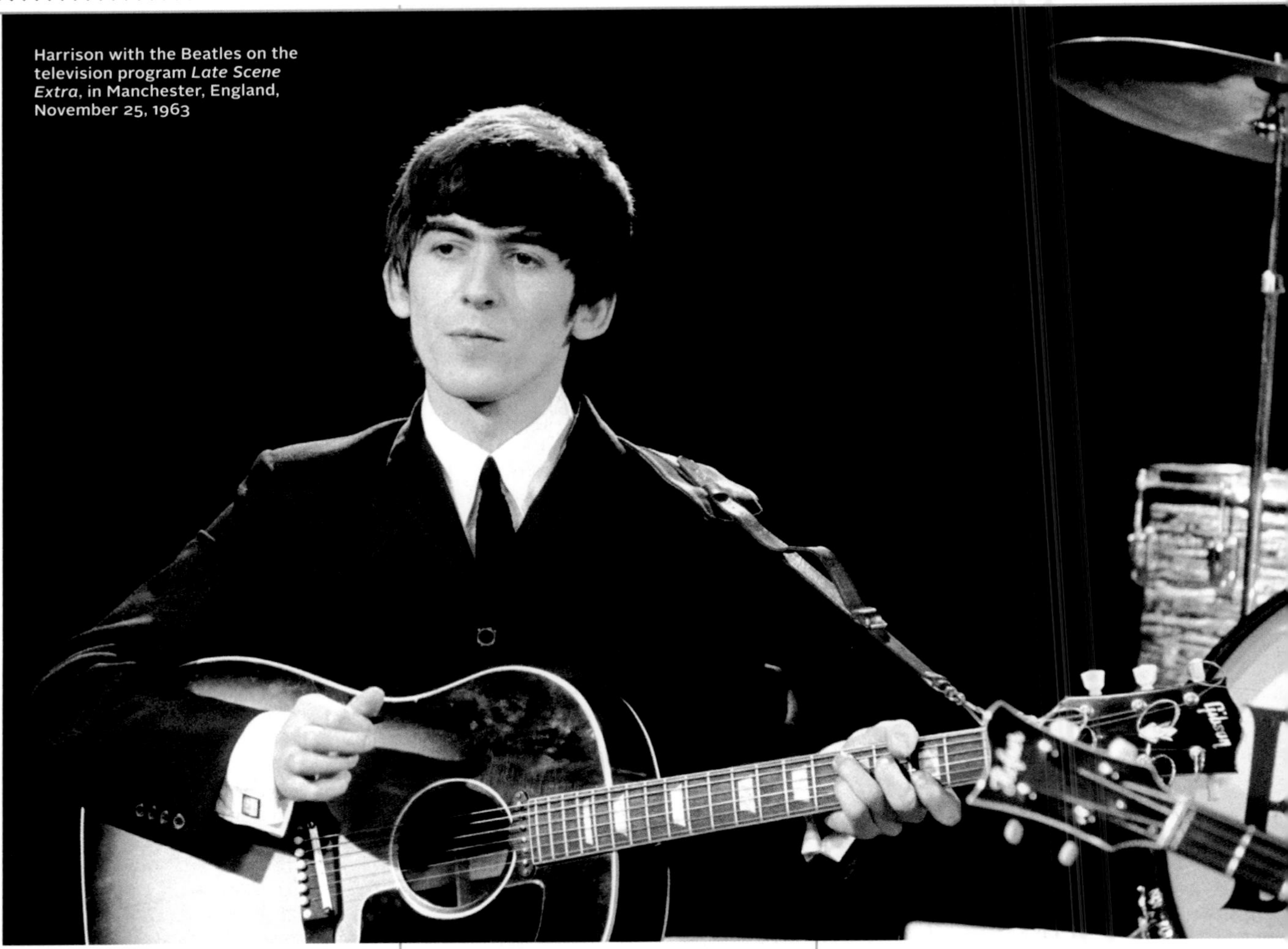

Harrison with the Beatles on the television program *Late Scene Extra*, in Manchester, England, November 25, 1963

BOB THOMAS/GETTY IMAGES

Indian music by sitar master Ravi Shankar. "I went out and bought a record, and that was it," he recalled. "I thought it was incredible." Harrison met Shankar in 1966 during one of the sitarist's London visits, and subsequently received lessons from him. Shankar not only became a lifelong friend of Harrison's but inspired him to pursue writing on the sitar, which resulted in Harrison writing three more songs—"Love You To," "Within You, Without You" and the groundbreaking "Lady Madonna" B-side, "The Inner Light"—that utilized Indian classical instrumentation.

As the Beatles moved into their final years as a band, George Harrison was growing as a musician. Having indulged his interest in Indian music, he began veering off in an entirely new direction with his guitar playing. While his contemporaries like Eric Clapton and Jimmy Page developed a rock style based on traditional blues guitar, Harrison continued to look East for his inspiration. He drew into his guitar-playing style the microtonal slurs and sustaining notes of the sitar and eventually employed a slide to facilitate his technique.

"Whatever you listen to has to come out someway in your guitar playing," Harrison told *Guitar World* in 1997. "I do think Indian music influenced the inflection of how I play, and certain things I play have a similar feeling to the Indian style. Ravi Shankar did bring an Indian musician to my house once who played classical Indian music on a slide guitar. And, yeah, he did play runs that were precise and in perfect pitch but so quick. That was a real inspiration."

The change in Harrison's sound was due not only to his change in technique but to a change in equipment. In the early years of Beatlemania, Harrison mostly wielded a Gretsch Duo Jet and Rickenbacker Chet Atkins Country Gentleman and Tennessean. The warm twanging tones of the acoustic-electric guitars were well suited to the group's combination of rhythm and blues and country-western-inspired music. As of 1965, however, Harrison began to favor solidbody guitars, which delivered greater sustain. From *Rubber Soul* forward his guitars included a Gibson SG Standard, a Fender Stratocaster, a Rosewood Telecaster and a Les Paul given to him by Eric Clapton, his friend since 1964.

As Harrison's guitar style came to maturation in the Beatles' final years, so did his songwriting. Between 1968 and 1970, he wrote some of his best and most popular songs, including "While My Guitar Gently Weeps," "Here Comes the Sun" and, his only Beatles song to be released as a single, "Something." Even so, Harrison still had to compete with Lennon and McCartney to get equal time for his songs.

"It wasn't easy, sometimes, getting up enthusiasm for my songs," he said. "We'd be churning through all this Lennon/McCartney, Lennon/McCartney, Lennon/McCartney. Then I'd say, 'Can we do one of these?' " When the group gave his 1968 masterpiece, "While My Guitar Gently Weeps," a less-than-enthusiastic reception, Harrison put his foot down. "I thought, This is really a good song, it's not as if it's shit.' " The next day, he invited Clapton to accompany the group in the studio to record the track. "Which he did. And everyone behaved and the song came together quite nicely."

But episodes of discord were becoming more frequent, and by 1970 the Beatles were history, torn apart by legal problems and each member's desire for greater autonomy. Even as the band members went their separate ways, it was Lennon and McCartney who continued to command the most attention, quickly releasing solo albums and carrying on a public spat both in the media and in their songs.

So it was a shock when Harrison turned out what is arguably the best—and at its original three-disc length, certainly the longest—solo album by a former Beatle. Released in 1970, *All Things Must Pass* is Harrison's declaration of independence, a surfeit of introspective and quasi-religious songs—including "What Is Life?" "Wah Wah" and his smash debut single, "My Sweet Lord"—that showed how little the Beatles had utilized Harrison's growing talents as a songwriter in their final years.

To help him record this backlog of material, Harrison assembled an all-star backing group that included Eric Clapton, Ringo Starr and producer Phil Spector. Also present was a trio of musicians—keyboardist Bobby Whitlock, bassist Carl Radle and drummer Jim Gordon—who would in the following months join Clapton to record the rock milestone *Layla and Other Assorted Love Songs* under the name Derek and the Dominos.

"I was really a bit paranoid," Harrison said in 1975 about this time period. "There was a lot of negativism going down [*in the Beatles*]. I felt that whatever happened to my solo album, whether it was a flop or a success, I was going out on my own just to have a bit of peace of mind. For me to do my own album after that—it was joyous. Dream of dreams. Even before I started the album, I knew I was going to make a good album because I had so many songs, so much energy."

Swept along by the success of "My Sweet Lord," *All Things Must Pass* reached No. 1 in Britain and the U.S. shortly after its release in late November 1970. From its suggestive title to its cover photo of Harrison surrounded by a quartet of reposing gnomes, *All Things Must Pass* signaled his emergence as a bona fide musician and songwriter.

As 1971 began, George Harrison was everybody's favorite former Beatle. His popularity reached an all-time high in August 1971 with the Concert for Bangladesh, a benefit to raise money for what was then a territory of East Pakistan. A brutal military crackdown had led 10 million of its people to flee for India, resulting in a vast humanitarian crisis. Instigated by Harrison's old friend Ravi Shankar, the Concert for Bangladesh consisted of two benefit shows held on August 2, 1971, at New York City's Madison Square Garden. Among the musicians Harrison recruited were many familiar faces associated with *All Things Must Pass*, as well as one particularly special guest—Bob Dylan.

Harrison had met Dylan on several occasions in the early Sixties, when Dylan was a young folk-rock firebrand. Their bond was forged in 1968, when Harrison paid a visit to Dylan at his home in New York's Catskills. Increasingly private and withdrawn following a nearly fatal motorcycle accident in 1966, Dylan warmed to Harrison, and the two composed "I'd Have You Anytime," one of the many standout tracks on *All Things Must Pass*. Dylan was still keeping a low profile at the time Harrison organized the Concert for Bangladesh, and though he made rehearsals for the show, Harrison didn't know until literally the last moment if Dylan would actually perform at the concerts.

"He never committed himself [*to play*] right up until the moment he came onstage," Harrison recalled. "I had a list, sort of a running order, that I had glued on my guitar.

> **"GEORGE WANTED TO JOIN US BECAUSE HE KNEW MORE CHORDS, A LOT MORE THAN WE KNEW. SO WE GOT A LOT FROM HIM."**
>
> —JOHN LENNON

When I got to the point Bob was going to come on, I had 'Bob' with a question mark. I looked over my shoulder to see if he was around, because if he wasn't I would have to go on to the next bit. And I looked around, and he was so nervous—he had his guitar on and his shades. He was just coming! So I just said, 'My old friend Bob Dylan!' It was only at that moment that I knew for sure he was going to do it. And after the second show he picked me up and hugged me and he said, 'God! If only we'd done three shows!' "

The show and its subsequent concert album and film were a major success, raising 8 to 10 million dollars for the impoverished country. Unfortunately, legal wrangling kept the money tied up in an escrow account for years. Harrison had to comfort himself with the knowledge that he had, at the very least, made Westerners aware of the suffering in Bangladesh and music's potential to improve the human condition.

Surprisingly, what appeared to be a promising solo career for Harrison came slowly to a halt. He was still capable of producing the occasional hit, as he did with "Living in the Material World," "Give Me Love (Give Me Peace on Earth)," "All Those Years Ago" and "Got My Mind Set on You." In 1988, he joined Dylan, Roy Orbison, Tom Petty and the Electric Light Orchestra's Jeff Lynne in the short-lived Traveling Wilburys, and cowrote the group's hit "Handle with Care." But for much of the Seventies and Eighties, Harrison refrained from making music. Instead, he indulged his interest in filmmaking, producing Monty Python's *Life of Brian* and the indie hit *Withnail and I*.

Harrison's last years were spent in semireclusion. He emerged for the Beatles' *Anthology* project, for which he teamed up with McCartney and Starr to record "Real Love" and "Free as a Bird," a pair of songs created from the late John Lennon's rough home demos. Likewise, he helped promote the group's 1999 *Yellow Submarine Songtrack*.

Sadly, in his final years, Harrison garnered headlines for his personal tragedies rather than for his music. In 1999 he was almost murdered by a deranged man who attacked him in his home with a knife and punctured his lung. A longtime smoker, Harrison overcame throat cancer in 1998, but in 2001 it was revealed that he had an inoperable form of brain cancer. Despite attempts to stave off the disease—including last-ditch efforts at radical treatment in New York City and Los Angeles—Harrison succumbed to it on the afternoon of November 29, while at a friend's house in Los Angeles.

It is our good fortune that much of his best work is readily available, including the Beatles' catalog and a selection of his solo albums. Harrison reissued an expanded and remastered version of *All Things Must Pass* in 2001, and a remastered *Concert for Bangladesh* album was posthumously released in 2005.

In the tributes that followed his death, George Harrison was mourned as a gifted guitarist and musician, as a charitable man of God, and as one who, at 58, died too young. Undoubtedly, Harrison in his last days drew from the well of Indian religious philosophy that had given him strength and faith throughout much of his life. Over the years, he spoke many times of his belief in reincarnation and the grace with which he hoped to meet his fate. To those grieve who his demise, Harrison might have offered this passage from his 1980 autobiography, *I Me Mine*:

"Funny how people say: 'You've only one life, Squire.' I've given up saying 'You've got as many as you like, and more, even ones you don't want.' But it's true. We have." ◆

# THE BALLAD OF JOHN

Yoko Ono and some of John Lennon's closest collaborators examine the solo career of the man who taught the world to imagine.

BY ALAN DI PERNA

JOHN LENNON 1940–1980

John Lennon in 1967

## A MOOD OF ANTICIPATION

surrounded the December 1970 release of John Lennon's first solo album. The Beatles had just disbanded, and the Summer of Love had given way to a winter of political discontent as the Vietnam War raged on. Lennon had recently divorced his first wife, Cynthia, and married avant-garde artist Yoko Ono. Nothing less than a major statement was expected from the man who had always been considered the Beatles' resident intellectual.

And Lennon delivered. *John Lennon/ Plastic Ono Band* opens on a suitably dramatic note: with the ominous tolling of church bells. A death knell for the Beatles? For the Sixties? Perhaps the bells are meant to recall a death that devastated John Lennon when he was 17 years old. Over pealing piano chords, John's plaintive voice sings one of the most momentous opening lines in all of rock: "Mother, you had me, but I never had you."

The naked emotional force of these words jolted through rock culture like an electric current. Every self-respecting Beatles fan knew Lennon's story. How his parents had divorced at an early age and how he'd been raised by his aunt. How his mother Julia was killed in an automobile accident just as John was becoming close to her once again. But to hear him sing about all this was painful. The coda, in which Lennon repeatedly screams "Mama don't go, Daddy come home," was particularly disquieting. No rock lyric had cut that close to real life before.

Many songs on the *Plastic Ono Band* album were a direct outgrowth of primal scream therapy, an intensive course of psychological treatment, which John and Yoko underwent in 1970. Patients who go through the therapy are led through a process of shedding their layers of psychological defenses and confronting the unresolved crises of their early lives by literally "screaming the pain away." The *Plastic Ono Band* album is primal scream therapy transformed as art.

"It is classic rock at its best," Yoko Ono says of the album. "The starkness of that record is very different from the kind of sound that people were used to hearing from the Beatles. I think it was very appropriate for John's first solo album."

*Plastic Ono Band* served clear notice that John Lennon's identity as a solo artist would be dramatically different from his role as Beatle John. By the time he stepped out on his own, Lennon had grown weary of the escapist fantasy that had been central to Beatles mythology ever since *A Hard Day's Night*. Largely abandoning the well-turned love conceits and hallucinogenic imagery of his Beatles years, John began writing in plain words about topics ranging from politics to painfully personal issues. His solo catalog is one grand exercise in seeing just how much truth can be loaded onto the classic verse/ chorus/bridge rock song format. The experiment didn't always work: Lennon's version of the truth sometimes swamped the three-minute musical vehicle that was his chosen medium. His notoriously incisive verbal wit occasionally deserted him in political contexts, giving rise to the empty sloganeering of tunes like "Woman Is the Nigger of the World" and "Power to the People." But even Lennon's less successful efforts were noble in their intent, and his triumphs provided rock with many of its most memorable and important songs.

> THE CODA, IN WHICH LENNON REPEATEDLY SCREAMS **"MAMA DON'T GO, DADDY COME HOME," WAS PARTICULARLY DISQUIETING.** NO ROCK LYRIC HAD EVER CUT QUITE SO CLOSE TO REAL LIFE BEFORE.

### *IMAGINE*

**ONCE, IN A** self-deprecating moment, Lennon described *Imagine* as a "sugar-coated" version of the *Plastic Ono Band* record. While its production is certainly sweeter than its predecessor's, *Imagine* has all the bite of *Plastic Ono Band*, particularly on tracks like "Crippled Inside" and "How Do You Sleep?" Lennon's withering indictment of his former bandmate and writing partner, Paul McCartney. At the same time, Lennon seems less defensive and scarred on *Imagine*, which gives rise to delicately beautiful classics like "Jealous Guy," "Oh My Love" and "How?" Led off by a title track that has become a great anthem of global consciousness, *Imagine* is Lennon's best-known and most loved solo work.

Drummers Alan White and Jim Keltner were among the musicians invited to the Lennons' stately English home at Tittenhurst Park, in Ascot, to cut tracks for *Imagine*. John had an eight-track studio (then state-of-the-art) built right off the kitchen. The musicians lived and worked in an idyllic, communal environment. "We'd all sit and have dinner together and then go back in the studio," White recalls. "I think I spent about eight or 10 days at his house. They were having building work done at the same time, so there were only a few bedrooms that were operational. I remember after we finished recording one evening, John wanted to watch a TV program. Eric Clapton, [*bassist*] Klaus Voormann and I were all in the studio that day. There was only one TV working in the whole house and it was in John's bedroom. So we all laid on his bed and watched this TV program. It was all very homey like that."

As with the *Plastic Ono Band* album and the 1969 "Instant Karma!" single, Lennon shared *Imagine*'s production

Lennon performing at Madison Square Garden in New York City on August 30, 1972

On the set of *A Hard Day's Night*

duties with Ono and the legendary Phil Spector, whose mid-Sixties hits for groups like the Ronettes and Crystals had been hugely influential on Lennon. Yet, even with a record-making mastermind like Spector in attendance, Lennon was clearly in charge. Beatles studio lore has tended to paint Paul McCartney as decisive and aggressive in the studio and Lennon as impulsive, with little patience for the small details of recording. But as demonstrated on the *Lennon Anthology*, the 1998 box set of his unreleased demos and studio outtakes, Lennon could be a confident and decisive figure in the studio. Right until the end of his life, he made records the old-fashioned way: live in the room, counting down takes, leading and supporting his players through every step of the process.

"I think [*the*] box set proves John was an incredible producer and arranger," Ono says. "He didn't need anybody else. He was very clearheaded and quick to notice, 'That musician's not playing what he should.' You'll notice that he's kind of instructing them. In his solo years he really wanted to prove that he could do it on his own, now that he was no longer with the other three [*Beatles*]."

"John was the kind of person who you knew had a strong leadership instinct as soon as he walked in the room," says White, who played drums on many early Lennon solo recordings and concerts. "In the studio he always had things very well planned out. Before we cut 'Imagine' and all the other [*tracks*], John would show us all the lyrics for each of the songs, so that everybody who was playing on it knew exactly what the message of the song was."

"Imagine" originally had a prominent—intrusive, perhaps—harmonium part. White recollects that the decision to lose the harmonium came fairly early in the recording process, and that it didn't take too long to arrive at a definitive master take of what would come to be the song that is most closely identified with the post-Beatles Lennon.

**"IN HIS SOLO YEARS HE REALLY WANTED TO PROVE THAT HE COULD DO IT ON HIS OWN, NOW THAT HE WAS NO LONGER WITH THE OTHER BEATLES."**

*—YOKO ONO*

Keltner had been staying at Clapton's house, working on material by Clapton and Steve Winwood, when a call came through from Phil Spector inviting him to Lennon's sessions. "John would generally have little sheets mimeographed for us that had all the chords and the basic structure of whatever song we were working on," Keltner recalls. "We would refine it in our own way, for our own needs. He would play it and sing it for us, generally one time. And then we'd start recording. The structure of his songs was so complete that they kind of played themselves. Working with John, it was very clear, when you'd hear the song, what had to happen. John was very demanding of guitar players especially. Being a guitar player himself, he would lean on them more."

White moved over to vibraphone when Keltner came in to play drums on "Jealous Guy." "Just for [*acoustic*] separation, I played the vibraphone in the bathroom, which was really tiny," says White. "John had a bathroom right off the studio and I had to leave the door open about a three-inch crack when they were cutting the track out there."

Keltner also played drums on "I Don't Want to Be a Soldier," a track that Lennon and his band had been struggling with. (An earlier take of the song, with Jim Gordon on drums and Keltner on percussion, appears on the *Lennon Anthology*.) "I had the advantage of watching Jimmy [*Gordon*] struggle with it and making up my own part in my mind," says Keltner. "It was a quirky kind of phrasing that John was known for. He'd do funny, odd time signatures that he didn't realize were odd."

A drummer who has played with just about everyone in the rock pantheon, Keltner rates Lennon "one of the greatest ever" on rhythm guitar: "John had impeccable time. Most of the really great artists I've worked with have been like that: Neil Young, George Harrison when he plays rhythm, Ry Cooder... When John was on rhythm guitar, you didn't have to worry about the groove; you were home. He was amazing with that. And that's where his confidence lay—he knew. When he said he was the greatest guitar player, that's what he meant. And he was right. You just watch all those Beatles live performances and listen to that groove. That was coming from him. All the rest of it was gravy. That's what all the great rock and roll bands are like. The groove comes straight from the rhythm guitar."

Keltner's participation on *Imagine* proved to be the beginning of a long-term working partnership and friendship with John and Yoko. He would go on to play on

(PHOTO BY K & K ULF KRUGER OHG/REDFERNS

four more Lennon solo albums, plus many of his concert and television appearances. "Very shortly after *Imagine*, John and Yoko moved to New York, and they called me once they'd settled there," Keltner remembers. "They told me they wanted me to continue working with them. They said, 'We're not sure what we're gonna do, but we want you to do it with us.' From there on, I was just on a cloud the whole time."

## SOME TIME IN NEW YORK CITY

**LENNON'S THIRD SOLO** album reflects the profound changes—geographic, political and domestic—that he and Yoko experienced after *Imagine*. The Lennons went to New York late in 1971 to search for Yoko's daughter, Kyoko, who'd been abducted by her father, Tony Cox. Despite the unhappy circumstances that brought them to New York, they ended up loving the city that had been Ono's home before she met Lennon. "I would always be telling John about the life I had in New York City," she says. "And that sounded much more exciting for him than what he was experiencing then in Kenwood [*the Beatles-era home he'd shared with his first wife, Cynthia*], or wherever. And once we came to New York, we just kind of decided to live here. We went from living in a beautiful, palatial house at Ascot to a little two-room bedroom apartment on Bank Street [*in Greenwich Village*]. And we were saying, 'This is great!'"

The Beatles' fame had made Lennon a virtual prisoner in a succession of English mansions, unable to move about freely in public for fear of being recognized and mobbed. In New York City, he found he was able to roam the streets readily and undisturbed. He eagerly took to Greenwich Village's active, colorful street scene and befriended singer/activist David Peel, who'd earlier become the toast of the East Coast hippie scene with his songs "Have a Marijuana" and "Up Against the Wall, Motherfucker." The radical left-wing movement in America, which had coalesced in opposition to the Vietnam War, was at the forefront of youth counterculture in the early Seventies. The Lennons, who'd always had deep political commitments, plunged headfirst into "the movement." Radicalism became an all-consuming passion for them, as primal scream therapy had once been.

"All our work was like a diary," Ono says. "First we were doing personal things about each other and the experiences we'd had, but then political concerns became a part of our lives. So it just came out like that. That's another part of the diary, I suppose."

It was Yippie (Youth International Party) leader and Chicago Seven trial defendant Jerry Rubin who got the Lennons together with their new backing group, Elephant's Memory. John and Yoko embraced this hirsute bar band from upstate New York but brought in Jim Keltner as "insurance." "John and Yoko liked Elephant's Memory because they were a real street punk type of band," Keltner says. "They liked their energy. They were a good bunch of guys, and we had fun. But John and Yoko wanted me there too, as a little cushion."

With Yoko Ono, walking on Central Park West in New York City, on April 2, 1973

BOB GRUEN

With the newly christened Plastic Ono Elephant's Memory Band, Lennon and Ono recorded *Some Time in New York City* (1972), an album of well-intentioned but generally less-than-inspiring political songs that John later said he was sorry he'd released. "That one, we both kind of regretted," Yoko admits. "When we were doing it, we thought it would be great to make it like a newspaper—put it out really quick, and with songs that were like newspaper articles, all about what was happening right then. We felt the whole thing should have a rough quality, like newsprint." The concept was carried over to the album's cover art, which was laid out like a daily paper. "We thought it was an interesting idea. But nobody got it. So I felt awful. Sales were bad, et cetera. It made things kind of difficult for us. The success of *Imagine* was soon forgotten. So of course we regretted it. The funny thing is, in 1985 I was invited along with other artists and religious leaders to Moscow by Gorbachev. And *Some Time in New York City* was one of the biggest hits there. All of the kids knew that album. And I thought, All right, John! Are you listening today?"

Ono says political songs were the only type of musical material she and John would actively co-write: "We were very independent of each other. The only time that we were open to creating together was when it was a political cause—when it wasn't artistic. [*laughs*] Like 'Luck of the Irish' and a lot of the songs on *Some Time in New York City*. That sort of thing was okay, but if it was artistic, we felt, 'It has to be mine or yours.' One of us would have to take creative responsibility for the artwork from beginning to end."

The Lennons' political activism cost them dearly. As was later proven in court, they became the object of FBI surveillance, illegal phone tapping and general harassment. In March 1972, an order was issued to deport Lennon from the U.S. on the basis of an earlier minor drug conviction in England. It was the start of a difficult and protracted legal battle that would take a tremendous emotional toll on John and Yoko.

## MIND GAMES

**BY 1973, THE** Lennons were ready to enter a new phase of their artistic and personal lives. They'd found a new home in the Dakota, a luxury apartment building on Manhattan's Central Park West; Tittenhurst was sold to Ringo. In addition, the Elephant's Memory Band were dismissed, having outlived their usefulness.

"We were not really good at finding people to work with," Yoko admits. "You can hire session musicians, but I think both of us were too big headed to create a band that we could move along with. I mean

Elephant's Memory were pretty good; they were very funky. But you see, John wanted to move on; he didn't want to use the same band. So with *Mind Games*, he used a different group of people."

Among the players drafted for the album were New York session guitar ace David Spinozza and pedal steel great Sneaky Pete Kleinow, who imparts a country rock feel to tracks like "Tight A$," a style that was certainly a departure for the solo Lennon. Lyrically, the album strikes a balance between the political and the personal, a mix that is generally more satisfying than *Some Time in New York City*'s stridently one-dimensional polemics. "Free your mind and society will follow" seems to be the message of *Mind Games*. This idea comes across most eloquently on the title track. With its descending major-scale chord progression and "love is the answer" chorus, "Mind Games" is reminiscent of Lennon-penned Beatles classics like "All You Need Is Love." Included on the *Lennon Anthology* are two fascinating early drafts of the song, both of them simple piano-and-vocal cassette demos. Each version's chorus is pretty much in place, but one takes an all-too-familiar "I'm sorry, Yoko" tack in the verses, while the second employs the shopworn Sixties slogan "Make love, not war" as a verse lyric. Somewhere between the demos and the final master, Lennon found a lyrical approach that deftly avoids both those sand traps.

"I still get a tear in my eye when I hear 'Mind Games,'" Jim Keltner says. "I remember listening to the playbacks with John, and I kept singing this high part to him. John started singing it, too. And later on, when I heard the finished record, he had put that line into the string part."

Shortly before the release of *Mind Games* in November 1973, the once inseparable Lennons stopped living together. The move was apparently instigated by Yoko. It's a rare woman who, for the greater good of her marriage, not only sends her husband off on a yearlong binge but also appoints an attractive young woman to accompany him. But that is exactly what Ono did. Lennon departed for Los Angeles with his and Yoko's longtime personal assistant, May Pang. The two became lovers, and Lennon embarked on a dark period of his life generally known as the Lost Weekend. "[*Yoko*] don't suffer fools gladly," Lennon later quipped vis-à-vis his banishment from the Dakota, "even if she's married to him."

## ROCK 'N' ROLL

**IN LOS ANGELES,** Lennon quickly fell into a routine of nightly booze-ups with a coterie of rock star wastrels that included singer-songwriter Harry Nilsson, Who drummer Keith Moon and Ringo Starr. At the same time, Lennon was working at A&M Studios with Phil Spector on an album of Fifties rock and roll classics that would emerge two years later as the *Rock 'n' Roll* album. Lennon had entered into the project to avoid a lawsuit: In his song

Backstage at Madison Square Garden with Elephant's Memory and Phil Spector (front), in August 1972

BOB GRUEN

In a New York City diner, March 1975

**“ WE WERE VERY INDEPENDENT OF EACH OTHER. THE ONLY TIME THAT WE WERE OPEN TO CREATING TOGETHER WAS WHEN IT WAS A POLITICAL CAUSE—WHEN IT WASN'T ARTISTIC. ”**

*—YOKO ONO*

“Come Together,” from the Beatles album *Abbey Road*, Lennon paraphrases a line from Chuck Berry's “You Can't Catch Me.” Threatened with legal action by Morris Levy, Berry's music publisher, Lennon cut a deal: he would record an album featuring a few songs to which Levy held copyrights, and Levy would drop the lawsuit, content with the publishing revenue he would receive from sales of a John Lennon album. That was the idea, anyway.

“The sessions could have been absolutely brilliant,” Keltner says. “But toward the end of each evening, it would just waste away because of the drinking and the drugs all of us were taking, including Phil. By the end of the night, John would be singing all slow and slurry. ‘Just Because’ [*the album's closing track*] is a perfect example of that. It started off early in the evening with a really great tempo, great feel, good vocal. And by the time it was done, it was just a real parody of a drunken John Lennon with a bunch of drunk musicians all playing live. I mean at one point, John was singing [*drunken voice*], ‘Just because you fuckin' think you're so fuckin' great *agggghhh...*’”

While this particular outtake doesn't appear on the *Lennon Anthology*, the box set does include examples of verbal repartee among Lennon, Spector and the other musicians as they persistently fumble the intro to “Just Because.” There's a sad moment when Lennon jokingly predicts he's going to “live to be a 99-year-old-guru.” At another point, he's heard to yell, “Keltner, control your prick!” Jim Keltner says he can't remember the remark or its context. Given the quantity of intoxicants being consumed, it's a miracle anybody remembers anything.

“John would buy one of those big gallon bottles of Smirnoff [*vodka*] and bring it to the session,” Keltner recalls. “One night I was following him through Hollywood on the way to the studio. May was driving this rent-a-car and John was in the passenger's seat. I was behind them in my Corvette. At a stop sign, I pulled up next to them and he hands me, through the window, this big gallon jug. Man, we could have ended up in jail so easily. It almost broke my arm trying to get the jug into my car. I had to take a big swig out of it so John could see I was keeping up with him. Or trying to keep up with him. I could never go anywhere near the kind of drinking he did. Then we got to the studio and I'd go over and check the bottle once in a while. And he damn well drank almost half of it. Half a gallon of vodka, man. John could drink. He could really drink enormous amounts of booze. He and Harry [*Nilsson*] were legendary with their drinking.”

Keltner was present on the evening of the infamous “Kotex incident,” when Lennon walked into the Troubadour, a Los Angeles rock club, wearing a women's sanitary napkin on his head. The evening began, the drummer recollects, “at a restaurant called Lost on Larrabee,” Larrabee being a West Hollywood street near the Troubadour. Also present were Lennon's lead guitarist at the time, Jesse Ed Davis, L.A. Record Plant co-owner Gary Kellgren plus various wives and dates. “After we finished eating, we were all pretty drunk,” Keltner says. “We went downstairs to the bathrooms. All the guys went in the men's room. Except John—he went in the women's room. You know, just being silly. And he came out with a Kotex stuck to his forehead. All the guys fell out. We thought that was the funniest thing we'd ever seen. The women were all giggling and thinking he was really silly. But then, he didn't take it off. And we were encouraging him to keep it on, like ‘Ah, you should walk into the Troubadour like that, man.’ We were being really stupid. And he was John Lennon, so nobody stepped in and said, ‘No, take that off.’ And so we walked into the Troubadour.”

The initial elation of alcohol invariably gives way to darker moods, as Keltner observed one evening after a session with Lennon at A&M: “Jesse [*Ed Davis*] was John's partner in crime, only because Jesse was an unmarried guy who loved trouble. He was crazy himself. He would always volunteer to be with John, like, ‘I'll take care of him; don't worry,’ because, amazingly enough, John didn't have a bodyguard in L.A.—unlike Phil.

“But this one evening Jesse drafted me to help him with John, saying, ‘Get in the car with us. You take one side and I'll take the other,’ 'cause John was starting to freak out. He was so drunk that he was yelling and screaming at everybody. He was yelling ‘Yoko!’ at the top of his lungs. Somebody put May in John's lawyer's car. And I was in the back of this Cadillac with John in the middle and Jesse on the other side, and we were trying to hold him down, because he was trying to kick the windows out of the car. He had these big cowboy boots on. John was very strong when he was drunk. He shoved me down to the floor of the car and was pulling my hair and just kicking the windows. He was shoving and hitting Jesse. And the whole time he's yelling at the top of his lungs, ‘Yoko! I want Yoko!’

BOB GRUEN

In the studio, in 1972

And screaming, 'You know who the fuck I am?' He was just out of it completely.

"So we got him to his attorney's apartment, got him inside and sort of calmed him down. I remember leaving and Jesse stayed with him. That night, he completely trashed the man's apartment. There were so many times like that. He trashed [*record producer*] Lou Adler's house. He even uprooted a little palm tree by the front door."

Things eventually got so wild at A&M that Lennon and his crew were kicked out of the studio. Work resumed at the L.A. Record Plant, but the group was soon sent packing. "We got kicked out of the Record Plant because Phil shot his gun off in the canteen," Keltner reports. "He shot his gun at the floor and it ricocheted up into the ceiling. Gary Kellgren and Chris Stone, the studio owners, both decided that was that. We were outta there."

Relations between Spector and Lennon eventually deteriorated, and Spector disappeared with the master tapes. Whenever Lennon had worked with Spector in the past, Yoko had always been present as a third producer. But out in L.A., without her tempering presence, fueled by gallons of Smirnoff and God knows what else, the two rock icons came to a masculine clash of egos.

"I told John it wouldn't work," Ono says. "He said when he was in L.A., 'I think I'm gonna do this thing with Phil.' I said, 'John, I don't think you should do that.' He said, 'Don't worry about it, don't worry.' But I just knew it wasn't going to work. And of course he called me later and said, 'Yeah, you were right—again.'"

Throughout their separation, John and Yoko spoke daily on the phone, sometimes as often as 20 times a day. Although they were physically apart, they continued to be involved in each other's lives. But from 3,000 miles away, even a woman of Yoko Ono's strength and determination couldn't control the events unfolding in L.A. John had to live through it by himself and for himself. One musical artifact on the *Lennon Anthology* sums up this period, and illustrates Keltner's point about how tempos would slow down as the evenings wore on and the musicians got drunker. It's a version of the Ronettes' "Be My Baby," taken at an incredibly sluggish pace. Given the impossibly draggy tempo, Lennon's vocal degenerates into camp histrionics.

"There's something about his voice that makes me feel so hurtful," Yoko says of the track. "Because you hear his pain. It's so sad. I felt so guilty. But also I know—or maybe I'm just telling myself this—that it could not have been any other way. What can you do? I didn't know it was going to be such a short life."

Lennon eventually got the L.A. tapes

BOB GRUEN

back from Spector and finished the album without him, recutting many of the tracks at the Record Plant in New York City. The finished album remained unreleased through 1974, during which time Lennon recorded and released his fourth solo album, *Wall and Bridges*. When finally released as *Rock 'n' Roll* in February 1975, it showed Lennon's considerable prowess as a singer of Fifties rock material. But it is the chaos of his personal life that lends a desperately urgent edge to many of his vocal performances on the disc.

## WALLS AND BRIDGES

**STILL SEPARATED FROM** Yoko, Lennon returned to Manhattan in 1974. Settling into an apartment on 52nd Street with May Pang, he began work on what would become the *Walls and Bridges* album. He was far more sober than he had been in L.A. "John had a tremendous sweet tooth," Keltner says. "And—partially in lieu of his drinking, I think—he had this massive bar of Hershey's chocolate that was like three feet across that he kept in the freezer at the studio. It was huge, kind of like the Smirnoff bottle."

*Walls and Bridges* tracks like "Scared" and "Nobody Loves You (When You're Down and Out)" reflect the bitterness of the Lost Weekend and Lennon's growing disillusionment with the music business. The title of the album's major hit, "Whatever Gets You Thru the Night," is drawn from an Alcoholics Anonymous slogan. An early take of the song appears on the *Lennon Anthology*: competent but lackluster, the performance offers hardly any hint of the song's potential. That all changed when Lennon's friend Elton John came into the studio to sing and play piano on the track. "Nobody plays piano with that kind of abandon," says Jim Keltner. "Not back then they didn't, anyway. So Elton just brought his energy and made that song come alive."

"Whatever Gets You Thru the Night" was also the song that brought John and Yoko back together. Elton bet Lennon that the song would reach Number One and made Lennon promise to make a guest appearance at one of John's concerts when it did. As it happened, the song went to the top of the charts, giving Lennon his first solo Number One record. He honored his commitment on Thanksgiving evening, 1974, by joining Elton onstage at New York's Madison Square Garden to perform a few songs. Yoko had been persuaded to attend the concert, and when the couple met up backstage, they decided it was time to live together again.

Reunited, they embarked on a new domestic regimen, cutting out alcohol and drugs and going on a strict macrobiotic diet. They also attempted to have a child. Their previous attempts had been in vain and resulted in at least one miscarriage, but at long last they were successful. On October 9, 1975, Sean Taro Ono Lennon was born.

With a child to raise, Lennon decided to take a sabbatical from the music business. He devoted the next five years to raising his son and playing the role of "househusband" at the Dakota while Yoko attended to the couple's financial interests in the downstairs office, amassing a considerable fortune in real estate and "environment friendly" investments.

> **"WHEN JOHN WAS ON RHYTHM GUITAR, YOU DIDN'T HAVE TO WORRY ABOUT THE GROOVE. HE WAS AMAZING WITH THAT. AND THAT'S WHERE HIS CONFIDENCE LAY. HE KNEW."**
>
> *—JIM KELTNER*

Although he was out of the public eye, Lennon's creativity continued to find outlets, albeit domestic ones. The *Lennon Anthology* contains an intriguing cache of little comic songs and vignettes that John created on his two cassette decks during this time. "He was amusing himself," says Yoko. "But he was also kind of proud that he had a knack for doing that sort of thing. And also he needed an audience, which I was. We were both in this luxury prison here, comparing notes. And even when I wasn't there, he'd be recording things. I'd be downstairs doing the business, and when I came upstairs he'd say, 'Listen to this!'"

A large project that occupied Lennon during these years was the planning of a stage musical. "John was constantly getting involved in new media," says Yoko. "So he said, 'How about a musical?' And the title was *The Ballad of John and Yoko*. So predictable." She laughs. "He had ideas like, 'The first scene should be like this, and the second scene like that.' He wrote some of the songs first. 'Real Love' was going to be the scene where we first meet. Just really corny stuff, you know? [*In 1994, the three surviving Beatles overdubbed onto Lennon's home demo of "Real Love" and released the completed track on* The Beatles Anthology. *Lennon's demo appears in its original form on* John Lennon Anthology.] And I wrote 'Every Man Has a Woman Who Loves Him' for the musical. There were a few that I wrote for it and a few that he wrote. I think that some of them went into *Double Fantasy* [*1980*] and *Milk and Honey* [*1984*]."

## DOUBLE FANTASY

**WHILE VACATIONING IN** Bermuda in 1980, Lennon began writing songs at a fast pace. After a five-year break from his career, he decided it was time to start recording again. A plan was devised for making an album that combined songs written by John with a more or less equal number penned by Yoko. The title for this work, *Double Fantasy*, was taken from the name of a hybrid flower John saw in Bermuda.

For their coproducer, the couple chose rock vet Jack Douglas (Aerosmith, Cheap Trick) who had first worked with John Lennon as an assistant engineer on *Imagine*. "John made the *Double Fantasy* project easy," Douglas says. He sent me these incredible demos that he had recorded in Bermuda by bouncing between two Panasonic boom boxes. He told me to do arrangements for the songs. His demo for 'Watching the Wheels' [*included in the* Lennon Anthology *box*] was a Dylan type of thing. He wrote me a note from Bermuda saying, 'Can you make it more circular?' So the first thing I did in arranging it was slow it down. And I added a hammer dulcimer, to give it a more circular feel."

Douglas and Tony Davilio prepared charts from Lennon's song demos, and Douglas contracted a group of top New York session players including guitarists Hugh McCracken and Earl Slick, and bassist Tony Levin. There was one catch: During rehearsals, the players were not allowed to know who the artist was. "I said to them, 'I can't tell you,'" Douglas recollects. "But some of the guys guessed after a few days. All the rehearsals were done with me and the band alone. The deal was we were gonna make this record, but nobody was going to know about it. John was insecure about how the whole thing was going to work out, having been away so long. So I took the charts to the rehearsal hall. I sang the songs and the guys played the charts. For the last rehearsal, the address I gave them was the Dakota. That was the first official time that they knew who the album was for."

The initial meeting between Lennon and the musicians went well, Douglas recalls: "We ran through all the songs. And as we were leaving John suddenly said, 'Stop. Wait one minute, Jack. I've got one more tune. I just wrote it.' There was a Fender Rhodes piano parked right by the entrance to the apartment. John sat down at it and played 'Just Like Starting Over.' The next day, we went in the studio and began by recording 'Starting Over.' Instead of going right to charts, I thought it would be a good way to get the chemistry going between John and the whole rest of the band. We worked it up pretty fast."

Hugh McCracken has the distinction of having played guitar with all four former Beatles. "John was really spontaneous and quick," is how McCracken characterizes Lennon. "[Double Fantasy] was the first time I remember working with an artist who was ahead of the engineer. The engineer is always ready to roll tape, especially on a project like that, but a lot of times John would be ready to roll and nobody else would. Keeping up with John was a task—a delightful one."

At first, the recording sessions for *Double Fantasy* were top secret. "I deliberately picked the old Hit Factory [*recording studio*] on 48th Street," says Douglas. "It was way out west between 9th and 10th avenues. I figured we could get in and out of that studio without anyone noticing us. The deal was, if anybody told anybody what was happening, the project would simply stop. After a month of working, John said, 'You know what? This is good. Let's let everybody know what's happening.'"

As the project evolved, Douglas and Davilio's original charts were tightened and modified. McCracken recalls going over to the Dakota several times for informal arrangement sessions with Lennon, Douglas and keyboardist George Small. "A lot of ideas came out of that. I'd play something and John would say, 'That thing.' 'What thing?' 'That thing you just played. Yeah, that.' And I would jot it down. As a guitarist, John was very free. He wasn't the kind of guitarist who had a library of licks. But he was very creative."

Life in the studio with the Lennons was very much an extension of their lives at the Dakota. "While we were doing *Double Fantasy* in the studio, of course Sean would be there all the time," Yoko says. "When John first went in the studio, he put Sean's picture up on the TV screen over the mixing board. That's how things were gonna be."

All the musicians and other people involved in the project had to turn in their birth dates, in order to be cleared by one of the Lennons' astrologers, according to Jack Douglas. "No one was rejected," he adds. Drugs and alcohol were banned from the studio. Sushi and macrobiotic food were catered in. "But the pizza and cheeseburgers were in the maintenance shop," Douglas says, and winks. "It used to be that guys would go off and smoke a joint. In this case, all the junk food was delivered to maintenance. John would say, 'I have to go to the bathroom.' And you'd see him running into the maintenance room and there'd be a slice of pizza in there, or a cheeseburger with everything on it. I mean, man does not live by sushi alone."

The mood in the studio was apparently upbeat. "I could bring a session to a halt in a second," McCracken says, "if I played some old rock and roll song from the Fifties. John and I were the same age and both grew up on that stuff. So no matter what we were doing, John couldn't resist playing some old song like that, whether it was Chuck Berry or Buddy Holly or whatever."

At one point, Douglas brought the members of Cheap Trick into the studio to cut some tracks. The producer had worked with the influential power pop band on their first two albums. "I thought it was a perfect marriage," he says. "They were deeply influenced by John's music and could lend a kind of contemporary feel to the album." Cheap Trick guitarist Rick Nielsen, bassist Tom Petersson and drummer Bun E. Carlos cut two tracks for *Double Fantasy*: Yoko's "I'm Moving On" and John's "I'm Losing You." The latter track is included in the *Lennon Anthology*, a rough-and-ready reading of the tune that rocks considerably harder than the version on the album.

It was Ono, according to Douglas, who vetoed the idea of using the Cheap Trick tracks. "She thought they were just some band I was trying to give a boost to," says the producer, "even though they'd been quite successful and were in the process of making an album with George Martin, ironically enough. But John was not one for arguing with 'Mother' [*Lennon's affectionate name for Ono*]. So we just played the Cheap Trick version into the headphones for Hugh and Tony and the guys. And that's how we got it."

All told, the sessions went on for four or five months, by the end of which time Lennon, Ono, Douglas and the band had not only completed *Double Fantasy* but also cut several tracks for an additional album. These included the hits "Nobody Told Me" and "Stepping Out." As it turned out, these songs were first heard under far sadder circumstances than anyone intended—after John Lennon's death, on the posthumous *Milk and Honey* album.

Lennon spent the last day of his life in the recording studio, with Yoko and Jack Douglas. December 8, 1980, is a day that

Onstage with the Beatles at Ernst Merck Halle in Germany, June 26, 1966

K & K ULF KRUGER OHG

In New York City, October 25, 1974

PHOTO BY DAVID GAHR/GETTY IMAGES

Douglas will never forget: "We were at the Record Plant, doing 'Walking on Thin Ice.' And we were going to meet the next day to master it at Sterling [*mastering lab*]. John wasn't even supposed to be in New York. He was supposed to be in Bermuda. So I'd booked another session. John called me up and I said, 'I thought you were in Bermuda.' He said, 'No, I'm not staying away. I'm on a roll now. Let's go in and finish that track of Yoko's, "Walking on Thin Ice." That track can be so brilliant. That's gonna be the one where the critics are finally gonna say, 'Yoko, we didn't take you seriously enough.'"

The Lennons and Douglas had spent about two weeks before that building up the track by overdubbing onto an eight-bar tape loop. "So I told John, 'Okay,'" Douglas recalls. "And he had me move my previously booked session to later at night, like a nine P.M. starting time. So I started working with John and Yoko at about one or two in the afternoon—just the three of us in the control room. John and I played instruments. Sometimes we both played the same instrument. We had an absolute blast. Yoko laid this beautiful poem over it and we finished the track.

"Normally, I used to ride home with John every night after we finished up in the studio. I live three blocks from the Dakota, on Central Park West. But that night I was going to another session. So I just said good night to him. He got on the elevator and said, 'I'll see you at nine A.M. tomorrow.' I said, 'Okay, I'll see you there.' John had a big smile on his face. We were so happy with the track. David Geffen had been by that day. He was thrilled. The record was going well. It was just a big up. It ended on a big up."

Forty-five minutes later, Douglas' wife came running into the studio where her husband was working. She'd been out strolling on the Upper West Side and heard a commotion. John Lennon had been fatally shot in front of the Dakota.

"I wonder quite often whether John might have known he was going," Yoko Ono says. "Because there was that 'Watching the Wheels' kind of resignation in a lot of his work at the end. Although he did have plans, obviously. He was saying, 'Let's go on tour.' He had tons of ideas in the sense of moving on and doing new things. Still doing music, but in new ways."

There were plans for Lennon to do an album with Ringo Starr, according to Jack Douglas. And many of the musicians who played on *Double Fantasy* had already committed to touring with Lennon, who had begun to do drawings of stage sets. "He was even planning to do new versions of 'She Loves You' and 'I Want to Hold Your Hand,'" Jack Douglas says. "He'd already played them for us. His new renditions of those songs exist somewhere, because I recorded everything that went on in those rooms."

While many of John Lennon's solo recordings did not have the massive and instantaneous cultural impact of the Beatles' records, Yoko Ono feels that, ultimately, Lennon's individual achievements outshine those of his former band:

"The Beatles definitely did change society in the latter half of the 20th century. But I think John really went a step further in communicating how to change. Not just having fun, you know? In the Sixties, people learned that loosening up, having fun and being nice to each other is better than being morally strict with each other like in the Fifties. The Sixties were definitely brought on by the Beatles, in a way. And I think they were great. But John was giving some kind of directional communication that further changed our lives—in the sense that men started to feel it was all right to be vulnerable and cry. And of course feminism was greatly helped by John: the househusband thing. It's kind of normal now for husbands to have more interest in the family. And 'Imagine,' as you know, is now a worldwide anthem. So I think there's a lot that John did single-handedly." ◆

Hendrix onstage at the Marquee Club in London, March 2, 1967

# WILD THING

Forty-three years after his death, *Guitar World* looks beyond the myth and presents the true story of rock's great electric guitar genius, Jimi Hendrix.

BY ALAN DI PERNA

JIMI HENDRIX 1942–1970

# OF ALL THE GREAT SIXTIES

guitar icons—Beck, Clapton, Page, Townshend—Jimi Hendrix is by far the most enigmatic. His career as a rock star lasted a scant four years, cut short prematurely by his death 43 years ago at age 27. In his time, he was notoriously reticent in front of interviewers' microphones—the king of the trippy non sequitur. Put it down to a consciousness radically altered by psychedelic drugs, the caution of a black man in a white world, or the natural inclination of a highly accomplished musician to say it all through his music, Hendrix liked to leave people guessing.

The celebrated psychologist Jacques Lacan thought that we all undergo a primordial identity crisis in early life when our parents confer a name on us. What to make, then, of the child christened Johnny Allen Hendrix on December 7, 1942, and renamed James Marshall Hendrix some four years later? Perhaps this was what lay at the root of the reticence, playful verbal evasiveness and seemingly fluid sense of identity possessed by the man who went on to find fame under the name Jimi Hendrix.

Contrary to what some would have you believe, Jimi didn't come from outer space. He came from Seattle. Growing up there, he quickly discovered an affinity for the guitar. Being left-handed, he took to stringing conventional guitars upside down and playing them that way. Among his strongest early guitar influences were bluesmen like Muddy Waters, B.B. King, Elmore James and Buddy Guy. His resemblance to the latter is uncanny at times. And Guy remembers being approached by Hendrix at a club date one evening during the Sixties.

"Jimi said, 'Can I tape what you're playing?'" Guy recalls. "And I said yeah. Somebody had a portable tape recorder on 'em and Hendrix got down on his knees and just stayed there at the corner of the stage. So Jimi gave birth to something that originally came from Buddy Guy. And I know if Jimi was here, he'd be the first one to tell you that."

Hendrix started playing semi-professionally while still in high school. After a year in the Army Airborne Division—he was honorably discharged after being injured on his 26th parachute jump—the guitarist embarked on a journeyman career as an R&B sideman on what was then known as the Chitlin Circuit—small, predominantly Afro-American clubs throughout the South. He changed names once again. As Jimmy James, he backed such R&B notables as Sam Cooke, Solomon Burke, Hank Ballard, B.B. King, Jackie Wilson, Wilson Pickett and Ike & Tina Turner. Hendrix would later remember this period as a time of poverty, struggle and constant ripoffs. But it was also a tremendous musical education—one that extended to the recording studio, where Hendrix cut some minor sides with a number of artists, including R&B greats the Isley Brothers (then just at the start of their career) and Little Richard (then on a downslide from his mid-Fifties burst of glory as one of rock and roll's boldest originators). Completists might want to collect these recordings, but they're pretty much just anonymous session work.

**"JIMI WAS FRUSTRATED BEFORE HE DIED BECAUSE, I THINK, THE PUBLIC DIDN'T UNDERSTAND HIM. HE WAS SO CONFUSED AS TO WHICH WAY TO GO."**

*—PRODUCER EDDIE KRAMER*

By 1966, Hendrix had landed in New York City's age-old bohemian neighborhood, Greenwich Village, where folk music and rock were intersecting in a big way. He was fronting his own group, Jimmy James and the Blue Flames. By this point, his act had begun to include stage tricks like playing the guitar behind his head, a move he'd appropriated from bluesman T-Bone Walker. But during that same period Hendrix also recorded and performed with aspiring soul singer Curtis Knight—a situation that would later lead him into legal and contractual hassles of major proportions. Like name changes, litigation was a constant in Jimi's life. After Hendrix hit it big in 1967, some of the Curtis Knight recordings were issued under the titles *Get That Feeling* and *Flashing*. By that point, these albums had become something of an embarrassment to Hendrix, who'd already changed his style considerably.

## SWINGING LONDON

**IT WAS IN** Greenwich Village that Hendrix was discovered by former Animals bassist Chas Chandler, who'd decided to try his hand at artist management. In September 1966, Chandler relocated Hendrix to London. Legend has it that the guitarist decided to rechristen himself Jimi Hendrix during the plane ride over, giving the everyday name Jimmy an exotic new spelling. Shortly after arriving in London, Chandler and Hendrix began auditioning sidemen for a new group to be centered around Hendrix's vocal and guitar work. They opted for the power-trio lineup that was then being popularized by Eric Clapton's new band, Cream. British drummer Mitch Mitchell—a veteran of Georgie Fame and his Blue Flames—was recruited into Hendrix's band. The bass slot was awarded to another Englishman, session guitarist Noel Redding. The new group quickly set about taking Swinging London by storm.

In late 1966, San Francisco's Haight-Ashbury scene was still a few months away

TOM COPI/MICHAEL OCHS ARCHIVES/GETTY IMAGES

Gibson

from breaking out worldwide. And things moved so fast in the late Sixties that a few months were like a few years on today's rock scene. So London was the undisputed capital of the pop culture universe. Rock musicians, visual artists, fashion designers and models partied all day and all of the night with British aristocrats and gangsters. It was in this highly charged, intensely creative atmosphere that the Jimi Hendrix Experience exploded. They adopted Swinging London's freewheeling attitude. And its look—billowing shirts with elaborate ruffles and boldly colored frock coats in the "electric dandy" style popularized by Brian Jones of the Rolling Stones.

The Hendrix Experience also adopted the sound of Swinging London—the highly amplified, feedback drenched guitar style that was then being pioneered by Clapton, the Who's Pete Townshend and then-Yardbirds Jeff Beck and Jimmy Page. Townshend had been incorporating feedback into the Who's music since 1964, and had developed an assertively violent form of performing on the guitar that culminated in smashing the instrument to shards at the end of each set. It was Townshend who had worked closely with London music shop proprietor Jim Marshall in developing the first 100-watt Marshall amp head and speaker cabinet stack. He'd played a similar role developing the Hiwatt amp with Dave Hill. And sure enough, shortly after arriving in London, Jimi Hendrix paid a call on Pete Townshend.

"The first time I met Jimi, the Who were recording at IBC [*studios*]," Townshend recalls. "Chas Chandler brought him in to meet me, and Jimi was covered from head to foot in dust. He looked like he'd just come out of what we call a skip in London—where you put builders' rubbish. He was very, very scruffy and his military jacket had obviously seen better days. His skin was bad. He was very pale. He was immediately nervous and shy and couldn't speak. He didn't speak. I just put my hand out and said, 'I've heard a lot about you.' 'Cause he'd been signed to our label. [*The Experience were signed to the Who's Track Records in the U.K.—Ed.*] And Chas said, 'Jimi wants to know what kind of rig to buy.' And I said, 'Well, you catch me at a strange time, 'cause I'm just shifting from Marshall to Sound City [*which later became Hiwatt*] and at the moment I'm using both.' Chas said, 'Well, that's what we'll do too.'

"A couple of days later," Townshend continues, "the Who and the Jimi Hendrix Experience appeared together at the Saville Theater, which was owned by the Beatles' manager, Brian Epstein. I think it was the first rock concert to play there. Jimi opened for us. And he had exactly the same rig as me—the sample [*prototype*] amplifiers in the same kind of arrangement. And I actually felt like I'd given too much away."

One of the most ill-informed and ubiquitous platitudes said about Hendrix is that he was ahead of his time. In fact, few musicians were ever more completely *of* their time than Jimi Hendrix. And that doesn't detract

**EVERYONE IN LONDON'S ROCK PANTHEON—FROM THE BEATLES AND STONES DOWNWARD—PAID COURT TO HENDRIX AT THOSE EARLY SHOWS.**

Hendrix, Redding and Chandler (in the engineer's booth) in a London recording studio, October 1967

PHOTO BY BRUCE FLEMING/GETTY IMAGES

in the least from his accomplishments. Mozart borrowed liberally from Hayden and J.C. Bach; he worked completely in the musical idioms of his day, but that doesn't make him any less a genius. In fact, the more you learn about the composers and music of Mozart's time, the more you appreciate what was utterly unique about him. And so it is with Jimi Hendrix. In fact, one reason why he seems the quintessential rock icon to many fans is that his work incorporated nearly all the major stylistic elements that went into the making of rock music during the classic Fifties and Sixties period. Hendrix had first-hand involvement in R&B, blues, folk and post-British Invasion English rock. His ears took it all in. And while he appropriated plenty from his contemporaries, he also brought his own arrestingly original tonal and melodic sensibility to what he'd learned from these influences.

When he hit London, Hendrix was even playing the same kind of guitar that Pete Townshend was using at the time—a Fender Strat. But by reversing the strings on a conventional right-handed Start, Hendrix altered the physics of the instrument. The heavier-gauge low strings were now interacting with pickup pole pieces intended as transducers for the high strings—and vice versa. This imparted unique sustain characteristics that Hendrix incorporated into his overall approach. His playing style was less chordal than Townshend's, more reliant on single-note riffs. But the riffs he played tended to have the singing cadences of vocal lines, as opposed to, say, the bluesy bursts of Clapton's guitar solos from the same period. In this regard, Hendrix is actually closer to Beck than Clapton or Townshend, to whom he is more frequently compared. And while Hendrix is generally thought of as the king of heavily distorted, loud guitar, he also employed clean tones of striking subtlety and beauty. In the recording studio, he would become one of the first great architects of guitar arrangements, masterfully overdubbing watery textures colored by wah-wah and other effects to occupy precise slots in the sonic spectrum.

Onstage, Hendrix's act was clearly indebted to Townshend. But he brought a whole new dimension to that as well—in a word, sex. With his pelvis thrusting and his tongue going like some non-stop cunnilingus machine, Hendrix's every stage gesture was more explicit than merely suggestive. At one moment, his guitar was a phallus. Next moment it was his lover, whom he eagerly bestrode. Back when he was playing the Chitlin Circuit, Hendrix had obviously paid close attention while backing sex-charged performers like Little Richard and Tina Turner.

The Jimi Hendrix Experience in Germany: (from left) Mitch Mitchell, Hendrix and Redding

No wonder all the English guitarists felt threatened. Jeff Beck remembers seeing Hendrix sit in with Eric Clapton during a gig at the London School of Economics: "Eric was up there doing his stuff in front of all the girlies, and along comes Jimi, who sits in and upsets the whole apple cart—playing with his teeth, behind his head, doing almost circus tricks with the guitar. Even if it was crap—which it wasn't—it got to the press. People wanted that. They were just starved for theater and outrage. I figured, Alright, that's it for me. None of us realized that someone was going to come along and whip the carpet out from under us in quite such a radical way."

Everyone in London's rock pantheon—from the Beatles and Stones down—paid court to Hendrix at those early shows. They were surprised to find a quiet, almost painfully shy person at the heart of all the hoopla.

"He would never raise his voice above a whisper," says Beck. "It was all in his facial expressions and his hands: unbelievable comedy and profound statements just by the raising of an eyebrow. The guy was on a big-time roll. He'd come from being a low-keyed sideman for Little Richard. Can you imagine the poverty and God knows what else? And suddenly he was recognized and whisked all over England in the wake of the Beatles and Stones, who were still active then. All of a sudden, he's on every radio and every TV show, turning out unbelievable singles and pissing all over everybody. He must have felt like Jack the Lad. And he was!"

## ARE YOU EXPERIENCED

**IN THE MIDST OF** this meteoric rise, the Jimi Hendrix Experience began recording the singles and other tracks that would make up their debut album, *Are You Experienced.* The first of these was "Hey Joe," a Billy Roberts composition that had already been covered by the Byrds, the Leaves and the Standells. These versions were fairly well known to serious rock fans at the time, although Hendrix preferred a less familiar recording of the song by Tim Rose. "Hey Joe" was part of the standard garage band repertoire of the day, as were several other songs performed live by the early Experience, including "Wild Thing," which had been a hit for the Troggs, and "Gloria," which had been taken to the top of the charts by Van Morrison's band Them, and by American one-hit wonders the Shadows of Knight. Like many garage bands of the day, the Hendrix Experience even took on Bob Dylan's epic hit "Like a Rolling Stone."

As always, though, Hendrix brought his own sensibilities to these covers. Taking Tim Rose's cue, he performed "Hey Joe" at a slower tempo than most other bands, weaving in a graceful guitar/bass unison line and glints of six-string sparkle. Work on that track actually began while the Experience were still hunting for a record deal. It was the first of Hendrix's many collaborations with his longtime engineer and eventual co-producer, Eddie Kramer.

"When we were recording this, we had no money," Kramer says of "Hey Joe." "Chas at one point sold his bass or put it in hock or something to get some money to record. They tried this track a few times. I have a hilarious outtake of this. It's the first time Jimi actually sang it. He was reading the words and cursing and laughing."

Working during downtime at several London studios, including De Lane Lea, CBS, Pye and Regent Sound, the Hendrix Experience also cut "Hey Joe's" B-side, "Stone Free," and completed rough tracks for their second single "Purple Haze"/"51st Anniversary." ("Purple Haze" would become the lead track for the *Are You Experienced* album.)

On securing a record deal, the group moved over to Olympic Studios, where Kramer was a staff engineer. Olympic was then the hottest new studio in Britain's capital, and would soon become home to the Rolling Stones, Traffic and other members of Swinging London's pop aristocracy, not least among whom were the Jimi Hendrix Experience.

"Once we got into Olympic, Jimi really got a chance to stretch out," says Kramer. "The sounds became deeper."

When it was first released in May 1967, *Are You Experienced* was hailed as one of the most important debuts of the year. The Experience seemed to arrive simultaneously with psychedelia. By this time, the San Francisco hippie scene had broken out worldwide. In America, teenagers and college age kids were growing their hair long, affecting a looser, more colorful way of dressing and engaging seriously with Eastern spirituality, radical politics, pacifism, free love and what were regarded as mind-expanding drugs such as marijuana and a substance at the time relatively new to the American public called LSD.

*Are You Experienced* was embraced as an ideal soundtrack to all these activities. "You'll never hear surf music again,"

Onstage at the Fillmore East

Jimi's slowed-down voice pronounces on the album's big instrumental track, "Third Stone from the Sun"—a public service announcement that rock music had left its "teenage entertainment" phase and had embarked on a new era of greater emotional depth and serious musicality. The cover art for *Are You Experienced* featured a solarized photo of Jimi, Noel and Mitch decked out in their best Swinging London finery and viewed through a fisheye lens, which at the time was a stock representation of one visual phenomenon peculiar to the LSD experience. For those who didn't get the point, the slightly cheesy back-cover copy advised that the album would "put listeners' heads into some novel positions," and that "You hear with new ears after being Experienced." "Purple Haze" was greeted as a hymn to lysergic transcendence and became the name for one highly popular variety of acid. The album's track, with its trippy backward tape effects, seemed to describe the transformational effects of dropping acid. "Not necessarily stoned," Hendrix intones, "but beautiful." It was all a little more heavy-handed than the Beatles' *Sgt. Pepper's Lonely Hearts Club Band*—released that same year and also regarded as a big LSD album—but nobody seemed to mind.

In fact, that was just the point. The Experience came on heavier than San Francisco bands like the Jefferson Airplane, Grateful Dead and Quicksilver Messenger Service, heavier than folk rockers like the Byrds and Buffalo Springfield. Heavier than anyone, in fact. Which gave it a kind of instant accessibility that those other bands didn't quite possess. This was true proto-metal. And the Experience, along with Cream, were at its vanguard.

Other big tracks from *Are You Experienced*, including "Fire" and "The Wind Cries Mary," show that Hendrix was still very close to his R&B roots. A huge part of Hendrix's appeal at the time stemmed from the fact that he was arguably the first black musician to present himself in a completely white rock context. The American Civil Rights movement of the mid Sixties was generally applauded by the free-thinking, white, middle-class hippie youths who formed Hendrix's first audience. But there was a long way to go in terms of the races actually coming together. Most white kids still listened to R&B songs in cover versions by white performers. Emboldened by collecting Stones, Animals or Young Rascals records, a few adventurous Caucasians crossed the color line into real R&B. But it really was a different culture. The shiny suits and tight horn arrangements favored by many R&B artists just seemed old-fashioned to a lot of white hippie kids. Hendrix, however, blew away all these boundaries.

A few years earlier, the Paul Butterfield Blues Band had made their mark as the first racially integrated blues group. But they were a relatively underground phenomenon compared to the Jimi Hendrix Experience. And they weren't about sex. There's no denying that Hendrix's early persona and stage shows tapped deeply into white culture's fascination with and fear of the black man's storied sexual prowess. "Purple Haze" is punctuated with vocal "oohs and aahs" that sound like they'd been lifted from a low-budget porn soundtrack. Another *Experienced* classic, "Foxey Lady," sports Hendrix's immortal mating call, "Here I come baby, I'm comin' to *gitcha!*" From today's post-feminist perspective, it sounds like a line from a bad "bodice ripper" romance novel. But back in the 1967 pop market, it worked like a charm. Hendrix became a major sex symbol for a new era of freedom when mixed-race couples were starting—albeit just barely—to gain social acceptance. The standard joke at the time was that girls ventured backstage at a Jimi Hendrix concert in hopes of a sexual encounter, while the boys wanted to meet Jimi and ask him what kind of guitar equipment he used so they could get girls too.

Maybe they weren't focusing on the right equipment, however. Soon a pair of groupies/souvenir collectors called the Plaster Casters would begin amassing molded impressions of rock stars' erect—or, in some cases, semi-flaccid—members. The Plaster Casters' handiwork made it clear that guitar playing wasn't the only area where Jimi left his competition in the dust.

So here was Hendrix—a quiet, gentle guy who just happened to be hung like a cart horse. No wonder he never lacked for girlfriends. But Jimi could also use quietness as a form of passive aggression, as Pete Townshend learned backstage at the Monterey Pop Festival in June 1967. This was the first big gathering of the hippie counterculture, featuring musical artists as diverse as Otis Redding, Ravi Shankar and Janis Joplin. It also marked Hendrix's triumphant return to the States.

"Jimi was on acid," Townshend recalls. "And he stood on a chair. I was trying to get him to talk to me about the fact that I didn't want the Who to follow him onto the stage. I was saying, 'For fuck's sake, Jimi, it's bad enough you're gonna fuck up my life, I'm not gonna have you steal my act. That's the only thing I've got. You're a great genius. The audience will appreciate that. But what do I do? I wear a Union Jack jacket and smash my guitar. So give me a break. Let us go on first.' But he was just playing the guitar and ignoring me. I thought he was kind of teasing me. But Brian Jones told me later that he was just fucking *completely* whacked on acid. So John Phillips [*festival promoter and singer with the Mamas and the Papas*] flipped a coin and it came down in my favor. I said, 'Right—we're going on first.' But I wasn't angry at Jimi. I loved him very, very much. After Monterey, I got to know him a little in L.A. And suddenly—

Performing in 1969

Onstage at the Royal Albert Hall, on February 24, 1969

PHOTO BY K & K ULF KRUGER OHG/REDFERNS/GETTY IMAGES

maybe it was a different bunch of drugs he was using—but he was very, very affectionate and friendly to me."

### AXIS: BOLD AS LOVE

**BEFORE 1967 WAS** over, the Jimi Hendrix Experience were back at Olympic Studios in London—disciplined by over 180 live shows and elated by the success of *Are You Experienced*. By December of that same year, they had emerged with what is arguably the most polished gem in the Hendrix catalog: *Axis: Bold as Love*. The cover art—gorgeous in its original 12-inch gatefold release format—enshrines Jimi, Noel and Mitch among the many-armed deities of the Hindu pantheon. The serene mood and soothing colors of the artwork reflect not only hippie culture's fascination with Hindu mysticism, but also the kaleidoscopic mastery of the music waiting within the sleeve.

Jimi Hendrix blossomed as a songwriter on *Axis*, crafting sardonic little vignettes ("Wait Until Tomorrow," "Castles Made of Sand") and conjuring up fantasy worlds of shimmering imagery and prismatic guitar textures ("Bold as Love," "One Rainy Wish"). *Axis* finds the Experience in top form. Chas Chandler and Eddie Kramer were growing more confident in their production and engineering roles.

"Chas Chandler was definitely in charge of production," Kramer recalls. "Without Chas' help, I don't think Jimi could have done what he did. I think Chas was an unsung hero in the whole career of Jimi Hendrix. He really helped Jimi develop. He was the man with the patience and fortitude to help him with his songwriting, to give him books on science fiction to fire his imagination, and to sit with him day after day in his apartment and let him be creative. Chas had a vision of what it would take to put Jimi on top, because Chas came from this background of the three-minute pop song with the Animals. In a way, that restricted Jimi. But I think it was a good kind of restriction. Because it forced Jimi to think, Okay, if my ideas are out here—six-feet wide—I have to make them three-feet wide: gather all that information and compact it into a little three- or four-minute piece. That produced some amazing results."

By this point, Hendrix was well into his collaboration with pioneering guitar effects designer Roger Mayer. Kramer cites *Axis*' "Spanish Castle Magic" as one of the first songs to employ Mayer's Octavia pedal, the primordial octave divider, on guitar:

"Roger was very much a part of what we were doing, whether it was on a daily basis or whether he came in once a week," Kramer notes. "He always had some kind of new box that Jimi was experimenting with. Roger would always be in there with his soldering iron, trying to give Jimi something different, with a bit more of an edge. He was only too willing to experiment. All the wah-wah pedals were highly hot-rodded. The octave doubler, wah-wah, fuzz...they were all very much custom-made for Jimi."

> "JIMI WAS ON ACID. AND HE STOOD ON A CHAIR. I WAS TRYING TO GET HIM TO TALK TO ME ABOUT THE FACT THAT I DIDN'T WANT THE WHO TO FOLLOW HIM ONTO THE STAGE."
>
> —PETE TOWNSHEND

But perhaps *Axis*' single biggest audio innovation was its brash use of stereo tape flanging. That's the effect that makes the guitar solo coda to "Bold as Love" sound like it's ascending into the stratosphere, bringing the original album release to an appropriately hallucinogenic conclusion.

### ELECTRIC LADYLAND

**LIKE ALL PERFECT** moments, the serenity of *Axis* proved short-lived. Relations within the Experience were growing strained—particularly between Hendrix and Noel Redding, who was beginning to feel under-compensated financially for his work in the band. In January 1968, on tour behind *Axis*, a heated argument broke out between Hendrix and Redding. Jimi spent the night in a Swedish jail after wrecking the hotel room where the altercation had taken place.

All the touring and rampant drug use were starting to take their toll. Under these strained circumstances, work began on the Jimi Hendrix Experience's third and final album, the epic double-LP *Electric Ladyland*. It took a year to make, which by Sixties standards seemed an unreasonably long amount of time. Just to hedge their bets, the group's record label put out *Smash Hits*, a repackaging of tracks from the first album, combined with the non-album B-sides from the first four singles.

Meanwhile, sessions for what would become the *Electric Ladyland* album moved from Olympic in London across the Atlantic to New York, where the project settled in at the newly opened Record Plant, the first in a new breed of hip, rock-oriented recording facilities. In the process, Chas Chandler walked out on the project and resigned as Hendrix's manager, frustrated at how much time it was taking to complete the album.

"Jimi was back in his home country and he wanted to stretch out," says Kramer. "He had the success of the first two albums behind him; he loved to jam and party and be creative. But I think the hangers-on became a problem. They became a problem for Chas. And certainly for me. Sessions would be tough because Jimi couldn't say no to his buddies. He invited everybody into the studio. He'd have invited the street sweeper and the cleaning lady and the record company president if he could."

On a few tracks, Hendrix began moving away from the core Experience lineup and instrumentation, adding congas, sax, flute and organ to the album's sonic palette. While Hendrix was generous to a fault—he once gave a Porsche to a casual friend—he was also demanding in the studio. Kramer remembers him losing patience with guitarist Dave Mason, then a member of the successful rock group Traffic, during the tracking session for Hendrix's cover of Bob Dylan's "All Along the Watchtower":

"Jimi had shown the chord progression to Dave, and Dave just couldn't get the damn thing right. And Jimi was yelling at Dave, 'Why are you screwing up, man?' Jimi got very upset, I remember. On most of the sessions I'd done with him, mistakes had been very rare occurrences."

Traffic's leader, Steve Winwood (formerly with the Spencer Davis Group and later to play with Eric Clapton in Blind Faith before going on to a stellar solo career) played organ on the live-in-the-studio "Voodoo Chile," as did Jefferson Airplane bassist Jack Casady. According to Kramer, Hendrix ran into those players at Steve Paul's Scene club one night and brought them back to the Record Plant. (Jazz guitar great Larry Coryell was there

PHOTO BY MICHAEL OCHS ARCHIVES/GETTY IMAGES

too, but declined to play on the session.)

"It was a good example of what I called 'planned jamming,'" says Kramer. "The whole thing wasn't as casual as you might think. Jimi directed everything, saying, 'Here, play this. Do that.' It was all worked out in his mind. He found some great players, and they rose to the occasion."

*Electric Ladyland* is one of the great rock double albums—a work that shows all of Hendrix's varied musical strengths. There are concise, well-crafted songs in the manner of *Axis* ("Crosstown Traffic," Redding's "Little Miss Strange," "House Burning Down.") and tight R&B numbers like the Earl King cover "Come On" and the title track, "Have You Ever Been (To Electric Ladyland)." But there are also looser, more jam-based tracks ("Rainy Day, Dream Away," "Voodoo Chile") and wondrous, otherworldly soundscapes, such as the feature-length suite that closes side three: "1983 (A Merman I Should Turn to Be)"/"Moon Turn the Tides... Gently Gently Away." Many of the tracks featured pioneering experiments in stereo panning and 3D audio imaging that greatly enhance the album's overall mood of cross-genre experimentalism.

The original album graphics reflected the album's dynamic of pop cohesiveness vs. freeform open-endedness. On the front there was a shot of the Experience in their old Swinging London regalia. The back cover was a grainy closeup of Hendrix in concert, his face bathed in orange and red hues from the stage lighting, his eyes closed and lips parted as if in mid-orgasm. The gatefold inner sleeve included an abstract prose piece by Jimi, "Letter to the Room Full of Mirrors," written in the free-association style his hero Bob Dylan had used on several of his album sleeves.

In all, *Electric Ladyland* is a glorious last hurrah for the Experience, who broke up shortly after its release.

## BAND OF GYPSYS

**BY THE END OF 1969,** all the great Sixties rock groups had either broken up or changed direction. The Beatles, Cream, Big Brother and the Holding Company (Janis Joplin's band), the Yardbirds and Buffalo Springfield had all called it quits. Dylan and the Byrds had gone country. The Stones had quit horsing around with psychedelia and gone back to their bluesy roots. The Who had gone operatic. The Kinks had turned to the British music hall tradition. The Doors were monkeying with saxophones. The Jefferson Airplane had gone political.

The mood of youth culture had shifted dramatically. The hippie thing was over. During a Rolling Stones concert at Altamont Speedway in California, an audience member had been stabbed to death by a mem-

Performing at the Marquee Club in London, March 1967

ber of the Hell's Angels, who had been hired as security guards. Despite protest marches and eloquent outcry against U.S. military involvement in Vietnam, the war dragged on. The anti-war and civil rights movements were turning militant.

In the midst of all this, Jimi Hendrix was trying to forge a new musical identity. As he'd done during the *Electric Ladyland* sessions, he used jamming as a vehicle for exploring new musical directions. In 1969, the Jeff Beck Group played a two-week residency at the Steve Paul Scene club in New York. Hendrix would often jump onstage for an extended encore jam. Jeff Beck couldn't help but notice Hendrix's energy-depleting lifestyle at the time:

"He did burn the candle [*at both ends*]. I couldn't keep up. We went out one night, after we'd finished up at the Scene. We'd already played two hours of raving rock and roll, with him coming on for the encore. Then we went to the New York Brasserie to have something to eat. And somewhere else after that. At four A.M. he said, 'Let's go back to the hotel.' I thought, Thank God; he'll fall asleep and I'll go off home. But instead, he'd start playing music and we'd go out somewhere else at five o'clock. This kind of thing was just an everyday occurrence with him. I'd be history for two days afterward, and he'd still be at it."

Hendrix had begun jamming with his old Army buddy Billy Cox. The two had played together in several bands during those dues-paying days before Hendrix hit it big in London. Mitch Mitchell had also begun to hang out with Jimi once again. With Cox and Mitchell, Hendrix put together a band called Electric Sky Church (also sometimes billed as Gypsys, Suns and Rainbows), which also included rhythm guitarist Larry Leeds and percussionists Juma Lewis and Jerry Velez. He played several dates with this lineup, including the Woodstock Festival in May 1969. But, much like its name, this collection of players never really jelled. It's no coincidence that Jimi's signature number from Woodstock became his unaccompanied solo guitar performance of "The Star Spangled Banner."

Jimi was happy to reconnect with Cox and Mitchell, but the past was also coming back to haunt him in less agreeable forms. Legal hassles stemming back to the old Curtis Knight days had reared up once again. They proved to be the catalyst for Hendrix's short-lived Band of Gypsys, consisting of Jimi, Billy Cox and former Electric Flag drummer Buddy Miles, who'd also played on *Electric Ladyland*.

"The deal with the Band of Gypsys was that Jimi had a contractual problem to rectify, and Buddy and I stepped in to help him out," Billy Cox told *Guitar World*'s Andy Aledort in 1999. "Jimi said, 'Man, they're gonna sue me for five million dollars,' or something like that. I said, 'Why don't you give him an album?' [*i.e., the proceeds from the sale of the album would be awarded to settle the lawsuit.*] A couple of days later Jimi said, 'You're right. Let's give him an album.' Mitch was Jimi's first choice for a drummer. But Mitch was in England. Buddy was readily available."

Entrepreneur Bill Graham booked the Band of Gypsys into the Fillmore East to play four shows—two each on New Year's Eve and New Year's Day of 1969–70. These tracks were duly recorded, then edited and mixed at a funky New York studio called Juggy's Sound. Today, *Band of Gypsys* is hailed as a classic live album,

PHOTO BY RAY STEVENSON / REX USA

> **“CLAPTON WAS UP THERE DOING HIS STUFF IN FRONT OF ALL THE GIRLIES, AND ALONG COMES JIMI, WHO SITS IN AND UPSETS THE WHOLE APPLE CART—PLAYING WITH HIS TEETH, BEHIND HIS HEAD, DOING ALMOST CIRCUS TRICKS WITH THE GUITAR.”**
> —JEFF BECK

particularly by connoisseurs of extended guitar improvisation. But in its time, it was not so universally acclaimed. Coming after the carefully crafted Experience studio albums, it seemed a disappointment to many Hendrix fans. The album's rough-edged quality, particularly on the standout track "Machine Gun," did reflect the militant mood of the times, but the Band of Gypsys were simply not as good a live band as the Experience in their prime. While Buddy Miles could lay down a fat groove, he lacked Mitchell's finesse. To many who had followed Hendrix's career since 1967, *Band of Gypsys* just seemed a throwaway: a hastily assembled live album. Which, of course, is exactly what it was. There are indications that Hendrix himself felt this way.

"I don't know that it was something Jimi liked 100 percent," says Eddie Kramer. "I think he was disappointed in some of the excessive [*vocal*] warbling of Buddy Miles. There was a tremendous amount of editing done on it. There was a huge amount of jamming and stuff that didn't quite fit on the record. The editing was a little untidy at points. But having said that, I think it's a wonderful example of Jimi being able to play with a reasonable amount of freedom."

The next Band of Gypsys appearance proved to be their last. The group had only gotten to the second number of their January 28 set at New York's Madison Square Garden when Hendrix abruptly announced, "I'm sorry, we just can't get it together," and walked offstage.

### THE CRY OF LOVE

**LIKE HENDRIX'S EARLIEST** years of life, his final days were fraught with confusion over identity. The dawn of the Seventies turned out to be a tricky time for him. Critics and hipsters were starting to say he'd "lost it." Meanwhile, he was starting to break through to a new audience, but there was a problem there too. While the hippie dream was dead as a doornail, the *Woodstock* film documentary had finally spread the gospel of long hair, psychedelic drugs and hard, improvisational rock music to the less-urban reaches of middle America and to more-conservative sectors of the youth population. So there was a new bunch of kids clamoring for Hendrix. They were generally a little younger and less "tuned in" than the original Hendrix audience, so they were essentially playing catch-up on the musical developments of the late Sixties. Which means they still expected Hendrix to do the "wild man of Borneo" guitar-humping act that had wowed Swinging London four years earlier. Hendrix was understandably weary of all this and eager to move on to a performance style that was more about music than theatricality.

At the same time, Hendrix was under pressure from militant groups such as the Black Panthers, who'd labeled him a traitor to the cause of black liberation, a sellout to the white world. The dissolution of the Band of Gypsys—Hendrix's only all-black group since his Chitlin Circuit days—certainly didn't help him on that front. It was the beginning of the age of political correctness. Hendrix had been more comfortable during the more freewheeling Sixties, when he could pursue his musical muse unencumbered by political agendas.

"Jimi was frustrated before he died because, I think, the public didn't understand him," says Eddie Kramer. "He was so confused as to which way to go."

In the midst of all this turmoil, Hendrix was pushing himself hard. He was trying to get together a new band and album, and build his own recording studio. The latter was an especially ambitious undertaking for that time period. A few rock stars like Paul McCartney, Mick Jagger and Pete Townshend had home studios. But Hendrix was planning something far more elaborate. While construction was underway at Electric Lady Studios—Hendrix's state-of-the-art dream factory down in the heart of Greenwich Village—the guitarist was hard at work on his new album uptown at the Record Plant. An overdub session for the latter-day Hendrix classic "Room Full of Mirrors" left a lasting impression on Carlos Santana. Then a young guitarist whose star was just rising in the wake of Woodstock, Carlos had been invited to hang with Jimi in the studio.

"They were continuing with what they had been recording the night before," Santana recalls. "It was take 25 or some ridiculous number. And it was 'Room Full of Mirrors.' The amplifiers were facing the control room glass and Jimi was facing the amps with his back to the glass, 'cause he didn't like anybody to see him playing. They rolled the tape and Jimi got on it. The first 10 or 12 bars were like, 'Wow, this is brilliant,' But then he just started going beyond the track—like Sun Ra, Screaming Jay Hawkins and Sonny Sharrock all rolled into one. What he was playing had nothing to do with

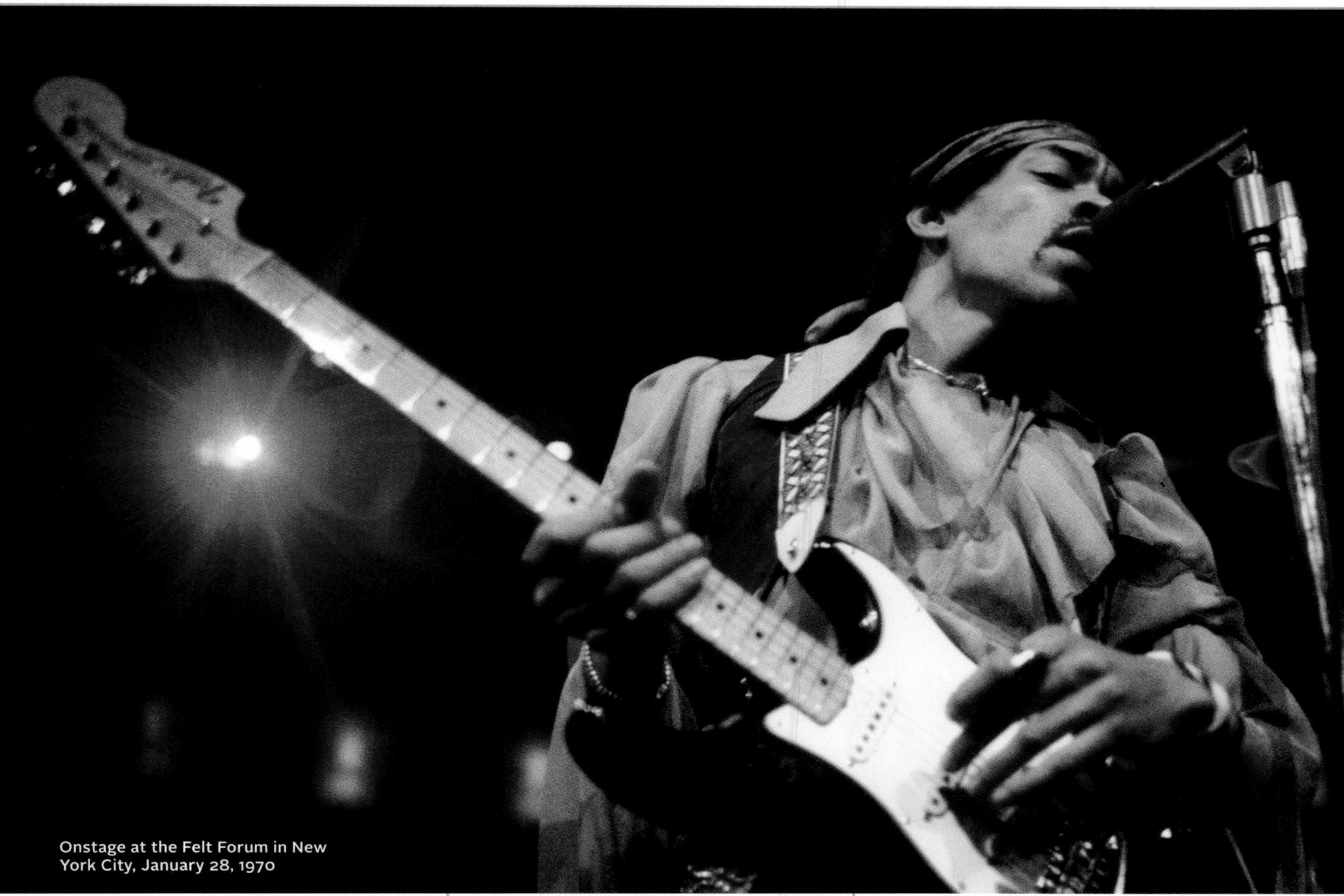
Onstage at the Felt Forum in New York City, January 28, 1970

the track anymore. I could see the engineer and producer look at one another like, Yeah, better go in there and get him. So two roadies go in the studio. They each grabbed Hendrix by one of his arms and pulled him away from the guitar and amp. And it was like one of those movies where the person's eyes are bloodshot and he's foaming at the mouth. It hit me like it would hit you if you were in the room when somebody was having an epileptic attack. I've heard of drooling when you play a solo, but never going into complete, possessed spasms."

By May 1970, Hendrix had moved his sessions into Electric Lady, working in Studio A while construction of studio B was being completed. He only got to make music in the studio he'd labored so hard to build for three months, from May to August 1970. Tracks he worked on during that period include "Dolly Dagger," "Night Bird Flying," "Straight Ahead," "Astro Man" and the aforementioned "Room Full of Mirrors." The official opening party for Electric Lady was held on August 20. Seven days later, Hendrix flew to London before embarking on some European dates.

Sad to say, things did not go well in Europe. Billy Cox had a bad acid trip, which left him behaving erratically. Hendrix's own psychological and physical condition was poor as well. He was thin, and patches of premature gray had started to appear in his hair. By several eyewitness accounts, he was out of it on drugs a lot of the time. There were violent incidents in hotel rooms. When a show in Denmark went badly, Hendrix told his audience "I've been dead for years." He was booed in Germany.

Back in London, Hendrix fared better at an informal jam with ex-Animals singer Eric Burdon and his band War at Ronnie Scott's jazz club. It was to be his last public appearance. Two days later, Jimi Hendrix was dead, having choked to death on his own vomit some hours after ingesting a combination of sleeping pills and red wine.

The recordings that Hendrix had been working on just before his death have come out in several forms over the years. Audiences at the time first heard 10 of these recordings on the *Cry of Love* album, released in March 1971. Some of the songs had been mixed when Hendrix was alive. Others had been completed after his death by Eddie Kramer and Mitch Mitchell. Over the following three years, more of the final Hendrix studio tracks emerged on *Rainbow Bridge* (which included the successful radio song "Dolly Dagger"), *War Heroes* and *Loose Ends*. Rock fans at the time were keenly aware that these were pieces of unfinished work by an artist who had been groping for a new direction. All this was well reported in the rock press in the early Seventies.

Given Hendrix's vulnerable psychological state during his final days, his experimental working methods and his general tendency to play life's hand close to the chest, one can only speculate as to how these recordings might have fit into the album that Jimi never got to complete. Today, latter-day Hendrix compositions like "Izabella" and "Ezy Ryder" are analyzed in tones of hushed reverence in the pages of magazines such as *Guitar World* and others like it. At the time of their release, however, these songs were nowhere near as well known or loved as Hendrix favorites like "Purple Haze" or "All Along the Watchtower."

Jimi would have been glad to see that his last works have come to be so greatly appreciated. That's one pretty safe conjecture. ◆

Bo Diddley circa 1957 in
New York City

# THE BEAT GOES ON

Bo Diddley changed rock and roll with a primal rhythm that will forever bear his name.

BY ALAN DI PERNA

BO DIDDLEY 1928–2008

# ROCK AND ROLL LOST ONE

## of its greatest originators, primordial architects and all-around wildest performers on June 2, 2008, when Bo Diddley succumbed to heart failure at age 79 in his Archer, Florida, home. His Fifties recordings for Chess Records' Checker label helped ignite the original rock and roll revolution, and his influence has been profoundly felt by every subsequent rock generation.

"It's a good day, because I've walked on the planet at the same time as Bo Diddley," Billy Gibbons said on hearing of Bo's passing. The ZZ Top guitarist is just one of many rock guitarists who took a major cue from Bo Diddley's unique style. "The simple and humorous artistry that accompanied the creation we all know as 'the Bo Diddley beat' is a resounding testament to someone who knew how to touch us in a rock and roll way. Many times Bo made a point to say, 'I'll always be around.' And we know he will."

The musical and sociological phenomenon known as rock and roll burst from two great rhythmic wellsprings. One was the amped-up 12-bar shuffle: Forties R&B gone hog wild and driven right off the road by Chuck Berry and Little Richard. The other was something even more primal, darker, deeper and dangerous sounding. The throbbing Bo Diddley beat has always seemed timeless: an orgiastic pulse, an inextinguishable life force that leads back to humankind's earliest roots on the African continent.

So it is fitting that the man the world knew as Bo Diddley was born Ellas Otha Bates in the deep South—McComb, Mississippi, to be exact, about 15 miles from the Louisiana border. In later life, Bo sometimes boasted that many of his relatives came from the Louisiana territory around New Orleans, that great source of Creole culture and the only American locale where enslaved Africans were allowed to keep their drums and thus preserve their native rhythms.

The child destined to reinvigorate those rhythms as rock and roll was mainly raised by his mother's cousin, Gussie McDaniel, who changed his name to Ellas McDaniel and brought him to Chicago when he was 6.

Young Ellas started out on violin but soon switched to guitar. By some accounts, he became fascinated by the instrument after hearing the great bluesman John Lee Hooker, another deeply elemental player who could work endless rhythmic voodoo out of a single root chord.

While Ellas was attending Foster Vocational School he built his own electric guitar, taking a Gretsch neck and electronics and fitting them onto a rectangular, cigar box–shaped body that would become one of Bo Diddley's iconic trademarks. Like the man's music, the simple shape was like a minimalist art statement—the guitar distilled down to its most essential geometry.

His other great trademark was of course his name, acquired in 1955 when he released his first recording, "Bo Diddley." There are varying accounts as to origin of this *nom du disque*. Billy Boy Arnold, Bo's harmonica player at the time, claims to have made it up, but most people associate it with the diddley bow, a simple homemade instrument consisting of a piece of wire stretched between two nails on a board. Many of the legendary bluesmen, too impoverished in their youth to afford a guitar, claimed to have taken their first musical steps on such an instrument.

> **" MANY TIMES BO MADE A POINT TO SAY, 'I'LL ALWAYS BE AROUND.' AND WE KNOW HE WILL. "**
>
> —*BILLY GIBBONS*

True or not, there's a kind of poetic justice in this attribution, since the beat unleashed on that momentous first single is very much a diddley bow rhythm: vigorous syncopations on a simple tonic base. It's similar to the Afro Cuban *clave* rhythm and thigh-slapping street beat called hambone. Bo said he picked up the distinctive rhythmic pattern in an African American church. The Bo Diddley beat is all of these things and more: an essential rhythm of the African Diaspora, and Bo articulated it that way on his discs. The instrumentation on "Bo Diddley" and follow-up classics like "Pretty Thing," "Hey Bo Diddley" and "Mona" is tribal in its simplicity. Drummer Clifton James sticks mainly to the toms, eschewing the more European military tonality of the snare drum. And a key member of Bo's lineup was maracas player Jerome Green, a guy shaking hollow gourds filled with beads, which is about as tribal as it gets.

Bo Diddley's unique contribution to this rhythmic heritage was to *electrify* it. The electric Spanish guitar had come along in the Twenties as a jazz instrument. But Bo liberated it from the dense jazz chord clusters that never sounded so great once those early electrics started distorting. Rather than fighting distortion, Bo was one of the first guitarists who figured out how to use it to great musical advantage, via simple chord progressions and voicings. Many times his guitar was tuned to an open E chord, which he'd barre as needed with one finger.

Along with distortion, Bo Diddley was one of the first electric guitarists to exploit the rhythmic potential of tremolo. He claimed to have made his first tremolo unit by himself, out of automobile parts and a clock spring. The pulsating tremolo on Bo Diddley's classic recordings drifts in and out sync with the main beat, creating hypnotic polyrhythms. Bo's other trick was that he didn't use a bass guitar or bass fiddle on many of his sessions. This simplified lineup did much to liberate the rhythmic interplay between the guitar and drums. This freedom was later taken up by later great bass-less rock and roll bands like the Cramps, Flat Duo Jets, Yeah Yeah Yeahs and White Stripes.

Bo's rhythmic savvy was matched by a colorful and clever knack for lyrics. The

Diddley (right) with bandmates, including Norma-Jean Wofford, a.k.a. "the Duchess," (left) in New York, circa 1958

badass protagonist of "Who Do You Love?" "walks 47 miles of barbed wire, has a cobra snake for neck tie" plus "a house made out of rattlesnake hide with a chimney made of a human skull." Bo Diddley's imagery came from sources as diverse as nursery rhymes and street slang. One of his best-selling singles, "Say Man," drew from the African-American oral tradition called "the dozens," a kind of playfully ritualized trading of imaginative insults that was a major source for both early blues and more recent hip-hop.

Bo Diddley possessed one of those highly active minds that was always tinkering with something—words, beats or music gear. In 1958, he went to Gretsch and asked them to build him a better version of his homemade rectangular guitar. Gretsch responded with the limited-edition Big B model and the curvy Jupiter Thunderbird, which Billy Gibbons revived years later as the Billy Bo Gretsch. Gibbons also got the idea for ZZ Top's famous furry guitars from the cover of Diddley's 1961 album, *Bo Diddley Is a Lover*.

The sacred rock and roll combination of wild guitars and pretty girls also traces back to Bo Diddley, who in the late Fifties started performing with a female co-guitarist. Peggy Jones, a.k.a. "Lady Bo," was the first to fill this role, but her successor Norma-Jean Wofford, a.k.a. "the Duchess," is perhaps better known. These were some of the earliest female musicians in rock.

Bo himself was a distinctive performer: a stocky black man with thick-rimmed eyeglasses, a bowtie and plaid jacket, wiggling his knees and rearing up on his toes while furiously down-stroking his cigar box guitar. It was a little too "outside" for some of the Fifties record buying public. Or maybe Bo was just too "black" for mainstream American culture of the time. Whatever the reason, he often felt that he never received all the credit he deserved.

But his fellow musicians took notice right from the start. Early on, Buddy Holly copped the Bo Diddley beat in his song "Not Fade Away," as did Johnny Otis in his tune, "Willie and the Hand Jive," later covered by Eric Clapton. The Bo Diddley influence can be felt on tracks as diverse as the Who's "Magic Bus" and the Smiths' "How Soon Is Now."

But musicians weren't the only ones influenced by Bo Diddley. Guitar manufacturer Hartley Peavey credits Bo as the inspiration for his Peavey Electronics empire. "In 1957 I went to a Bo Diddley concert in Laurel, Mississippi," Peavey recalls. "And from then on I wanted to be a guitar player. I begged my father to give me an electric guitar but got nowhere with the request. So I ended up modifying a classical guitar for steel strings and building my own pickup. And I built an amplifier out of junk parts. I'd decided I wanted a big amp with four 12-inch speakers in it, like Bo's."

Bo Diddley first toured England in 1963 and was a huge influence on the British Invasion. The Rolling Stones covered "Mona" and the Yardbirds had a massive hit with Bo's "I'm a Man." Jeff Beck's double-time outro solo on the Yardbirds track culminates in some rhythmic scratching that surely derives from Bo.

Down through the years, rock musicians never forgot Bo Diddley. Players as diverse as Leslie West, Albert Lee, Alvin Lee, Roger McGuinn, Joe Cocker and Billy Joel turned out to perform on Bo's 1976 *20th Anniversary* album. In 1979, the Clash tapped Bo Diddley to open for them on their first American tour. The Rolling Stones' Ron Wood toured with Bo Diddley in the Eighties under the sobriquet "the Gunslingers." And in 1987 Bo Diddley was inducted into the Rock and Roll Hall of Fame by his long-time admirer, Billy Gibbons.

Bo Diddley's 1996 studio album, *A Man Amongst Men*, would prove to be his last, although nobody knew it at the time. It is a fittingly solid sendoff, with guest spots from Wood, Keith Richards, Jimmy Vaughan and Richie Sambora, among other guitar luminaries. But Bo's health began to decline in his later years. He became diabetic and in May 2007 suffered a stroke, followed by a heart attack that August. When he passed away in June 2008, he was at home, peaceful and surrounded by many of his family members.

The extended family of rock and roll will also mourn him. Every one of us who has ever found an identity, a paycheck, some solace or a source of joy and strength in rock and roll music owes a huge debt of gratitude to Bo Diddley. ◆

# STIR IT UP

Bob Marley awakened the world to the power of reggae music and the soul-affirming teachings of the Rastafarian movement. Thirty-two years after his death, his lead guitarist and friend Junior Marvin pays tribute to Marley's music, life and legacy of peace.

BY ALAN DI PERNA

BOB MARLEY 1945–1981

"JAH HAS SPARED MY LIFE to do things that I never dreamed of before." That's what Bob Marley told his lead guitar player Junior Marvin in 1977. At that time, Marley was already a legend. The release of his 1973 album *Catch a Fire* had ignited a worldwide fascination with reggae music—the sound of Kingston, Jamaica's Trenchtown ghetto—and with Marley's culture of the Rastafarians: dreadlocked men and women of color who took the Ethiopian emperor Haile Selassie as their messiah, one whose coming had been prophesied by the early 20th century black leader Marcus Garvey. The Rastas' copious, sacramental use of ganja certainly resonated with the college crowd and others, as did their message of universal love and black liberation.

But most of all it was Marley himself who captivated music fans worldwide. A handsome young man with a leonine mane of dreadlocks and a gift for making sheer musical poetry out of the ghetto's hard realities, he seemed like a Jamaican Bob Dylan, Jimi Hendrix, John Lennon and Che Guevara all rolled into one gargantuan musical spliff. Throughout the Seventies, college dorms, motor vehicles, apartment blocks, dancehalls, clubs, suburban homes and mansions were rocking to Marley anthems like "Get Up Stand Up" and "War," party classics like "Lively Up Yourself" and "Trenchtown Rock" and poignant love songs like "No Woman No Cry." Eric Clapton himself had covered Marley's ganja outlaw saga "I Shot the Sheriff." The man was huge.

But on the evening of December 3, 1976, Marley had received a brutal wake-up call. Seven gunmen broke into his home and opened fire, in what was most likely a politically motivated assassination attempt. A bullet grazed Marley's rib and passed through his arm. Another bullet lodged between the scalp and skull of his wife, Rita. Just an inch lower and it would have entered her brain. Marley's manager Don Taylor took four in his leg and another in the base of his spine, his body acting as a shield for his employer. Other members of Marley's band, the Wailers, miraculously escaped being struck by the hailstorm of bullets that riddled the walls of Marley's home with holes, like the scene of some gangland hit. Yet no one was killed.

A devout Rastafarian, Marley recognized the hand of Jah at work in his life once again. "Bob was very much in high spirits and very happy to be alive," Junior Marvin says. "He felt like he got a second chance to live, and it was like every second from that point onward counted for him. He wasn't going to take anything for granted."

As a result of the attempt on his life, early 1977 found Marley in virtual exile in London and in need of a new guitar player. His former lead guitarist, Donald Kinsey, had been present when the gunmen opened fire, narrowly escaping with his own life. He'd gotten on the first plane back to the States, never to return.

Of course Bob Marley was no stranger to Britain's capital city. He had pounded the pavements of London back in 1973, when an earlier record deal with CBS had gone sour. He'd ultimately landed at the door of Island Records, headed by entrepreneur Chris Blackwell. A leading light of the Jamaican industry, Blackwell had formed Island Records in Jamaica in 1959. He'd spearheaded the careers of artists like Jimmy Cliff and Millie Small and was a major rock mogul with acts like Traffic, Jethro Tull, King Crimson, Emerson Lake & Palmer and Free, all of whom recorded for Island imprints. It was Blackwell's support, clout and savvy that helped bring Bob Marley's music and message to the world in 1973.

**THE ASSASSINATION ATTEMPT HAD MADE BOB KEENLY AWARE THAT HE WASN'T GOING TO BE AROUND FOREVER. AND THERE WAS SO MUCH WORK YET TO BE DONE.**

Blackwell came to the rescue once again in 1977, bringing Jamaican-born, London-bred Donald Hanson "Junior" Marvin Kerr into the fold. An up-and-coming player at the time, Marvin had worked with guitar icons like T-Bone Walker and John McLaughlin and had done sessions for Blackwell ranging from reggae greats like Toots Hibbert and the Heptones to British folk legends Fairport Convention and U.K. bluesman Keef Hartley.

"I'd just played guitar on Steve Winwood's first solo album, *Arc of a Diver*," Marvin recalls. "Chris Blackwell heard the disc and said to Winwood at a party, 'Man, your guitar playing has come a long way.' Steve told him, 'Thank you, but actually it was this British Jamaican guy who lives in Ladbroke Grove. His name is Junior.' Blackwell said, 'Junior? I know Junior.' "

Marley was eager to get back into the studio. He had plenty of material that he was itching to get down on tape. The assassination attempt had made him keenly aware that he wasn't going to be around forever. And there was so much work yet to be done. All over the world, the poor and the marginalized were still being brutally oppressed. War and intolerance continued to bring suffering all around the globe. If Bob Marley wanted to make the world a better place through his music, he knew he needed to work even harder and accomplish even more than he'd already achieved.

What he couldn't have known in 1977—although perhaps he might have sensed it on some intuitive spiritual level—was that he only had four more years to live. On May 11, 1981, his life was brought to an end not by bullets but by cancer.

A great deal of Marley's legacy rests with the work he accomplished between 1977 through 1981. Although he'd been a professional singer and musician since 1962, the music of Marley's final four years is informed by a level of intensity not quite

Performing in Santa Barbara, CA, 1979

heard on his earlier recordings. His message of unity, liberation and One Love becomes more urgent, and the sound and scope of his music becomes more universal. In this relatively short time span, he produced four of his greatest studio albums: *Exodus*, which was named best album of the 20th century by *Time* magazine, *Kaya*, *Survival* and *Uprising*, along with the powerhouse live album *Babylon by Bus* and a string of concerts that literally made history around the world.

As Marley's lead guitarist, Junior Marvin was an integral part of the momentous final chapter in the life of a legend. While Marvin has gone on to work with an impressive roster of reggae stars including Burning Spear, Culture, Bunny Wailer, Alpha Blondy, Rita Marley, Judy Mowatt and Sly & Robbie, the years he spent with Marley hold a special place in his heart. He still vividly recalls driving through the streets of London in Chris Blackwell's Rolls-Royce on February 14, 1977—Valentine's Day—going to meet Marley for the first time. Blackwell hadn't told the young guitarist whom they were en route to meet, but Marvin figured it must be someone important, so he'd brought his guitar along with him.

"Chris took me to Chelsea," Marvin recalls. "We went to a big house on Oakley Street. We walked in the door and there's this man with big, big dreadlocks standing there, with his back to us. When I looked at him, he had a big aura around him, shining like a rainbow. I thought, It's gotta be Bob Marley. It just came to me. He turned around and he had a big grin on his face. Bob Marley looked at me, shook my hand and said, 'I've been hearing a lot about you. They call you the Jimi Hendrix of London.'

"I said, 'No way. There's only one Jimi Hendrix, and I'm nowhere in his league.' Bob goes, 'Well, people seem to think you are.' I thanked him for the compliment, and Chris said, 'I brought you here because Bob needs a guitar player. He's working on two albums at the same time, *Exodus* and *Kaya*."

Marvin was invited to take out his guitar and jam. "Bob was playing acoustic guitar," Marvin recalls. "His keyboard player Tyrone Downie was on bass and I was playing lead guitar. We jammed on 'Exodus,' 'Waiting in Vain' and 'Jamming.' Bob was constructing those songs at that time, getting ready to do the vocals and perfect them. He and Tyrone were singing. At the end of the jam, he slapped five with me and said, 'Welcome to the Wailers.' "

But there was one complication. That very morning, Marvin had received a phone call from Stevie Wonder, who also wanted Marvin to join his band. This was a major dilemma, as both Marley and Wonder were major heroes for the young player. "I called all my school friends," he says, "and all my musician friends. I called my mom and my uncle who ran a sound system in England. I said, 'What would you do if you were in my position?' They all said, 'Bob Marley is from Jamaica and you were born in Jamaica. You gotta support your countryman.' And, believe me, that's how the decision was made. I also felt it was important to go with Bob because reggae was, at that time, a new form of music that is very inspirational and has a strong message."

Marvin had just joined what is arguably, and may well always be, the greatest reggae band of all time. On drums and bass were the sibling rhythm section of Carlton "Carly" and Aston "Family Man" Barrett, who are to reggae what the Funk Brothers are to Motown. Seasoned veterans of the Jamaican studio scene, they'd even played on Toots and the Maytals' 1968 track "Do the Reggay," the song that gave the music its name. Along with Tyrone Downie on keyboards and Marley's old Rasta friend Alvin "Seeco" Patterson on percussion, the band was also blessed with the angelic backing vocals of the I-Threes: Judy Mowatt, Marcia Griffiths and Bob's wife, Rita Marley, each one a Jamaican hit maker in her own right and collectively a trinity of voices that shone like a halo around Bob's dreadlocked crown.

With Marvin onboard, this reggae dream team repaired to Island Records' Hammersmith rehearsal studio to tighten things up. From there they went on to Island's Basing Street recording studio, in London. They'd block-booked three months at the facility. They had two entire albums to record.

"We recorded about 30 songs," Marvin says. "Bob had the songs for each album in different folders. Between the logistics of touring, rehearsing, studio availability and everyone's schedules, it was better that we recorded two albums at the same time. Because the songs were all ready and the concepts and ideas were all ready."

Marvin's comment sheds light on a key aspect of Bob Marley's personality. While the world tends to regard Rastafarians as stoned-out layabouts, Marley was anything but. He was a man with a mission, a mission from Jah. Highly motivated and hard working to an almost extreme degree, he was known by his band members as "the first one on the bus."

"He was a workaholic," Marvin says. "Bob slept only four hours a day. He was very motivated and very focused on what he was doing, writing over 100 songs a year and taking the best album out of them. So his success wasn't by chance or luck. It was pure hard work on his part. Everyone in the band was influenced and motivated by that."

As sessions at Basing Street got underway, Marvin introduced one more obsessive into the mix. Guitar electronics guru Roger Mayer had designed custom effect pedals for Hendrix, Page, Beck and the Isley Brothers, among others. Mayer had befriended Marvin around 1974, and Marvin's first move upon joining the Wailers was to contact Mayer, then in New York, with a request to buy him a guitar suitable to this prestigious new gig.

"I could afford it," Marvin says. "Bob gave me some money. Roger went to Manny's Music in Manhattan and chose a Strat out of about 100 guitars and shipped it to me within a couple of days. And that's what I played on *Exodus*."

Beyond that, Marvin brought Mayer into Basing Street to assist with the sessions. "I introduced Roger to Bob, and of course Bob loved him right away, because Bob found out that Roger had done Jimi Hendrix's guitar sounds, and Bob also loved Jimi Hendrix."

At Basing Street, Mayer immediately set to work tweaking Marvin's Strat, Family Man's 1972 Fender Jazz Bass and Marley's circa 1972 Gibson Les Paul Special. He also designed custom effect pedals for the group, much as he'd done for Hendrix and others before. "You listen to the Wailers from 1977 onward and you listen to the Wailers pre-1977, and you will hear the difference," Marvin says. "Part of that is down to Roger Mayer."

Bob Marley's iconic Les Paul Special, with its black P-90 pickup configuration is an odd one, indeed. Small-block fret inlays were not commonly used on this particular model. The neck and headstock binding are also anomalous and seem like some kind of custom job. The gold-plated Tune-o-matic bridge clearly isn't original. All other hardware is made of nickel. Marvin claims it was Mayer who did many of the modifications to Marley's Les Paul Special, including its large, oval, metal toggle switch plate and custom metal pickguard.

**IF YOU HUNG WITH BOB MARLEY, YOU WERE GOING TO EAT HEALTHY, SMOKE GOOD HERB, REHEARSE FOR HOURS ON END AND PLAY SOCCER.**

"The design on Bob's guitar, with the silver plate, is Roger's design," Marvin says. "I was there when Roger designed it. He did things to Bob's guitar that nobody knows. And you can't find it. If you go in the circuit board looking for what was done, you'll never find it. Roger showed me the secret of how they can't find it. He made me swear not to tell anybody what he did."

The year 1977 was a momentous one in many regards. Against a backdrop of severe worldwide economic recession and racial tensions, an anarchistic new form of music called punk rock burst out of London and New York with debut albums by the Sex Pistols, Clash, Television, Richard Hell and others. In Jamaica, the song "Two Sevens Clash" by the reggae group Culture was taken as an end-of-the-world prophecy, stopping traffic and closing down the banks and government offices on July 7 (7/7/77).

Into this charged environment came *Exodus* by Bob Marley and the Wailers, arguably Marley's finest disc ever and a work that mirrored the turbulent times from a fascinating new angle. The cover art, by longtime Marley art director Neville Garrick, is eloquent in its simplicity: stark red lettering shadowed in black, like some ancient Biblical inscription, against a gold background. The graphics are rich in Rastafarian imagery, the Lion of Judah symbolizing the Rasta belief that they, and black people generally, are the Lost Tribe of Israel, dispossessed of their homeland, wandering in bitter affliction. The back cover lettering echoes a line from the title track, "Exodus: Movement of Jah People," a reflection of the Rastas' Garveyite faith in repatriation, the glorious day when black people shall return in triumph to the African homeland.

The album casts its hypnotic spell right from the first track, "Natural Mystic," with its protracted fade-in, like a vision arising from the mist. Over a slow, deep-skank groove, Marley delivers a prophetic lyric, echoing passages from the Biblical Book of Revelation. "This may be the first trumpet, might as well be the last."

Junior Marvin's evocative lead guitar lines contribute much to the track's mystical vibe. Pumping his Strat through a Fender Twin, he spins out hypnotic blues riffs that curl around Marley's vocal like incense smoke swirling about a golden idol. "I really went for a blues feel on 'Natural Mystic,'" he says. "I drew on what I learned from playing with T-Bone Walker, but also my love of Albert King, B.B. King and Buddy Guy."

The track's long, slow fade-in was Chris Blackwell's idea. "Chris came in one day and said, 'How can we get people who put this CD on to automatically turn the volume up and keep it up?'" Marvin recalls. "We decided that we would fade the intro in. So people would think, Oh I need to turn my system up, it's too low. Once you'd turned it up and the drums come in and blast you, you'd be pinned to the back of your chair and go, 'Wow, lovely.' And that's the magic of 'Natural Mystic.' It was very cleverly put together by Chris and the band."

A militant mood predominates side one of *Exodus* in its original vinyl release. "Heathen" takes no prisoners, and "Exodus" is one of Marley's most powerful tracks ever. Tyrone Downie's kinetic Clavinet line conjures the energy of mass migration, the pilgrimage out of Babylon back to the African homeland, the Biblical wicked kingdom reincarnated as modern corporate mechanized society with its greed-ridden economics of oppression. The horns ring out like a call to battle.

But Marley lightens the mood considerably on side two, which kicks off with the funky reggae classic "Jamming." "Bob was a big James Brown fan," Marvin says. "So what I played on guitar was kind of James Brown, but reggae style. It had a kind of R&B-ish dance feel, especially on songs like 'Exodus' and 'Jamming.' That was the

Bob Marley and the Wailers arriving at the Odeon Theatre in Birmingham, England, 1975

beginning of a new style of incorporating dance funk into reggae. And 'Heathen' was the beginning of incorporating rock into reggae. And 'Waiting in Vain' is more melodic. I tried to play a little like George Benson on that, kind of jazz."

The latter song exemplifies Marley's smooth way with the romantic ballad style of reggae known as lover's rock. Bob's fondness for the ladies is well known. His marriage to Rita was an open one, and he also fathered children with the Jamaican model Cindy Breakspeare and a virtual harem of other women, including Pat Williams, Janet Hunt, Janet Bowen, Lucy Pounder and Anita Belnavis. "He was the king and they were his queens," Marvin says, laughing.

From romantic love, the theme turns to universal love as *Exodus* draws to a close with one of Marley's best-known songs, "One Love," which is paired with a rendition of the Curtis Mayfield spiritual "People Get Ready." The phrase "One Love" is often heard in Rasta culture. It can be used as a greeting, or as part of the proverbial phrase, "One love, one heart, one aim, one destiny," alluding to the belief in the essential unity of all humanity that was central to Marley's message, as Marvin recounts.

"Bob would say all the time, 'My father is a white Englishman, my mother is a black, African Jamaican. My job is to bring black and white together through music as my vehicle. If I can't do that with my life, then I don't want this life.' He had no negativity. Like he said, the Rastaman vibration is positive. We don't preach negativity. We preach one love. We look for the truth and love."

*Exodus* was a huge success immediately upon its release. In diversifying his musical style on the album, Marley was reaching out to an even wider audience than he'd reached up until that point. Endeavoring to bring his message to every corner of the world, he and the Wailers embarked on a vigorous round of touring.

"My first show with Bob was in Paris," Marvin recalls. "I was a little, like, Please don't let me make any mistakes tonight! At the end of the show, Bob slapped me five because he liked what I did. And then the second show was at the Rainbow in London, and we made that film *Live at the Rainbow*. That first night, I felt like the band was a mountain and I was a part of that mountain. That's the feeling. Like my feet had roots going right through the ground and you couldn't move me if you tried. Everybody was connected. It was magic. Bob was on top of everything, perfectly woven with everything. Totally hypnotic. You felt like nothing would go wrong. Bob would rehearse us so much. At the end of rehearsal, you could play that thing in your sleep."

But the heavy rehearsals could be emotionally demanding. "Bob made me cry one time," Marvin remembers. "I thought I had a part down. I got it. Then he came up to me right in the middle of rehearsal and said, 'You think you can play my music?' I didn't answer him. I was like, 'What's he talking about?' He said, 'It's not just a matter of playing notes. You gotta *feel* it.' Tears came

Onstage in The Hague, Netherlands, 1977

out of my eyes, man. Down my cheeks."

The Wailers were a tight-knit unit on the road. Living up to his name, "Family Man" Barrett would cook Ital—natural—food for the group. If you hung with Bob Marley, you were going to eat healthy, smoke good herb, reason together on Rastafarian topics, rehearse for hours on end and play soccer. Marley was obsessed with the game, and his entourage included Jamaican soccer star Alan "Skilly" Cole, who would eventually become Marley's co-manager. But it was Marley who was captain of the team.

"One of Bob's nicknames was the Skip, which means the skipper of a soccer team, like David Beckham or something," Marvin says. "He was the guy who would go up there and get the goals. And as we know, he had a passion for soccer just like he had for music."

But soccer would prove to be quite literally Marley's downfall. He sustained a serious injury to his toe during one game while on tour for *Exodus*. A London doctor recommended that the toe be amputated, but Marley refused, maintaining that surgery was contrary to his Rastafarian faith. Over time, the toe would turn cancerous. And the cancer would spread to his lungs and brain, finally claiming his life.

Against doctors' advice, Marley insisted on continuing to tour immediately after his injury. He was in a great deal of pain, but determined to persevere with his musical mission. And he never held back, giving energetic performances, dancing vigorously on a toe that was literally killing him.

If he had any fear of death, it certainly wasn't in evidence on April 28, 1978, when Bob Marley and the Wailers headlined the One Love Peace Concert in Jamaica. A similar event, the Smile Jamaica concert in 1976, had precipitated the ambush that very nearly took his life. Smile Jamaica had been organized by Jamaica's ruling People's National Party (PNP), and it is generally believed that the attack on Marley, two days before the concert, was performed by the rival party, the JLP (Jamaican Labor Party). Marley demonstrated amazing courage by appearing at Smile Jamaica following the attempt on his life. With his assassins still at large and his arm in a sling and bloodstained bandage, he wasn't afraid to give would-be assailants another crack at him.

Politics is an extremely violent business in Jamaica. Elections generally take place amid a backdrop of heavy gunplay and gang-style hits, as rival factions endeavor to intimidate one another. Gang-related gun violence in America pales in comparison. Yet there was Bob Marley up on a Jamaican stage once again in 1978 at the politically themed One Love Peace Concert, attempting to reconcile Jamaica's two rival political parties.

"Believe it or not, that was my first concert in my home country," says Junior Marvin. "Can you imagine that?"

At the climax of the set, while the band vamped behind him, Marley invited PNP leader Michael Manley and JLP chief Edward Seaga onto the stage, enjoining them to shake hands in a show of unity and reconciliation. It was a highly charged moment, and one that nobody knew was coming.

"I'm 99 percent certain that it was a spur-of-the-moment thing on Bob's part," Marvin says. "Before that show, Bob had not slept for something like 48 hours. If you listen to his voice, there's a different tone that's never been there before. He had to fight to make sure his voice came out. When you go without sleep, your senses heighten and you start to pick up things from the universe. That's what happened with him. He was totally in a trance.

"He wanted to unite everybody in Jamaica as one people. Because the motto of Jamaica is 'Out of Many, One People.' And that was Bob's dream, to bring all people together—black, white, red, yellow, pink, blue, purple, no matter what color or creed. He started off by inviting Manley onto the stage, because Manley was in awe of Bob."

The release of *Kaya*, the second set of songs recorded at Basing Street, was timed to coincide with the One Love Peace Concert. The album takes its name from one of Jamaicans' innumerable appellations for marijuana, a fact underscored by the back cover illustration of ganja leaves growing from a half-smoked, burning spliff. The disc itself is predominantly centered around love songs, including the classic "Is This Love." Perhaps this focus on romance provided an apt respite after the heavy politics of *Exodus* and the One Love show.

If *Kaya* found Marley in a mellow, romantic mood, its successor—1979's *Survival*—is pretty much the polar opposite, perhaps Marley's most politicized and militantly Afrocentric work. Black unity is the theme. The cover art depicts the flags of 47 African nations at the time, over which is superimposed an antique drawing depicting the inhuman way in which captive Africans were packed into slave ships like so much human cargo.

The music is equally confrontational. Tracks like "Babylon System," "Survival" and "Africa Unite," call down the oppressors in no uncertain terms. And on "Ambush" Marley directly addresses the 1976 attempt on his life, contextualizing his personal survival alongside the black people through 400 years of slavery and post-slavery persecution.

But perhaps the album's best-known song is "Zimbabwe," written in celebration of that African nation's struggle for independence. Art merged with history on April 18, 1980, when Bob Marley and the Wailers performed at the Zimbabwe Independence Day festivities at the invitation of the new government. They played before an audience that included Britain's Prince Charles, India's Prime Minister Indira Gandhi and Zimbabwe's new prime minister, Robert Mugabe. Through Marley's efforts, reggae had become the official soundtrack of the pan-African liberation movement.

The scene inside Zimbabwe's Rufaro Stadium was frenzied and chaotic. About 20 minutes into the show thousands of gate crashers struggled to fight their way in, desperate for a glimpse at the man who had become a black saint in their eyes. Police used tear gas to control the crowd. Marley and the band had to vacate the stage until the fumes cleared. Some 45 minutes later, they took the stage and performed one of the most memorable shows of their eventful career. Sessions for the *Survival* album marked the return to the Wailers of two key members, keyboardist Earl "Wire" Lindo and guitarist Al Anderson. An American player, Anderson had gone off to work with Peter Tosh for a while, but was enthusiastically welcomed back into the Wailers fold. "I've known Al since I was 17 years old," Marvin says. "I first met him in New Jersey when I was playing with [*jazz organist*] Larry Young. Al would come and jam with us. Then I landed a job with T-Bone Walker. Al wanted to meet T-Bone and so decided to become my guitar tech. He took care of my guitar for me when I did a concert at Carnegie Hall with T-Bone Walker."

Anderson had played lead guitar on many of Marley's best-known earlier tracks, including "No Woman No Cry," "Lively Up Yourself," "Them Belly Full" and "Crazy Baldhead." Marvin says that the decision to bring Anderson back into the Wailers arose from a discussion the he and Marley had. "We decided that, in terms of stage presentation, Al could come and play all his solos that he did on the albums, I could play the solos from the albums I'm on, and the sound would be just like the records," he says. "I wouldn't have to try to duplicate what Al did and vice versa. Al and I got along. We didn't step on each other's toes musically. And Bob got the best of both worlds. We were perhaps the first reggae band in history with two lead guitar players. I think that Al Anderson is one of the best lead guitar players in the world."

> **"EVERY SONG WE DID WAS FOR EVERYONE ON EARTH."**
>
> —JUNIOR MARVIN

Bob Marley and the Wailers on tour were like a guerrilla commando unit, only with guitars instead of guns, following a strong but ailing leader and bringing a message of freedom all around the world. "We got to the point where we stopped thinking about money," Marvin recalls. "Money was there. Money was not the issue. The issue was how many more people can we take with us and how much can we do for the people. When I say people, I mean everyone on earth. Every song we did was for everyone on earth."

In May 1980, Marley and the Wailers played their largest concert ever, attracting over 100,000 people, in Milan, Italy. As in Zimbabwe, the crowd overflowed the venue's nominal capacity, eager to hear and see the man that people had begun calling the king and prophet of reggae music.

"The promoter expected 10 to 12 thousand people," Marvin says. "But when it reached 50,000, he went home. Then it reached 100,000 and went over that. People were hypnotized. Bob Marley drew more people than the Pope, the Italian papers said. We had a ball. But we were very disciplined. It never went to our heads. Bob always said, 'If there's one person out there or a million, we're gonna do the same show.' That was the attitude of the whole band."

It was on another overseas journey that Marvin cowrote the iconic Marley track "Could You Be Loved." "I gave Bob the guitar riff," Marvin says. "He heard me playing that rhythm and said, 'Can I have that riff?' I said, 'Sure.' And then he came back with the chorus, [*singing*] 'Could you be loved, and be loved.' Then Bob and I were with [*reggae singer*] Jacob Miller on Chris Blackwell's private jet. We were en route to Brazil to do the first promotion of reggae in that country. And the three of us completed the song."

"Could You Be Loved" is one of several standout tracks from the final album Bob Marley created in his lifetime, *Uprising*. It is perhaps his most overtly spiritual album, the work of a man reconciling himself with death. Songs like the blissfully joyous "Forever Loving Jah," evoke the promise of eternal life common to many faith traditions. Even the title, *Uprising*, seems to hint obliquely at resurrection while it carries connotations of revolution.

But the album's best-known and most loved track is the concluding piece, "Redemption Song." Intentionally or not, this poignant solo acoustic performance has come to possess the emotional resonance of a final farewell from Marley, an intimate, personal and reflective summing up of his life's work, once more casting his individual story against the backdrop of the journey of black people from slavery to liberation. The song, and the viral video of Marley performing it with his Ovation acoustic guitar, have become so iconic that it's hard to believe that Marley and the band toyed with several radically different alternate arrangements.

"We did a ska version in the studio with the whole band," Marvin says. In the end, though, Marley did the right thing with the song. "If you listen to the lyrics of 'Redemption Song,' " says Marvin, "Bob is cursing the slave masters for doing something they should not have done. But at the same time, he's forgiving them. And at the same time he's reeducating everyone. It's like a history lesson. If you listen to each word and study

With the Wailers in Holland, 1976

GIJSBERT HANEKROOT/REDFERNS/GETTY IMAGES

its meaning, you'll see what I'm saying. He's reminding you of history, but at the same time he's reminding you that we're not here to fight flesh and blood. We're brothers and sisters, all of us."

For Marley, the beginning of the end came on a Sunday morning, September 21, 1980. He was in New York, having recently played two triumphant shows at Madison Square Garden with the chart topping R&B group the Commodores. While jogging in Central Park with Skilly Cole, he suddenly collapsed.

"He'd had a stroke and was partially paralyzed on one side of his body," Marvin says. "Everybody heard about it and thought maybe he just wasn't getting enough rest. He was traveling a lot and doing a lot of interviews. He was working very hard and we thought maybe he just needed to cool down and relax a little bit. We prayed and hoped that it was nothing too serious."

The following Tuesday, on September 23, Marley and the Wailers were scheduled to play at the Stanley Theater in Pittsburgh. Although he was in bad shape, Marley decided to soldier on with the gig. But shortly before showtime, Skilly Cole called a backstage meeting with the band. He told them that this would most likely be their last concert with Bob Marley.

"We couldn't believe it," Marvin says. "We thought it was a freak thing and that he'd just had a mild stroke. But now we knew it was going to be the last show ever. The performance itself was phenomenal. We all tried to play the best we could ever play in our whole lives for that show. And now, 30 years later, they put it out."

The 90 or so minutes preserved on the two-disc *Live Forever* set are poignant in their intensity. The entire band plays at a level of ferocity and deadly precision not heard on any other live Wailers recording. Summoning every ounce of strength left in him, Marley turns in a courageous and inspiring performance worthy to be called a hero's farewell.

But after Pittsburgh he could go no further. The remainder of the tour was canceled. Bob spent time at a number of cancer clinics around the world, ending up at a facility in Germany run by Dr. Josef Issels. The cancer that had begun in his injured toe had now spread throughout his entire body. As a result of radiation therapy, his mighty lion's mane of dreadlocks had fallen out. That was the last time Junior Marvin saw him alive.

"I was in Germany for the last part," he says. "Al Anderson and a couple of other people from the band were there. Rita was there and Bob's mother. Bob was walking around with an IV drip. His stomach was all messed up from the chemotherapy. He couldn't digest things properly, so he was being fed intravenously. We all went to play soccer and Bob wanted to come and play with us, with the drip in him. While he was playing, the drip fell off. Of course we all panicked and went to find the doctor. The doctor was like, 'Bob, why are you playing soccer? You're not well and you've got this drip.' And Bob says, 'I want to live. Fight. Wake up and live.' He'd do anything within reason and truth to stay alive. That was the last time I saw him.'

Not long after, Marley recognized that the end of his life was at hand. Accepting his imminent death, he determined to draw his last breath in Jamaica. But he only made it as far as Miami, where his mother lived. "They put him on a Concorde, and I think he took a turn for the worse on that flight from Germany," Marvin recounts. "They didn't want him to die on the plane. They could be sued for millions. So they brought him to a hospital in Miami."

Bob Marley passed away on May 11, 1981, some 40 hours after leaving Germany. He was 36 years old. His body was carried back to Jamaica and given a hero's funeral. He was entombed with one of his guitars (accounts vary as to which one), a soccer ball, a sprig of cannabis and a ring that had belonged to Haile Selassie and had been one of Bob Marley's most prized possessions.

Although he's been gone 30 years now, Bob Marley's music and legacy remain very much alive. The 1984 Marley compilation *Legend* has become one of the biggest-selling releases in the entire history of recorded music. The Marley name and heritage are carried forward in this time by Bob's children Ziggy, Stephen, Cedella, Sharon, Julian, Ky-mani and Damien, all gifted singers and players in their own right.

"If you really simplify Bob's message down to its most basic meaning, I think you'll find it in the song 'One Love,'" Junior Marvin reflects. "He says, 'Let's get together and feel all right.' If we can all get together in harmony, then of course we're gonna be all right. But until that day we will have war and strife. So we're waiting for that day to come...patiently." ◆

# NEVERMORE

The life and death of Kurt Cobain, the man who saved the rock world.

BY ALAN DI PERNA

KURT COBAIN 1967–1994

PHOTO BY MICHEL LINSSEN/REDFERNS

# KURT COBAIN'S TRAGIC

demise will be remembered as a defining event—perhaps the defining event—of the rock and roll Nineties. As the leader of Nirvana, Cobain set the tone for rock music in this past decade. He was the premier icon of grunge, the raw, guitar-heavy, blunt-spoken style that will stand for all time as a signifier of the Nineties, much as glam does for the Seventies and psychedelia for the Sixties.

As a human being, Cobain personified the anxieties, frustrations and despair of his generation—kids from broken homes, young men and women facing a future of reduced economic expectations. A misfit within the institution called rock and roll, Kurt's punk values put him at odds with the rock stardom that the world was so eager to thrust upon him. As he declared in the sardonic "Radio Friendly Unit Shifter" (*In Utero*), "I do not want what I have got." Kurt Cobain's death—at age 27, of a self-inflicted wound to the head with a 12-gauge shotgun—denied a voice to a generation most in need of a champion, comforter and friend.

Born on February 20, 1967, Cobain was just eight when his parents divorced. Although almost universally associated with Seattle, he was actually from Aberdeen, Washington, a small, economically depressed logging town more than 100 miles from Seattle. "White trash posing as middle class," is how Cobain described his background to biographer Michael Azerrad in the latter's *Come As You Are: The Story of Nirvana*. By all accounts, Kurt was deeply and permanently hurt by his parents' divorce. After the split, he never really had a stable childhood home. At school he was diagnosed as hyperactive and given the drug Ritalin. He dropped out in the 12th grade. Cobain didn't fit in with the macho stereotype imposed on young males in Aberdeen. He had no use for hunting, sports or other "manly" pursuits, although he did enjoy getting high with the local stoners. He was harassed at high school for befriending a gay student. In later life, he would speak out vehemently against homophobia, sexism and racism.

Cobain demonstrated artistic ability at an early age, and his collages, sculptures and other artworks adorn many of Nirvana's records. Had he not become a musician, he might well have pursued a career in the visual arts. But when he was 14, his fate took another course: his father bought him his first electric guitar, which Kurt soon discovered he was most comfortable playing left-handed. Cobain's musical tastes developed along much the same lines as many musicians of his generation. His mother introduced him to the Beatles, the Monkees and other Sixties pop music when he was very young, but he moved on to bands like Led Zeppelin, Black Sabbath and AC/DC while still in his preteens. When punk rock finally made its way out to Aberdeen sometime in the early Eighties, Cobain embraced it eagerly. Years later, he would be embarrassed when relatives or childhood friends recalled him jamming to Iron Maiden records or drawing the Led Zeppelin logo on his bedroom wall. But it is precisely that combination of heavy metal and early Eighties punk (Black Flag, Flipper, etc.) that would later become known as grunge and have an extraordinarily powerful effect on the masses.

Cobain started writing songs soon after picking up the guitar. His first band, a trio called Fecal Matter, did not last long. But in 1986, he and bassist Chris (later Krist) Novoselic, a friend from Aberdeen High, teamed up to form the nucleus of a band that would eventually be called Nirvana. (Cobain had wanted to call it Skid Row at one point.)

> **"I WANTED TO F**KING BLOW MY HEAD OFF, I WAS SO TIRED OF IT."**
>
> —KURT COBAIN

By 1987, Cobain had moved to Olympia, Washington, a college town that was somewhat more bohemian than Aberdeen and about 50 miles closer to Seattle. Acquaintances from that time recall him as a quiet, reclusive guy who mainly stayed inside the apartment he shared with his girlfriend, working on his sculptures and collages. An inveterate haunter of thrift shops and swap meets, Cobain was perpetually buying old dolls and other semi-collectible junk, much of which he used in his artwork. He applied his thrift-shop aesthetic to his guitars as well and became infamous for playing a succession of battered old pawn-shop specials. But there was a practical angle to his obsession with six-string castoffs: affordable left-handed guitars are fairly hard to find and Cobain played with such angry violence that the Fender Jaguars and Jazzmasters that were his guitars of choice frequently needed replacing. (In the days before they were popularized by bands like Sonic Youth, Dinosaur Jr. and Nirvana, Jags and Jazzmasters could be had for very reasonable prices.) Shortly before his death, Cobain designed a signature model hybrid cross between a Jaguar and a Mustang for Fender.

Early in 1988, Cobain, Novoselic and drummer Dale Crover journeyed to Seattle to make a demo at Reciprocal Recording Studios with engineer Jack Endino, an important figure at the city's highly influential indie label, Sub Pop. The demo led to a deal with Sub Pop, and on June 11, 1988, with Chad Channing now on drums, Nirvana released its first single, "Love Buzz," a cover of an obscure song by Shocking Blue, the early Seventies Dutch group that had had a big hit with "Venus." A year later, Nirvana's first album, *Bleach*, came out on Sub Pop.

Cobain often said in interviews that he deliberately suppressed his more melodic, quirky, "new wave" side on *Bleach*. (Kurt often used the term "new wave" to describe everything from the Young Marble Giants and Gang of Four to the Butthole Surfers

PHOTO BY MICHEL LINSSEN/REDFERNS

Kurt Cobain recording at Hilversum Studios in the Netherlands, November 1991

Nirvana in 1991; from left, Kurt Cobain, Krist Novoselic and Dave Grohl

and Scratch Acid, all groups that had greatly influenced him.) His feeling was that this sensibility didn't really fit in with Sub Pop's early Seventies hard-rock aesthetic, as exemplified by Soundgarden and Green River, the group which later mutated into Pearl Jam.

Cobain's musical tastes were quite a bit broader than the noisy alternative fare championed by Sub Pop and similar indie labels. But coming from the rural wastelands of a place like Aberdeen, he could see where Nirvana fit in. "We're a perfect example of the average uneducated 'twentysomething' in America in the Nineties," Cobain told Michael Azerrad. "[*We're*] punk rockers who weren't into punk rock when it was thriving. All my life, that's been the case, because when I got into the Beatles, the Beatles had been broken up for years and I didn't know it... Same thing with Led Zeppelin."

But Cobain's sense of kinship with his age group went beyond music: "My story is exactly the same as 90 percent of everyone my age," he said. "Everyone's parents got divorced. Their kids smoked pot all through high school, they grew up during the era when there was a massive Communist threat and everyone thought they were going to die from a nuclear war. And everyone's personalities are practically the same."

Cobain was a reluctant, unwilling spokesman for his generation. He was uneasy with notoriety, even the underground notoriety that Nirvana gained on the strength of *Bleach* and its follow-up EP, *Blew*, also released in 1989. On the band's first European tour, a grueling low-budget trek with the band Tad, Cobain had what Sub Pop co-owner Bruce Pavitt has described as a nervous breakdown onstage in Rome, storming off stage, climbing into the rafters and screaming at the audience. Adding considerably to Cobain's unhappiness was his chronic, undiagnosable stomach pain, which began shortly after his move to Olympia and would torture him for the rest of his life.

> **"EVERYONE THOUGHT THEY WERE GOING TO DIE FROM A NUCLEAR WAR."**
>
> —KURT COBAIN

But Cobain's existence wasn't completely bleak. In 1990, he began a relationship with Tobi Vail, of the band Bikini Kill, a leader in the radical feminist *riot grrrl* movement. He apparently took his relationship seriously; by all accounts, he wasn't much of a casual womanizer. He told Michael Azerrad that he'd slept with only two women over the course of all Nirvana's touring. "I've always been old-fashioned in that respect," he said. "I've always wanted a girlfriend that I could have a good relationship with for a long time. I wish I was capable of just playing the field, but I always wanted more than that."

Nirvana's career began to accelerate at a heady pace during 1991. In April, they went to record with producer Butch Vig at Smart Studios, his recording facility in Madison, Wisconsin. Now perhaps best known as the drummer of the band Garbage, Vig was then an up-and-coming indie producer with well-regarded records by the Laughing Hyenas, Smashing Pumpkins, Firetown, Tad and

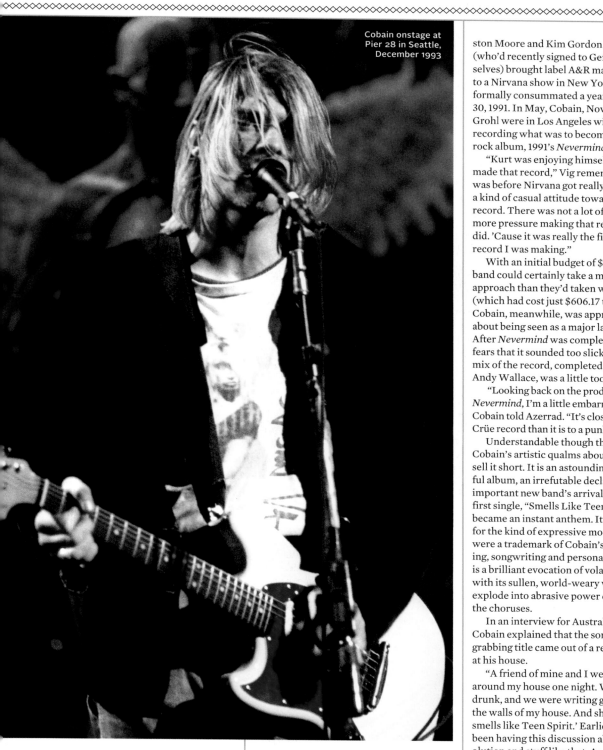

Cobain onstage at Pier 28 in Seattle, December 1993

PHOTO BY JEFF KRAVITZ/ FILMMAGIC, INC

Killdozer, among others. The recording of the song "Polly" that appeared on Nirvana's landmark *Nevermind* album came from the Smart sessions. Earlier versions of five other *Nevermind* songs—"In Bloom," "Dive," "Lithium," "Breed" and "Stay Away"—were also recorded during the week-long recording project.

A month after the Smart dates, drummer Chad Channing left Nirvana. He was replaced by Dave Grohl, a hard-hitting stickman from the Washington, D.C., hardcore scene. Grohl took Nirvana's sound to a new level of intensity. Once the "classic" Nirvana lineup was in place, a significant record deal wasn't far behind. Geffen Records had been taking an active interest in the band since April 1990, when Thurston Moore and Kim Gordon of Sonic Youth (who'd recently signed to Geffen themselves) brought label A&R man Gary Gersh to a Nirvana show in New York. A deal was formally consummated a year later, on April 30, 1991. In May, Cobain, Novoselic and Grohl were in Los Angeles with Butch Vig, recording what was to become a landmark rock album, 1991's *Nevermind*.

"Kurt was enjoying himself when he made that record," Vig remembers. "That was before Nirvana got really big. They had a kind of casual attitude toward making the record. There was not a lot of pressure. I felt more pressure making that record than they did. 'Cause it was really the first major label record I was making."

With an initial budget of $65,000, the band could certainly take a more leisurely approach than they'd taken with *Bleach* (which had cost just $606.17 to make). Cobain, meanwhile, was apprehensive about being seen as a major label sellout. After *Nevermind* was completed, he had fears that it sounded too slick—that the final mix of the record, completed by producer Andy Wallace, was a little too radio friendly.

"Looking back on the production of *Nevermind*, I'm a little embarrassed by it," Cobain told Azerrad. "It's closer to a Mötley Crüe record than it is to a punk rock record."

Understandable though they may be, Cobain's artistic qualms about the record sell it short. It is an astoundingly powerful album, an irrefutable declaration of an important new band's arrival. The disc's first single, "Smells Like Teen Spirit," became an instant anthem. It is a showcase for the kind of expressive mood swings that were a trademark of Cobain's guitar playing, songwriting and personality. The tune is a brilliant evocation of volatile emotions, with its sullen, world-weary verses that explode into abrasive power chording for the choruses.

In an interview for Australian radio, Cobain explained that the song's attention-grabbing title came out of a relaxed evening at his house.

"A friend of mine and I were goofing around my house one night. We were kinda drunk, and we were writing graffiti all over the walls of my house. And she wrote, 'Kurt smells like Teen Spirit.' Earlier on, we'd been having this discussion about teen revolution and stuff like that. And I took [*what she wrote*] as a compliment. I thought she was saying that I was a person who could inspire. I just thought it was a nice little title. And it turns out she just meant that I smelled like that deodorant [*called Teen Spirit*]. I didn't even know that deodorant existed until after the song was written."

Cobain worked notoriously fast as a lyricist. He'd write the words to his songs in

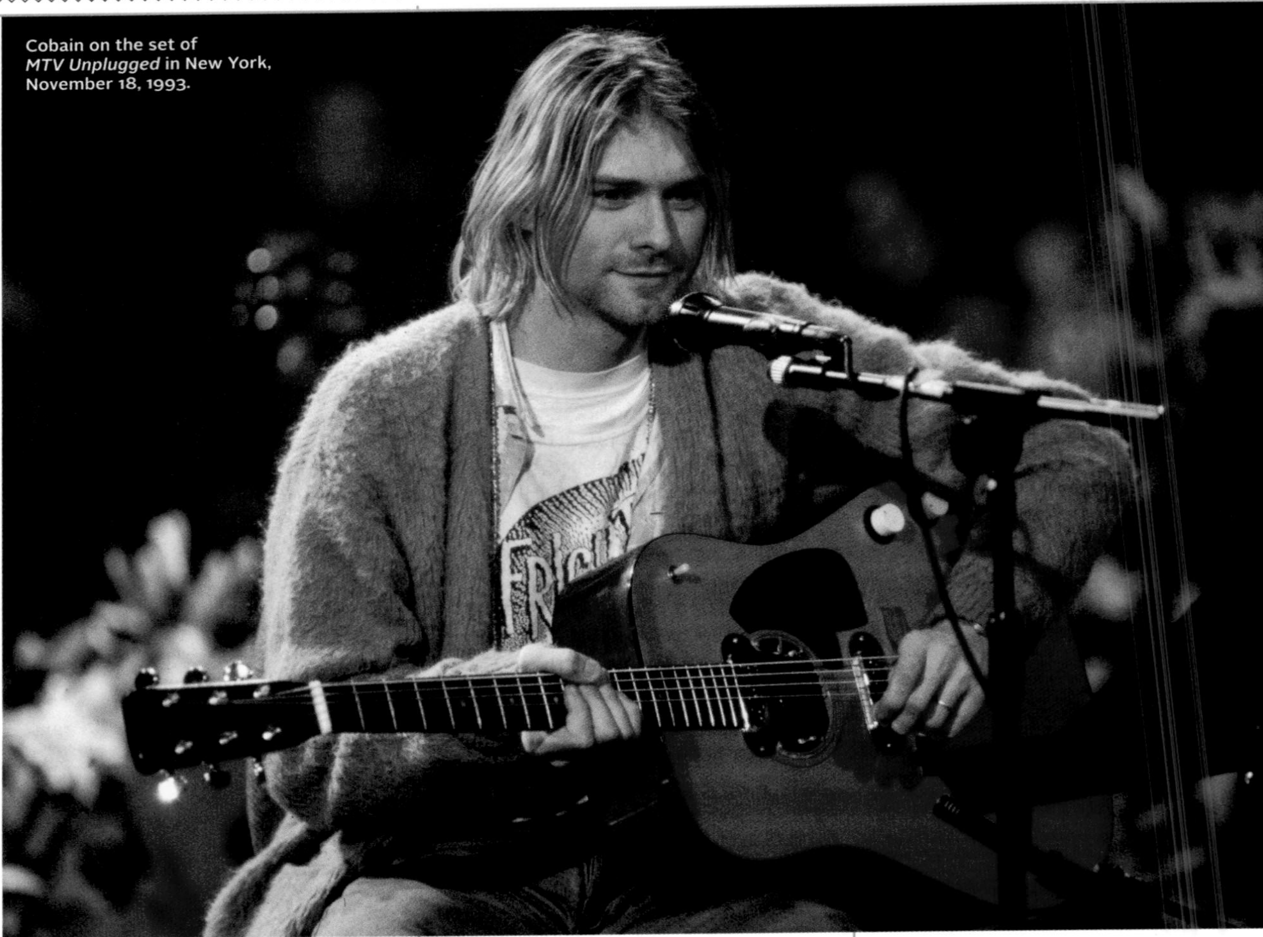

Cobain on the set of *MTV Unplugged* in New York, November 18, 1993.

PHOTO BY FRANK MICELOTTA/GETTY IMAGES

the car on the way to the studio, or even a few seconds before having to record a final vocal. But the unstudied, hasty quality of his lyrics are part of their expressiveness. His songs are like action paintings: kinetic, disconnected bursts of angry energy. He shifts from topic to topic in a manner that has been compared to a restless adolescent channel-surfing through the cable TV wasteland. It has been pointed out that Cobain's lyrics were inseparable from his plaintive, raspy vocal style. Nobody else could sing those words with quite the same effect. But it's equally true that Cobain's distinctive voice was inseparable from his guitar style. The voice and guitar in Nirvana rubbed against each another in an ever-shifting dynamic, like a couple making love, or fighting, or both at the same time, with Cobain's choppy guitar rhythms and grainy distortion welling up to dominate at one moment then slipping into subaqueous quietude the next.

The months following the release of *Nevermind* were turbulent ones for Cobain. Not only were there the pressures of sudden, massive stardom to cope with, but he also entered into two relationships that were to have a profound effect on him. One was with Courtney Love, longtime punk scenester and splashy frontwoman for the group Hole. The other was with heroin. Cobain and Love first met at a Nirvana club gig in 1989, but didn't become serious about each other until '91, after Kurt had moved to Los Angeles to record *Nevermind*. Love was often blamed for introducing Cobain to heroin, but he had experimented with the drug as early as his Aberdeen days. Cobain always insisted that he became a serious heroin user of his own accord, because it was the only thing that seemed to quell the terrible pain in his stomach. In describing this pain to Azerrad, Cobain made some seemingly rhetorical statements which later proved tragically prophetic: "Halfway through [*Nirvana's last*] European tour, I remember saying I'll never go on tour again until I have this fixed because I wanted to kill myself. I wanted to fucking blow my head off, I was so tired of it."

Cobain and Love were married on February 24, 1992. Their daughter, Francis Bean Cobain, was born on August 18 of that same year. Because of press reports—inaccurate, Love insisted—that she used heroin while pregnant, the Los Angeles Children's Services began proceedings to take the Cobains' daughter away from them. It was the beginning of a long and difficult legal battle that the couple ultimately won, in March 1993. But it wasn't only the law that seemed to have it in for the Cobains. Provocative, outspoken and confrontational, Love was disliked by many Nirvana fans who perceived her as a gold digger who manipulated the passive Cobain. Love often joked about being her generation's Yoko Ono.

But even in the midst of all these difficulties, Nirvana's career kept on skyrocketing, and Cobain continued developing as a songwriter. December '92 saw the release of *Incesticide*, a collection of previously unreleased rarities. Selections like "Hairspray Queen" and "Mexican Seafood" go back to that first Jack Endino–produced demo. The public finally got to hear some of the "new wave" side that Cobain had suppressed on *Bleach* and *Nevermind*. Meanwhile, at a much more advanced level, Cobain was writing songs for what would become Nirvana's final, and arguably finest, studio album, *In Utero*. Thanks to the band's success, Cobain was finally able to make pretty much the album he'd always wanted to make.

Influential alternative rock producer Steve Albini (Pixies, Sonic Youth, Jon Spencer Blues Explosion) was drafted to produce the disc. "The main reason we recorded *In Utero* with Steve Albini is that he is able to get a sound that sounds like the band is in a room no bigger than the one we're in now," said Cobain in a hotel room interview with British journalist Jon Savage. "*In Utero* doesn't sound like it was recorded in a hall, or that it's trying to sound larger than life. It's very in-your-face and real."

As a lyricist, Cobain had begun to move away from the last-minute, free-associative writing techniques he'd used in the past. "There are more songs on this album that are thematic," he told Savage, "that are actually about something, rather than just pieces of poetry. Like 'Scentless Apprentice' is about the book *Perfume*, by Patrick Suskind. I don't think I've ever written a song based on a book before."

The result of all these efforts is a far more diverse and adventurous album than Nevermind. Cobain's songwriting skills had become more focused and assured. "Serve the Servants" verges on Beatles-esque, while "Scentless Apprentice" is among the heaviest things Nirvana ever recorded. Tracks like "Rape Me," "Heart Shaped Box" and the stately "Pennyroyal Tea" showcased Cobain's unique sense of melodic phrasing: vocal lines of irregular length that generally resolved on the major third of whatever chord the singer happened to be strumming when the line ended. Cobain's words and cover art suggest a peacefully resigned acceptance of the life cycle, from birth to death. Even the album's more disturbing images of disease and pain seem appropriate elements of that cycle.

A similar mood of slightly eerie tranquility pervaded Nirvana's November 18, 1993, appearance on *MTV's Unplugged* and the album that was taken from it. The stage decor, with its heavy drapery, candles, flowers and muted blue lighting, was designed by Cobain himself. Seen in retrospect, the set design seems to foreshadow Cobain's death a few months after the *Unplugged* appearance. "Kurt seemed to like to take things and internalize them," says *Unplugged* producer Alex Coletti. "I'd heard that he was something of a visual artist. So beyond making sure he was happy with the stage set, since he seemed to show some interest in it, I thought it would be good if he had some creative input. He was pretty cooperative. He did specify that he wanted star lilies, which are these big white flowers. 'You mean like a funeral?' I asked. 'Yeah,' he said. I don't want to read too much into it, but that memory sure spooked me out a couple of months later."

"Kurt wanted something that would break away from just the normal, dull TV set," says Nirvana tour manager Alex MacLeod. "He didn't want it to look like just a bare stage. He had seen a lot of *Unplugged* shows before and felt they weren't really unplugged. His feeling was that a lot of the bands would just use semi-acoustic instruments and play their songs exactly the same way they would if they were doing a full show. He wanted to make Nirvana's *Unplugged* appearance slightly different, sort of a downbeat kind of set. Really laid back. To just go in and play a bunch of songs and, to some extent, make changes to the arrangements. They tried to stick to acoustic instruments as much as possible. Kurt wanted to make it something that would show a whole different side of the band."

Being asked to do *Unplugged* was a validation of sorts for Cobain, a confirmation of his arrival as a significant rock songwriter. The show has always been a tunesmith's forum, an opportunity to strip away the high decibels and let the songs stand on their own melodic and lyrical integrity. Resisting considerable pressure from MTV to focus mainly on big Nirvana hits in his performance, Cobain assembled a diverse set that included both well-known and lesser-known songs of his, as well as a few tastefully chosen covers.

> **"I'VE ALWAYS WANTED A GIRLFRIEND THAT I COULD HAVE A GOOD RELATIONSHIP WITH FOR A LONG TIME."**
>
> —KURT COBAIN

"It was the first time in a long time that I'd seen them so nervous about doing something," says Alex MacLeod. "Things had gotten to the point where they'd go out and play in front of 7,500 or 10,000 people, like [*very nonchalantly*] 'Okay, boom, let's do it.' But they were really nervous about doing *Unplugged*. Because they were really leaving themselves wide open."

The set turned out to be a rousing success. It was capped by a riveting version of "Where Did You Sleep Last Night," a traditional tune recorded by one of Cobain's musical heroes, the American folksinging archetype, Leadbelly. Having done pained, screaming justice to the death-haunted ballad, Cobain left the stage, never to return.

"I really tried to get him to do an encore," Alex Coletti remembers. "I had the other band members ready to do it. But Kurt just wasn't into it. I was just doing my job for MTV at that point, trying to get that one extra song in the can, to see if the night could produce one more gem. The pleading went on for about five minutes. Finally Kurt said, 'I can't top that last song.' And when he said that, I backed off. 'Cause I knew he was right."

If only Cobain's own life had been able to attain a similar sense of triumphant completion. The sad chain of events leading to his death probably began on March 4, 1994, in Rome, when Cobain fell into a near-fatal coma after taking some 60 sedative pills washed down with champagne. Although initially reported as an accident, the *Los Angeles Times* later stated that the overdose was in fact a suicide attempt and that Cobain had even left a suicide note. (The newspaper cited "sources close to the situation who asked not to be identified" as the basis for this statement.) Two weeks later, Courtney Love summoned police to the home she and her husband shared in Seattle. Following an argument with Love, Cobain apparently locked himself in a room with three or four guns (reports vary) and 25 boxes of ammunition. Love called in the law because she feared he intended to take his life. Cobain denied this, saying he merely wanted to be alone for a while. The officers confiscated his weapons, nevertheless. Cobain had begun to amass a collection of guns, for protection purposes, he said, while he and Love were living in Los Angeles.

By March 28, Cobain and Love had returned to L.A., she to work out some final details on the release of Hole's new album, *Live Through This*, he to check into a drug rehabilitation clinic. This was to be the last of several unsuccessful rehab attempts. Three days later, Cobain abruptly left the clinic and apparently flew back to Seattle. Fearing for his safety, Love hired private detectives who tried in vain to locate him. On the morning of April 8, his body was found at a home he owned in Seattle. An electrician who had come to work on the premises made the discovery. Medical experts determined that Cobain had been dead for several days.

Shortly before the death, reports that Nirvana planned to break up surfaced. In his suicide note, Cobain said, "I haven't felt excitement in listening to as well as creating music for too many years now. I feel guilty beyond words about these things." The note goes on to thank Nirvana's fans for their "letters and concern during the last years."

Among the many ironies associated with this brilliant artist's short, sad life is that while he was unable to conquer his own intense pain, his music helped millions of fans deal with theirs. ◆

Recording in 1972

# AGAINST THE GRAIN

Success didn't elude Rory Gallagher. He turned it away throughout his short, sad life. Now, in death, he's more successful than ever. *Guitar World* presents the story of the Irish rocker's demise and his posthumous revival.

BY ALAN DI PERNA

RORY GALLAGHER 1948–1995

Performing in London, 1972

# DEATH MADE JIMI HENDRIX,

John Lennon, Elvis Presley and Kurt Cobain seem even larger than they were in life. In a sense it deified them. But death also has the power to take artists who were mid-level stars, or even relatively unknown in their own time, and confer on them a radiant halo of posthumous glory. Musicians ranging from Robert Johnson to Nick Drake to Randy Rhoads have posthumously attained the widespread fame and cult-like devotion that they never lived to enjoy.

In the past couple of years, a sizable posthumous cult has grown up around Rory Gallagher, the Irish blues-rock guitarist, singer and songwriter who passed away on June 14, 1995. The past few years have seen an avalanche of retrospective product, including a double CD "best of" set, *Crest of a Wave,* culled from Gallagher's deep catalog of studio and live albums, plus numerous live DVDs including *Live in Cork* and the exhaustive five-disc set *Live at Rockplast* compiling three decades' worth of live appearances. There's plenty more in the vaults; Rory was a tireless live performer.

Gallagher certainly has all the prerequisites for posthumous deification. In his prime, he was a good looking lad, with a shaggy, nut-brown mane and a winning smile. And while not quite Beck or Hendrix at the fretboard, perhaps, Gallagher was an agile riffster whose scrappy, energetic style was punctuated by occasional bursts of fluid, six-string poetry. His playing was steeped in bluesy authenticity. Equally adept at electric and acoustic, slide and standard fretting, he brought to his guitar playing a boundless zeal that even years of hard touring and numerous career disappointments did nothing to diminish.

And, of course, Rory Gallagher possesses in spades the most important qualification for posthumous cult adulation: a sad life story. The tragedy of Randy Rhoads is all about the untimeliness of his death—that he was cut down while he was still quite young and had yet to really make his mark in the world. But the tragedy of Rory Gallagher is something different, a tale of a life filled with missed opportunities, unfortunate career decisions and misplaced idealism, all exacerbated by the usual demons of alcohol and drug dependency. Gallagher's fretboard prowess was all too often matched by unerring marksmanship when it came to shooting himself in the foot.

There always seems to be a surviving relative in the cults of dead rock stars, someone to tend the flame and collect the back royalties. In Randy's case it's his mother, brother and sister; in Jimi's case, his half sister. Rory Gallagher is survived by his younger brother, Donal. But while Randy Rhoads' or Jimi Hendrix's surviving relatives witnessed very little of their loved one's glory moments onstage and in the studio, Donal was Rory's closest confidant, tour manager and sometime business manager throughout his career. He saw it all.

"Rory never went for the brass ring the way other artists did," Donal says. "But he enjoyed being a musician. His enjoyment was to do it the way he wanted. He would have loved to have a Number One album in the States, but it all seemed so cynical and callous to him. After 25 tours, he had put in way more slog than a lot of the younger bands that came out of Ireland and gotten to Number One in America with little effort. I'd get angry about that. But Rory would point out that there were more brilliant guitarists than him who never got the attention they deserved either. It goes with the turf. 'I'm doing what I want to do and doing it the way I want,' he'd say."

Although he came up in Ireland rather than England, Gallagher had much the same musical influences and background as British musicians like the Stones, Beatles, Cream and Led Zeppelin. The early Fifties skiffle craze gave him his first exposure to American folk and blues idioms. Rory fell deeply in love with this music, which was popularized in the United Kingdom by artists like Lonnie Donegan, and would remain deeply devoted to it all his life. But like all of U.K.'s youth, he got swept away by the rock and roll explosion of the mid Fifties. He graduated from a toy guitar to a real one at age nine or 10, after his family had moved from Derry in northern Ireland to Cork in the south.

By age 15, Gallagher was playing professionally in an Irish showband, the Fontanas. Showbands were a uniquely Irish phenomenon. Donal explains, "Those bands would play five-hour stints at country dance halls, and they'd have to cover everything from country to comedy, the hits of the day and also the old-time waltzes and a variety of traditional Irish music. The band would also have to break down in smaller units, as guys went off on a 20-minute break for sandwiches."

Rory's penchant for good time showmanship—exhorting crowds to sing along or clap their hands—no doubt derives from his showband experience. But when the Merseyside boom brought the Beatles and other beat groups to the fore, Gallagher hijacked the Fontanas, stripped down the lineup and morphed the group into a gritty R&B-inflected outfit called the Impact. He persuaded the band members to relocate to London, at the time the epicenter of everything that was most hip in rock culture.

Donal says, "Rory would check out the Marquee, the Flamingo and various clubs, and see people like Georgie Fame, Alexis Korner and Steampacket, which was Long John Baldry's band with Rod Stewart. He immersed himself in that."

But he adds, the guitarist's own gigs at the time were more humble. "London having a huge Irish population, there were plenty of Irish dance halls for the Impact to play, particularly in the north of London." Hitmakers of the day like the Byrds, Kinks and Animals would play the same venues. "They'd come in and do a 20-minute set—a few of their biggest hits—and the Impact would be the support band. So Rory got to know guys like [*the Byrds'*] Roger McGuinn through that. But the showband thing had a stigma to it. They still had to play the waltzes and country music and wear a uniform."

So Rory took the Impact to Hamburg, Germany, to work the same rough, red-light-district clubs that the Beatles had worked a few years earlier during their rise to fame. By this time, the Impact were a three-piece. The format seemed to suit Gallagher, and he would employ it for much of his career. By this point in the mid Sixties, the power trio was an idea whose time had arrived. It was in Hamburg, according to Donal, that Rory first

MICHAEL PUTLAND/GETTY IMAGES

Performing in the U.K., 1978

rubbed shoulders with members of another up and coming power trio, Cream.

The Impact eventually morphed into another bluesy three piece, Taste, a group that recorded two studio albums and two live albums, albeit with a lot of personnel shifts in the rhythm section. Taste were serious contenders. They were favorably name-checked by John Lennon in a press interview at the time, and they played opening sets for Cream, Fleetwood Mac and John Mayall, among others, in Ireland and elsewhere. They were even tapped to be the support band for Cream's very high-visibility farewell performance at London's Albert Hall.

For that matter, Gallagher was himself invited to be Eric Clapton's replacement in Cream. The group's breakup had been set in motion by Clapton's decision to quit. Impressed by Gallagher's guitar playing, Cream's management approached him with an offer to carry on with Jack Bruce and Ginger Baker, still performing and recording as Cream. Many guitarists would have killed for that opportunity, but Gallagher turned it down. It was the first of several high-profile offers that he famously declined.

"It was very much a management thing—'Find somebody to replace Clapton!' " Donal says. "Rory was known to them, and they got on well. But Rory wouldn't have any of it. He said, 'Musically, there's no way I'd try and fill somebody else's shoes, especially Eric's.' " Had Gallagher made at least one album with Cream or even toured with them, he might have put his career into overdrive. "Yes, it would have been a fast track," Donal acknowledges. "But he felt that he would never be his own man."

Gallagher's tendency to "go it alone" was perhaps his tragic flaw. Withdrawn and shy, he was unable to trust others or to enter into truly collaborative relationships. "He was never a great one at interacting with people," Donal admits. "He was brilliant in front of an audience, but offstage it was a Jekyll-and-Hyde effect. He was bad at one-on-one relationships. He wouldn't even let the guy in to read the water meter or gas meter of his house. Even the band didn't get past the front door."

Gallagher soon got his chance to "go it alone" for real. Taste split up in 1970, amid a dispute with management, and Gallagher decided to carry on as a solo artist. "Basically, Rory went solo to get away from [*Taste's*] management," Donal says. "The backing guys stayed with the manager under the name Taste. Rory didn't want any further entanglement with the manager. He basically went with his own name because his previous band had been hijacked by the other members."

Gallagher released not one but two albums in 1971, *Rory Gallagher* and *Deuce*. He insisted on producing himself, and the results were mixed at best: flashes of brilliance amid bouts of plodding mediocrity. Gallagher seemed to have lacked any capacity for editing himself. For much of his career he operated on the somewhat simplistic assumption that he could simply walk into a recording studio and do his live show and come out with a great studio album. A live-in-the studio approach does work for some groups, and it may have even worked for Gallagher, but it's virtually impossible to self-produce this kind of album.

Gallagher's guitar tone on these early albums is an example of the problem. Unlike many power trio guitarists, he did not rely on massive Marshall stacks or huge amounts of distortion to fill the sonic space. Instead, and to his credit, he played his battered '61 Strat through a variety of small combo amps. But lacking production expertise, Gallagher was unable to create a proper distinctive sound for himself, and his guitar tone on *Rory Gallagher* and *Deuce* is thin and weak. Without any overdubs to fill in the picture—let alone much in the way of savvy drum miking, skillful signal processing and so on—the albums sound almost painfully anemic.

Tighter songwriting might have helped as well. While a decent tunesmith, Gallagher did suffer at times from a lead guitarist's tendency to string a bunch of riffs together, ad hoc, and hope they somehow add up to a song. In retrospect, Gallagher's first two albums might have been more judiciously edited down to a single release, with time taken for higher production values.

In effect, Gallagher was a great sideman who insisted on being a merely adequate front man. His prowess as an accompanist is amply demonstrated on the many side projects he participated in over the years. Perhaps the most notable was *The London Muddy Waters Sessions* disc, released in '72. The London Sessions were a series of recordings that brought great American bluesmen and rock and rollers of the Fifties together with the Sixties British rock stars who adored and emulated them.

The series had gotten off to a rousing start with the *Howlin' Wolf London Sessions*, featuring Eric Clapton, Steve Winwood and the Rolling Stones rhythm section of Charlie Watts and Bill Wyman. So it was a huge honor for Gallagher to be offered the lead guitar slot with Muddy Waters, the great patriarch of the electric Chicago blues style. Donal thinks that London blues kingpins Alexis Korner and Chris Barber recommended Rory for the *London Sessions* gig. For once, the introverted guitarist didn't say no.

"I think a lot of people were puzzled by the fact that it wasn't Eric Clapton again," Donal says. "But I recall a [*later*] *Playboy* magazine interview with Muddy Waters where he said Rory was closer to his style of music—the Chicago kind of sound with the bottleneck guitar."

As it was, Gallagher almost missed the first session. "He had a gig that night in Leicester, which is 100 miles from London," Donal says. "So Rory said, 'I'll be there as soon as I can after the gig.' I remember we really burned rubber getting back to London. Rory was upset. 'They'll kick me out; I'm so late,' he said. But when he walked in the studio Muddy was standing there with a glass of champagne for him. 'Glad you made it. Here, have yourself a drink.' An absolute gentleman."

Gallagher really shines on the Muddy Waters tracks. His soloing is concise, incisive and impassioned, his comping tasteful and rhythmically savvy. Performing with greats that include keyboardists Steve Winwood and Georgie Fame and Jimi Hendrix Experience drummer Mitch Mitchell, Rory has a well-defined space that he fills admirably, never overstaying his welcome and making his musical statement eloquently in the choruses allotted him. Gallagher's profound love of the blues is one of the most touching things about him. He'd clearly done his homework, and his deep affection never lost the innocent sincerity of a teenage love affair.

He also fared well on the *Jerry Lee Lewis London Sessions*, released in '73. The young Irish guitar wiz formed a deep bond with "the Killer," America's original rock and roll wild man. Perhaps it was the instinctual brotherhood of two hard-drinking men. Donal recalls one of the defining moments of the sessions.

"All went well at first," he says. "Jerry Lee was kept off the bottle. But then the producer said, 'Jerry, you're doing all the "Johnny B. Goode" type old rock and roll stuff. Let's try something different.' Jerry Lee said, 'You name it, I'll play it.' So the guy said 'Satisfaction' by the Rolling Stones, and Jerry Lee had never heard that track." Some of the musicians laughed when they heard this, which greatly upset Lewis. Rory, didn't laugh, however, and this earned him this singer's trust. Donal says, "There's a great photo from that session of Jerry Lee looking up into Rory's eyes and Rory singing to him. Rory was teaching him the words and melody to 'Satisfaction.' So there was a link between Rory and Jerry Lee. They got on quite well."

**ONE POSITIVE OFFSHOOT OF NOT BECOMING A ROLLING STONE WAS THAT GALLAGHER WENT ON TO MAKE TWO OF HIS FINEST ALBUMS, *AGAINST THE GRAIN* AND *CALLING CARD*.**

Gallagher did a lot of session work over the course of his career, most of it first-rate and much of it with musical heroes like Muddy Waters, English jazz trombonist Chris Barber and Lonnie Donegan. Rory seemed able to relinquish control to these elder statesmen in a way that he couldn't with his peers. Meanwhile, as he prepared to make his third solo studio album, 1973's *Blueprint*, he seemed to have been aware of the shortcomings of the first two discs. *Blueprint* marks the debut of a revamped and expanded lineup, with drummer Rod De'Ath and keyboardist Lou Martin—both from the band Killing Floor—joining forces with longtime Gallagher bass player Gerry McAvoy.

A ballsy, barrelhouse-bluesy piano-and-organ man, Martin proved an ideal foil for Gallagher, lending a sense of variety and interplay to the guitarist's solo work. The format on *Blueprint* and its successor, *Tattoo*, was still for the most part live in the studio, but Martin's contributions fleshed out the sound. The Martin/De'Ath/McAvoy lineup was the most stable of all Gallagher's backing bands. It stuck together for three years, during which time it recorded four studio albums and one live disc with Gallagher. Donal says, "Rory never actually took a proper vacation. He'd use his vacation time for songwriting, developing, and listening to other people's music. He didn't know what else to do with himself."

Nor did he take much interest in the typical distractions of life on the road. Donal says Rory didn't use recreational drugs, like marijuana, nor did he go in much for groupies. "The prettiest girls on the planet would be queuing up for him," Donal says, "and we were all hoping he'd meet somebody. But he never would. I think that he was so keen on becoming a professional musician from an early age that he basically blocked everything else out of his life. In his teenage years, he just felt that girlfriends were a drawback. He'd seen too many guys fight over girlfriends, and seen girlfriends split up bands. He denied himself. It was almost like a vocation in the priesthood: 'Music is my life and I don't want to have any distractions or dead weights.' Later in his life there were one or two women, but he never settled down. Frankly, as a family member, I was praying he would."

Like many solitary, creative and intensely driven people, Rory found a kind of companionship in the bottle that he couldn't find in interpersonal relationships, a buffer to help block out the outside world and an anodyne to dull the pain of isolation. Although alcohol wouldn't become a real problem for him until the Eighties, there were earlier signs of impending trouble. "He'd go off and have a binge of drinking," Donal recalls. "He'd lock himself in a room for three days, probably go through a few bottles and come out with a set of songs. Unfortunately the alcoholism gene that runs in families was certainly in our family."

Gallagher's personal issues certainly didn't impede his output in the Seventies. Indeed they may have been at the root of his compulsion to record and release discs. The album that many fans regard as the apotheosis of the Martin/De'Ath/McAvoy lineup was *Irish Tour '74*. Live albums were hugely popular in the Seventies. Everyone from the Who and Stones to Yes, Deep Purple, Peter Frampton and Led Zeppelin released blockbuster live discs during the decade, and live performance was certainly Galla-

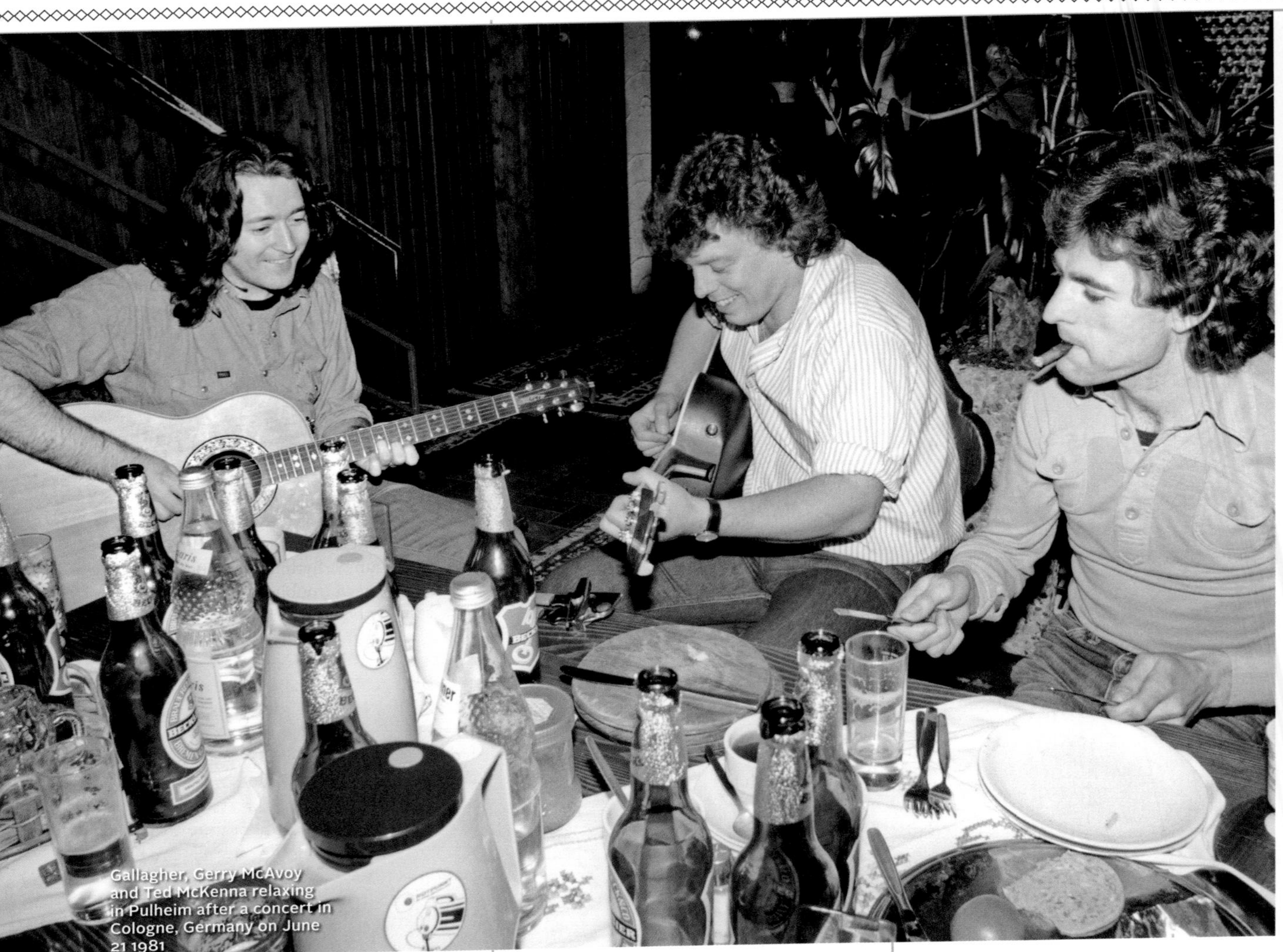
Gallagher, Gerry McAvoy and Ted McKenna relaxing in Pulheim after a concert in Cologne, Germany on June 21 1981

BRIAN COOKE/REDFERNS/GETTY IMAGES

gher's métier. Unable to connect with people very well in ordinary social situations, he may have treasured those few hours of rock and roll communion. And while *Irish Tour '74* didn't have a major impact in the States, it was the best-selling disc of Gallagher's career, worldwide.

Had *Irish Tour* been less successful, Gallagher might have responded differently to an offer that came in late '74/early '75 to join the Rolling Stones. Mick Taylor had just left the group and, as Donal tells the tale, Rory was the Stones' first choice for a replacement. The offer came quite informally—a phone call from Stones pianist Ian Stewart inviting Gallagher to "come have a blow and a jam session with the lads." The invitation was postponed several times, as the Stones were having problems with a new mobile recording truck they'd acquired at the time. Rory, meanwhile, had an important Japanese tour on the immediate horizon.

"Rory was naïve enough to think, Oh they only want to have a blow and a jam session. It's nothing serious," Donal says. "I was angry with him, to say the least."

Finally Rory got on a plane to Rotterdam with his Strat and a small, tweed, Fender Champ amp. The Stones had only provided one airline ticket, so Donal couldn't accompany his brother. According to what Rory later told Donal, he was met at the airport by none other than Mick Jagger, who put him in a cab and took him to a rehearsal space the Stones had occupied. There he was met by Marshall Chess Jr., head of the Rolling Stones' record label at the time, who reportedly said to Rory, "Welcome to the Rolling Stones. I knew it would be you. You're the guy for the job."

According to Donal, "Rory did four nights with them. The first night Keith didn't turn up. So Mick said to Rory, 'Can you give me a riff? I've got this song, "Start Me Up." ' And Rory said, 'Well, I'm working on a song.' So they worked it up. It's a legend that that album, [*the Stones'* Tattoo You] has different guitar riffs from different people. I think Rory referred to 'Miss You' as the other song they worked on. On the second night Keith came down and they got going. Keith liked Rory's style in the sense that Rory was into Hank Snow and the country guitar players as well as the rock and blues guitarists. So they obviously listened to the same records."

Parts of Donal's tales seem farfetched. The "Start Me Up" riff is very much dependent on Keith Richards' five-string, open-G guitar tuning, a configuration that Rory Gallagher is never known to have used. So one has to wonder where truth gives way to traditional Irish blarney in Donal's account. Still, it is theoretically possible that Keef's classic "Start Me Up" riff could have been derived from an earlier idea by Rory Gallagher. As to what happened next, the account becomes even more muddled.

"There was no coherence in the camp," Donal recounts. "Rory kept saying to Mick, 'Look what am I supposed to do about these Japanese dates? How long can you guys wait?' Mick said, 'Go and speak to Keith.' Mick and Keith weren't talking to each other at the time, which was another difficulty. The last evening, Rory went up to see Keith in his bedroom, but Keith was comatose. Rory spent the entire night up, going back every half hour, the door to Keith's suite being wide open.

Onstage at the Starwood in Hollywood, CA, 1974

BY GETTY IMAGES

Rory had to be on the plane back to Heathrow at 10 o'clock in the morning. Everyone else had gone to bed. There was no one else around. So Rory just packed his guitar and amp up, I met him with a suitcase at Heathrow airport, and we flew to Tokyo."

Donal was upset that Rory had let the opportunity to work with the Rolling Stones slip away. "I remember saying to Rory, 'All you had to do was ring and say, 'Postpone the Japanese tour.' We just would have sold more tickets in Japan, going back in six months' time. He said, 'I kept chasing for an answer and nobody seemed to know what was going on. It was a bit of a mess.' Maybe if he had rolled with it..." In the years afterward Rory turned down similar offers from Deep Purple and Canned Heat, but by then Donal knew enough not to be surprised by his brother's decisions.

One positive offshoot of not becoming a Rolling Stone was that Gallagher went on to make two of the finest solo albums of his career, *Against the Grain* released in '75 and *Calling Card* in '76. By this point, the Martin/De'Ath/McAvoy lineup had become a well-oiled machine. *Calling Card* also benefits from first-rate production work by Deep Purple bassist Roger Glover. For once, Rory was able to trust someone else with the production of one of his albums. Donal says, "We'd been out on a package tour with Deep Purple and Fleetwood Mac. On the road, Rory hit it off with Ritchie Blackmore and all the Purple guys."

*Calling Card* makes one wish Gallagher had been able to work with an outside producer more often. Engineered by the German wunderkind Mac (who'd later work with Queen), it is Rory Gallagher's best-sounding album. The playing is tight and the guitar tones beefy. There are proper overdubbed leads over chunky rhythm tracks. But by the end of the project, trouble had broken out, and Gallagher burnt yet another bridge.

"Rory wasn't happy with the mixes," Donal says. "He remixed the album with Chris Kimsey, who later did the Stones stuff, and that was annoying to Roger. But they never had rows—Rory just wouldn't talk to people. He said to me, 'No, that's not how I want the album to sound. I want it remixed.' And he'd pull it apart himself. It was difficult."

Gallagher was hardly in a position to be high-handed at that point. Bluesy hard rock bands were thick on the ground in the early and mid Seventies. Savoy Brown, Spooky Tooth, Nazareth, Ten Years After, Bad Company, Grand Funk Railroad, the James Gang...you couldn't throw a stick without hitting some guy with a shaggy Seventies mane riffing pentatonics into the ground. All these bands were competing not only with one another for attention, but also with more cutting edge—at the time—rock genres like prog, glam and fusion, not to mention popular non-rock genres like funk, disco and reggae. Solo artists like Alvin Lee and Peter Frampton had risen from the bluesy hard rock ranks to become major stars of the Seventies, proving that there was indeed a market for the "hot guitarist as singing/songwriting frontman" archetype. But Gallagher seems to have been blissfully oblivious to the fact that that's what it was—a market.

"Those other guys were prepared to act the superstar, and Rory wasn't," Donal says. "He wouldn't let the record company release singles from his albums. I remember when *Live in Europe* came out [*in 1972*], the executives from Polydor Records came down from a Washington gig with an edited version of the song 'Going to My Home Town.' They said, 'Polydor promise we'll take this to Number One.' And Rory nearly went through the roof, taking the Polydor guy with him. The idea of somebody editing his music...he just wasn't prepared to play that game. Even the guys in Deep Purple said, 'Look, you gotta do this. This is a hit single!' But Rory was terrified of becoming a novelty act. You release one hit single and the pressure is to follow it up with another hit single. And your next single becomes more important than your next album. I disagreed with Rory all along the way. For me, from tracks like 'Tattoo'd Lady' [*from 1973's* Tattoo] all the way through to 'Calling Card' [*from the 1976 album of the same name*], there were plenty of songs that would have been playable on the radio."

Gallagher's refusal to play the singles game demonstrates the extent to which he lived in his own private world. Perhaps his purist attitude derived from his early interest in folk music, that great bastion of anti-commercial sanctimony. Whatever the underlying logic, Rory was unable to perceive a single release as anything other than an intrusion on his divine right to solo uninterruptedly over 37 consecutive choruses of a 12-bar. In a way, this makes him the ultimate guitar hero. He was willing to commit career suicide to uphold the inviolable sanctity of the guitar solo.

Donal says the single release issue reared its head once again during the tense moments at the conclusion of the *Calling Card* sessions. "Chris Wright, who was one of the two bosses of Chrysalis Records, said, 'I'll tell you what. Put the album release back a year. We'll take the track "Edged in Blue," lop the guitar solo off and release that as a single. And we'll call the album *Edged in Blue* when it comes out.' Chris Wright is a music exec. I respected him. I went back to Rory and said, 'Look, this is proposed by the president of the company.' And, again, he nearly got on the phone to damn blast Chris for even thinking about it."

End-of-album-project jitters became an increasingly prevalent phenomenon for Gallagher as his career wore on. He'd completely recorded and mixed a follow-up to *Calling Card*, only to pull the plug at the 11th hour. "At the end, the lacquer [*master*] was cut and I was about to deliver it to Chrysalis, to do the whole listening thing with the execs," Donal says. "That morning, right in front of me, Rory said, 'You can't play it to anyone. I don't like the album.' And he dropped it in the [*garbage*] bin. I said, 'You can take time to remix it. Just let me play a couple of cuts to the label guys and send them on their merry way.' There were 75 execs flown in from all over the States. This was going to be Chrysalis' big push on Rory. I told him, 'Rory, you'll blow it with your record company if you do this kind of thing.' But he wouldn't compromise. He was just so depressed about it. So I had to go up to these guys with nothing to play, which didn't go down too well."

But the adventure wasn't over yet, as Donal discovered on returning to the L.A. hotel where he and Rory had been staying. "I got back from the meeting with the execs to find a message saying, 'Rory's in Cedars Sinai Hospital. But he's okay. Not to worry.' After I'd left, he'd gone off to see the Bob Dylan movie, *Reynaldo and Clara*, and he'd fractured his thumb in a taxi door. So it wasn't even possible to go back into the studio and re-record the album."

The mood was dour when the brothers returned to Ireland. "Rory seemed to get depressed at that time," Donal recalls. "One day he finally said, 'I want to change the lineup. I'm not happy with the band anymore.' He wanted to make a clean sweep, but I said, 'Look, at least retain the bass player, Gerry.'"

Exit Gallagher's most stable and successful backing band. Some of the material from the sessions Rory had trashed ended up on 1979's *Photo Finish* album, with Ted McKenna on drums. Gallagher had forged a friendship with Alan O'Duffy, a London-based engineer who worked on Paul McCartney & Wings' *Venus and Mars* album. He trusted O'Duffy enough to have him co-produce *Photo Finish* and its successor, *Top Priority*. Both are solid works of late-Seventies rock, but by that point it hardly mattered anymore. Punk rock had burst out of London and New York in a big way, charting a bold new direction for rock and roll. Meanwhile, Eddie Van Halen and Randy Rhoads were setting a new, less blues-centric course for hard rock and metal.

**GALLAGHER'S REFUSAL TO PLAY THE SINGLES GAME DEMONSTRATES THE EXTENT TO WHICH HE LIVED IN HIS OWN PRIVATE WORLD.**

Punk, in particular, declared war on Gallagher's whole style of presentation—the long rounds of guitar, keyboard, bass and drum soloing, the compulsory good-time audience participation, the all-too-casual and seemingly interminable bouts of guitar retuning between songs. Ironically, Gallagher liked punk. He'd attended the Sex Pistols' final gig in San Francisco and told his brother, "This is as close to Eddie Cochran as you're going to get." But apart from a vaguely new-wavy move or two in some of the songwriting from this period, Gallagher's music seems to have been as uninfluenced by punk as it had been by anything that had happened in rock since Cream had called it a day.

Gallagher's career and life took a turn for the worse in the Eighties. A hint of bitter irony creeps into some of his albums' titles. *Top Priority* was a somewhat mocking reference Chrysalis' promise that the disc would be their top marketing priority—despite the trashed masters, refusals to release singles and other drama Rory had put them through in the past. And the title of 1982's *Jinx* is fairly self-explanatory. By this point the substance abuse had begun to take its toll. Along with alcohol, Gallagher had become hooked on prescription tranquilizers.

"Where the 'medication'—for want of a better word—started to kick in was when Rory's fear of flying had flagged itself up," Donal says. "I think it was the pressure. He was wearing too many hats for his own good. He was being his own producer, his own songwriter, his own manager... With all the mental strain, the flying tablets probably relaxed him, so he began to take them for other purposes. And, of course, after a while they weren't strong enough, so he was constantly going back to the doctor and upgrading. Rory was very discreet about it all. He'd go swallow them in the bathroom."

Donal didn't gauge the extent of the problem until Rory began to have severe stomach pains and nausea. He says, "I managed to get him into a clinic, and the doctor there said, 'You realize the problem is not so much the alcohol. It's the pills.' And he lambasted the private doctor that Rory had for prescribing the amount of stuff he had. It wasn't any one prescribed tablet, it was the combination. Throw in alcohol and you're mixing a devil's brew."

In the final years of Rory's life, Donal became, quite literally, his brother's keeper. "I was acting as agent and manager and running an office," he says. "In the meantime, I'd gotten married and was trying to run my own life. Kids were coming. We'd clear time and take months off. But Rory was going to seed when he had time on his hands. You could see the emptiness in his life."

Donal settled his brother into a very nice modern house in London which had formerly been tenanted by Elton John, Dusty Springfield and John Mellencamp. "So it had great music credentials," Donal says. "I thought, Once I let him in there, maybe he won't have dinner parties as such, but at least he'll have people over. But he didn't invite anyone. Then maintenance of the house became a problem so I moved him out to a hotel. It was a very beautiful hotel. I knew the manager and he gave us a suite."

Rory may have spent some of the happiest days and nights of his final years at the Conrad, a luxury hotel in London's Chelsea Harbour. He would hold court at the hotel bar, hanging out with bands that passed through

Gallagher, Gerry McAvoy and Ted McKenna in Germany, 1981

BRIAN COOKE/REDFERNS/GETTY IMAGES

London and stayed at the hotel—every one from folk artists Martin Carthy and Bert Jansch to rockers like Gary Moore, INXS and Guns N' Roses. "Of course, Slash was a huge Rory fan," Donal says.

Rory even befriended the musicians who played in the hotel bar. But that's where things started to run amok. "The piano player was so out of it he couldn't play for the customers," Donal explains. "Or he'd be up in Rory's suite jamming with the drummer and bass player. My manager friend called and said, 'We've got to have the room back. This can't go on.' They had a building of apartments right across the street that they serviced. The hotel manager put Rory over there in this huge apartment. But he felt so isolated there and he got depressed and then he wouldn't see anybody."

Despite his declining physical and psychological condition, Gallagher completed two more studio albums, *Defender* in 1987 and *Fresh Evidence* in 1990. He managed to maintain a fairly active touring schedule into the early Nineties, although this became increasingly difficult. "The only cure for Rory was to keep him active, give him a schedule and give him a life," Donal says. "He didn't have a life when he was on the road, sadly."

But the touring brought pressure, and the pressure occasioned more abuse of tranquilizers and alcohol. The road and the live gigs—the very things that given purpose to Rory's life—were now killing him. "The last thing you want is to have your brother go out and make an ass of himself onstage," Donal says. "But we had to run the risk of doing that, or pissing off the fans. At one major London gig, Rory had obviously taken some tablets of some kind and washed them down with a brandy. He was fine before he went onstage. But within 20 minutes to an hour of being onstage he couldn't understand why his fingers had gone to jelly.

"On one of the last tours I broke into his dressing room, stole his baggage and made it look like a robbery in order to get at the medication and find out what was going on. I was shocked. His withdrawal symptoms were colossal. After a week or so, he sweated out the toxins from his body and got his appetite back. After three weeks he played better than ever. You'd turn him around, but you didn't want to risk him too long on the road. It was a very difficult call."

As the Nineties got under way, Gallagher was able to perform less and less frequently. Poor health forced him to turn down an offer to play on one of Mick Jagger's solo albums, among other gigs. Shortly after what would be his final performance, in the Netherlands, on January 10, 1995, Rory's liver failed.

"He was going in and out of a coma and I had to make the decision to have a liver transplant done," says Donal. "I'd never expected to be confronted with something like that. And the clock was ticking because we had to wait for a donor. You can't just buy a new liver."

Rory survived the initial 12-hour transplant surgery. But complications set in and there were numerous subsequent surgeries over an agonizing period of some three months. In the end, an infection he caught while in the hospital claimed his life. Donal Gallagher was at his brother Rory's side when he passed away in London, on June 14, 1995, at the age of 47.

"You can never say," Donal reasons. "Maybe it was a blessing in disguise. Who knows what kind of life he would have had if he had recovered."

The first signs of a revival of interest in Rory Gallagher and his music began in Europe, where he enjoyed greater popularity than he did in the States. A street was named after him on the outskirts of Paris. Many more tributes followed. "There was quite an outpouring from Germany and Ireland," says Donal. "People realized they missed a lot of good music."

Control of Rory's back catalog reverted to Donal in the late Nineties. All of the albums were remastered and reissued by BMG. "We didn't know what was going to happen," Donal says, "whether they were going to stiff or not. But within the first year, there were a million units of catalog sold."

And there's plenty more to come. Given Rory's unquenchable zeal for live performance, there are likely to be plenty of concert DVD releases in the future. "We haven't really tapped the BBC concerts yet," Donal says, "but we'll get there yet. Fortunately there's a whole vault full of live performance footage, which is great because young guitar players can study Rory's technique."

Gallagher himself would no doubt be gratified that his music has outlived the changing musical styles that kept him out of the Number One slot during his lifetime. There's some justice in the fact that he's found his place in the hearts of today's rock guitar subculture. He was always most comfortable among fellow musicians. ◆

# BELFAST COWBOY

When Gary Moore died in February 2011, the world lost one of its greatest electric blues-rock practitioners. *Guitar World* pays tribute to the fallen Irish guitar slinger.

BY TED DROZDOWSKI

GARY MOORE 1952–2011

**GARY MOORE LOOKED** and sounded invincible onstage. With a Les Paul slung at his hips, the Belfast-born whirlwind would close his eyes, grit his teeth and invest his entire soul in his incendiary playing. Sweat beaded around his trademark shag haircut as he'd rip through chorus after chorus of his iron-fisted fusion masterpiece "Parisienne Walkways" or the Celtic-swayed shredfest "Over the Hills and Far Away." And the snarling tone he'd craft while squeezing sparks from his Marshalls' howling speakers was among rock's boldest: grimy and articulate for his fusillades of single notes, and atom-smashing for his hard-chiseled chords.

Moore, who died in his sleep from a heart attack on February 6, 2011, belonged to the pantheon of blues guitar greats that came out of the United Kingdom during the Sixties. He arrived on the scene later than Jimmy Page, Jeff Beck and Eric Clapton, and though he never achieved their level of fame, he was their equal in technique, tone and touch. Perhaps it was a combination of his relative youth, his arrival in a less formative musical era or a subtle bias against his Irish ancestry that kept Moore from achieving their level of recognition.

Regardless, he left a legacy of more than 27 solo albums that document his trajectory from blues to hard rock to metal to fusion and back again to blues. These are supplemented by a handful of discs with Thin Lizzy, the original Skid Row and the fusion group Colosseum II, as well as collaborations with two-thirds of Cream's Holy Trinity, drummer Ginger Baker and bassist Jack Bruce.

"When it comes to rock and roll, Gary was fundamental in developing that twin-guitar, lyrical thing, like on 'Parisienne Walkways,' " Bob Geldof told BBC Radio, as word of Moore's death spread. "Axl Rose will say that without Thin Lizzy you don't get Guns N' Roses. [He was] just a great, great blues player, and absolutely one of the best."

Innovative guitar wrangler Reeves Gabrels, who ascended to a 13-year musical partnership with David Bowie and a solo career in the shadow of Moore's influence, concurs. "Gary was a beacon. When he played blues, it was from a rock point of view," he says. "Even when he was playing metal on albums like his own Victims of the Future, or playing rock with Thin Lizzy or Skid Row, he had such soul and feeling. He pushed me further. He had such speed and intensity in his right hand, and his vibrato was just ridiculous. And if you hear his albums in order, it's clear that there was a progression—he was always growing. How many guitar players live up to that?"

Joe Bonamassa, Metallica's Kirk Hammett, Thin Lizzy's Scott Gorham and Brian Downey, Def Leppard's Vivian Campbell, and scores of other heavy hitters also offered testimonials to Moore in the days after his passing. Brian Robertson recalled the daunting task of replacing Moore in Thin Lizzy—which Moore joined and left several times during the Seventies—in 1974. Moore had departed early during the recording of the *Nightlife* album.

"There was this track—'Still in Love with You,' " Robertson said. "I refused to replace Gary's original solos. They were the best solos I'd ever heard at that point and I wouldn't let anyone talk me into changing that."

And while Moore was revered for his electric playing, he also possessed stunning acoustic guitar technique, most recently heard in his beautifully sculpted contribution to the single "Sunday Morning" from blues maverick Otis Taylor's 2009 *Pentatonic Wars and Love Songs*. "I opened five tours for Gary in Europe, and sometimes we'd play traditional Irish music together while we were hanging around backstage," Taylor says. "He was amazing at that, of course. There was so much to his artistry that it's hard to comprehend what we've lost."

Moore was born in Belfast on April 4, 1952, and began honing his chops on a hand-me-down acoustic guitar at age eight. Although he was a lefty, Moore learned to play right-handed while digesting a musical menu that included Elvis Presley, the Beatles, the Shadows and Albert King. But it wasn't until he moved to Dublin as a teenager and witnessed Jimi Hendrix and John Mayall's Bluesbreakers onstage that Moore saw his future.

Blues legend Peter Green, who Moore met at a Bluesbreakers gig when he was 14, became his mentor. Green's highly original, melodic soloing and wicked vibrato gave Moore the template for his own style. When Green quit Fleetwood Mac in 1969 for a decades-long hiatus from the music business, Moore acquired Green's Les Paul, a shimmering-voiced 1959 Standard that's come to be nicknamed the Holy Grail for its majestic tone and history in the hands of both famed masters.

The Holy Grail was Moore's main ax for 37 years, starting with his first important band, Dublin blues-rockers Skid Row. In that group he began his long creative association with singer-bassist Phil Lynott, a childhood pal whom Moore would follow into Thin Lizzy and continue to write and record with until Lynott's death in 1986. Together, they composed "Parisienne Walkways" and other enduring tracks, including Thin Lizzy's 1979 smash "Sarah."

Moore moved from blues to hard rock with his first solo disc, *Grinding Stone*, in 1973, and subsequently joined the fusion group Colosseum II. That band built its sound on Moore's bare-knuckled approach to loud, electric jazz and revealed a sense of humor in song titles like "Dark Side of the Moog." After three high-flying albums that

Moore onstage with Phil Lynott in Birmingham, England, in April 1979

failed commercially, Colosseum II broke up.

In the early Eighties, Moore played on art-rock giant Greg Lake's two solo recordings and formed the group BBM with Ginger Baker and Jack Bruce. Along the way, he kept a parallel solo career in motion, yielding his metal masterpieces *Corridors of Power* and *Victims of the Future* in 1982 and 1983, respectively, along with 11 more discs. But with 1990's pivotal *Still Got the Blues*, Moore revealed his recommitment to the genre that had sparked his musical imagination. Among the songs on that album was a cover of Peter Green's "Stop Messin' Around," a tribute to Moore's mentor.

Moore's 11 subsequent studio CDs stuck mostly to his muddy roots, with the notable exception of 1994's bone-crunching and poetic *Around the Next Dream*, with BBM. But the bottom line is that Moore's playing was always best live. Onstage, with his eyes closed and his channels fully opened, he gave way to lengthy flights of improvisation where every part of his musical vocabulary had its say.

His most recent release was 2009's five-CD *Essential Montreux*. The box captures all of his virtues as an uncompromising player in performances at the famed Swiss festival from 1990, 1995, 1997, 1999 and 2001. Its 60 songs display the furious shredding of his hard rock and fusion eras, with both styles compacted into the anti-war epic "Out in the Fields," the last tune Moore wrote with Lynott, as well as the classics "Over the Hills and Far Away" and "Parisienne Walkways." But it's his raw-boned, big-toned nods to his blues heroes B.B. King, Otis Rush, T-Bone Walker, Freddie King and Green, that take center stage—which is exactly where Moore kept the blues in his heart until the end. ◆

Robert Johnson (left) with fellow blues musician Johnny Shines, circa 1935

# DEVIL IN THE DETAILS

It's said that Robert Johnson sold his soul in return for six-string mastery. But the truth behind the blues legend's archetypal mix of vice and virtuosity is complex, as his friend David "Honeyboy" Edwards explained just before his death in 2011.

BY ALAN DI PERNA

ROBERT JOHNSON 1911–1938

## SHORTLY BEFORE HIS DEATH

in 2011, bluesman David "Honeyboy" Edwards vividly remembered the first time he met Robert Johnson. It was on a plantation in Lake Cormorant, Mississippi, in 1937. Edwards heard tell of some hot players gigging locally that night. He got the word from Charles Dodd, who was Robert Johnson's half brother.

"Dodd had a country store at Lake Cormorant," Edwards recalled. "We talked a while, and he say, 'Cross the field there, Son House, Willie Brown and Robert Johnson playing tonight.' It was at what they call a juke house—big house, sold wine, whiskey, barbecue and stuff like that. I went over there, and that's the first time I met Robert."

It's amazing that there was a guy living and walking around in our digitized dystopia as late as 2011 who actually knew, hung with and, on many occasions, played guitar with Robert Johnson, a bluesman so revered today that he has become almost a mythological figure—a larger-than-life, folkloric legend on the order of Johnny Appleseed, John Henry, Joe Hill or Paul Bunyan. Johnson seems to come from another world. In the Thirties, the rural southern United States was a place where most African Americans lived a life of poverty under the harsh strictures of a segregated and frequently brutally racist society. For many people raised in post–civil rights America, it's hard to imagine such a culture on our own shores.

Most of us have come to Robert Johnson through the music of Eric Clapton, the Rolling Stones and other Sixties rockers who were profoundly influenced by Johnson's music and who have passed that influence on to subsequent generations. Thanks to these artists, Johnson songs like "Love in Vain" and "Crossroads" have become modern standards. Clapton has gone so far to say that his first discovery of Robert Johnson was "like a religious experience."

While the rock covers are wonderful, there's nothing like hearing Johnson himself. Via reissued recordings of his original 78-rpm phonograph discs, we can imaginatively and symbolically retrace the journey "Honeyboy" Edwards made all those years ago, across a dark field of changing cultural currents, to be charmed and mesmerized by the fleet-fingered guitar work and plaintive singing of a man whose music touches us in an intimate and oddly familiar way, and yet who simultaneously seems so utterly remote.

In many ways, Johnson was the original model for our modern guitar hero archetype: the good-looking traveling man who gets all the chicks and whose playing is so impossibly accomplished that he is surrounded by legends that he sold his soul to the devil in return for his supernatural musical prowess. That's just one of the reasons guitarists and music lovers around the world celebrated the 100th anniversary of Robert Johnson's birth in 2011. Edwards himself, along with fellow blues luminaries B.B. King, Hubert Sumlin, Charlie Musselwhite and Ruthie Foster, contributed to a tribute album and tour, *100 Years of Robert Johnson*, spearheaded by the popular jam band Big Head Todd and the Monsters.

It's all quite impressive when you consider that Johnson was pretty much a regional one-hit wonder in his own time who reportedly never bested the success of his 1937 debut record, "Terraplane Blues" (5,000 copies sold, according to some estimates). And it's something of a minor miracle that he is so well known and well loved today—all that we have from him are three photographs and 41 recordings, comprising multiple takes of some 29 songs recorded over a handful of sessions in 1936. It's much less than we have from blues contemporaries of Johnson's such as Tampa Red, Leroy Carr, Bessie Smith, Big Bill Broonzy, Lonnie Johnson, Memphis Minnie and Blind Boy Fuller.

> "ROBERT PLAYED HIS MUSIC, AND HE DRANK AND HE LIKED HIS WOMEN. HE WAS A NICE GUY. KINDA QUIET."
> —"HONEYBOY" EDWARDS

Yet, it is Johnson who survives as the great exponent of acoustic Delta blues, the only Thirties-era bluesman that many people today have ever heard. Every detail of his known photographs and 41 recordings has been analyzed, interpreted and debated with full forensic and academic rigor. Scholars and pundits have gone over every crease and detail of the natty pinstriped suit, tie, tiepin, pocket handkerchief, hat, shoes and socks worn by Johnson in his best-known photo, drawing inferences about Johnson's life and personality from this scant evidence. Guitar fiends pore over a photo of Johnson holding a Gibson L-00, studying the positioning of his long slender fingers on the fretboard and arguing endlessly about whether the guitar was his personal instrument or merely a prop used for this carefully posed studio portrait. The music, of course, has been studied in even greater detail. Entire academic dissertations have been written on minor variations among Johnson's multiple takes of songs like "Kindhearted Woman Blues," "Rambling on My Mind," "When You've Got a Good Friend," "Cross Road Blues" and "Me and the Devil Blues."

Johnson's work may well have been lost to us were it not for the work of a handful of folklorists who discovered, preserved and passed his music on to future generations. His early and dramatic death has also fueled much speculation as to what he might have accomplished had he lived longer, in much the same way that people speculate about Jimi Hendrix, Jim Morrison, Janis Joplin and Randy Rhoads.

"Robert Johnson didn't make too many records, but the stuff that he made, man, is livin'," said Hubert Sumlin, a participant in the *100 Years* tribute and longtime guitarist for Howlin' Wolf, another legendary figure who knew and was profoundly influenced by Johnson.

It's fairly certain that Johnson was born in 1911; the date May 8 is often given. He was born out of wedlock, shunted from one home to another and consigned to the care of various guardians during his childhood. Much like the young Jimi Hendrix, Johnson bore a number of names in his early life as his family situation shifted. At various points, he was called Robert Leroy, Little Robert Dusty and Robert Spencer before taking the surname of his birth father, Noah Johnson.

Robert Johnson's unstable and peripatetic childhood may lie at the root of the restless wandering he did for the short duration of his adult life, moving from place to place, never staying long, never getting too close to anyone, not even the many women with whom he took up. He is noted for having numerous relationships with women older than himself, who would take him into their homes, feed him and care for him. Freudians might well interpret this as a desperate search on Johnson's part for some kind of surrogate mother. In this connection, it's interesting that his first-ever recording paid

## ERIC CLAPTON

“Robert Johnson is the most important blues musician who ever lived. I've never found anything more deeply soulful than Robert Johnson.”

homage to a “Kind Hearted Woman.”

We know Johnson suffered poor eyesight and angered his father by being unwilling to engage in backbreaking farm labor. A naturally gifted musician who could play the jaw harp and harmonica as well as guitar, Johnson struck off on his own fairly early. By age 19, in 1929, he was already married, to the 16-year-old Virginia Travis, but his wife died in childbirth a little over a year later. The baby didn't survive either. Some commentators trace the profound note of death-haunted sadness in Johnson's work to this event. A year and one month after his first wife's death, Johnson wed Caletta Croft, whom he would eventually desert.

Around 1930, Johnson met three bluesmen who would become teachers, mentors and important musical influences. Son House and Willie Brown were both successful recording artists in the “race records” market aimed at African Americans. Both were friends and protégés of another key Delta blues musician and singer, Charlie Patton. The influence of these artists can be heard in Johnson's music. Brown is even cited by name in “Cross Road Blues.”

Son House, who lived to become a celebrated figure on the Sixties folk scene, recalled seeing Johnson with a seven-string guitar that he'd rigged up himself. While no audio recording or photographic evidence of this instrument survives, all eyewitness accounts of Johnson concur on his keen musical prowess. It was said he could hear a phonograph record just once and be able to play and sing the song with note- and word-perfect accuracy, even if the record had only been playing in the background while Johnson was engaged in some other activity.

“Robert was a funny kind of musician,” Edwards recalled. “He never did talk too much. He didn't do a lot of cussin' like a lot of musicians did. He was easygoin'. He played his music, and he drank and he liked his women. I never heard him cussin' and hollerin' like the other guys did. He was a nice guy. Kinda quiet, but he just had his ways, you know.”

Johnson spent most of the early Thirties as an itinerant musician, traveling throughout the South and even up North, playing at juke joints, parties and on street corners, consolidating his skills and repertoire. Like most African American entertainers at the time, he played not only blues but also vaudeville songs, ragtime, jazz and pop hits of the day. Then as now, a working musician had to play whatever people wanted to hear.

But blues is what the record companies wanted. Still in its infancy at the time, the record business had already discovered what would today be called niche marketing. They learned they could make money selling hillbilly music to rural white folks, mariachi to Mexican-American communities and blues to African Americans. Discs aimed at the latter population were known as race records. To serve all of these niche markets, the record labels sent recording teams out into the field to record local performers.

And so it was that Robert Johnson found himself in Room 414 at the Gunter Hotel in San Antonio, Texas, on November 23, 1936, for a series of sessions for ARC Records.

## KEITH RICHARDS

“If I could transcend time, Robert Johnson is the first person I'd want to visit, just to see how he managed to play like he did. The man was asking for trouble and didn't mind saying so. In all of his records, the man is asking for trouble all the way down the line. All his deals with the hellhounds and the bitches—one of them will get you. But if Johnson had lived into the era of the electric guitar, he'd have killed us all!”

IAN GAVAN/GETTY IMAGES (RICHARDS); CHRIS JACKSON/GETTY IMAGES (CLAPTON)

Producer Don Law had set up his recording gear in the room. Johnson was just one performer in a full roster of acts recorded on the week of the 23rd, taking his place in line among several mariachi bands, a hillbilly outfit, and Western swingsters the Chuck Wagon Gang. It is known that Johnson was positioned in the corner of the room facing the wall, much like a schoolboy who had misbehaved. This detail has excited much speculation. Some say it was because he was painfully shy. Others say he faced the wall so that the other musicians present couldn't cop his licks. Still others say that the placement was meant to take advantage of an acoustic phenomenon known as corner loading, which helps to enhance an instrument's bass frequencies.

That first session yielded two songs that have become standards, “I Believe I'll Dust My Broom” and “Sweet Home Chicago.” The former is one of many Johnson songs that exhibit a pronounced influence from the pianist and singer Leroy Carr, who was a major blues star at the time. Carr's 1928 hit, “How Long, How Long Blues,” was known to be one of Johnson's all-time favorite songs. The main melody for Johnson's recording of “Dust My Broom” comes from another Carr recording, “I Believe I'll Make a Change,” although it also reflects the influence of another popular bluesman of the day, Kokomo Arnold.

In adapting Carr's piano music to the guitar, Johnson also picked up the driving root-V-to-root-VI bass figure heard in "Dust My Broom" and countless other blues songs that use a shuffle rhythm. This left-hand figure is very natural for pianists, but it requires a bit of pinkie stretching to play on a guitar in standard tuning, making it somewhat difficult for a beginning player. Through Johnson, it was picked up by guitarists like Jimmy Reed and Elmore James, and it has become a staple of the blues guitar vocabulary.

The same bass figure grounds "Sweet Home Chicago," another blues standard that Johnson adapted from Kokomo Arnold's "Old Original Kokomo Blues" by way of an earlier recording by guitarist and frequent Leroy Carr accompanist Scrapper Blackwell. Along with its driving bass-string figure, the track exemplifies Johnson's gift for supple and artful turnarounds, graceful descending figures built around the V chord at the end of verses, and dramatic high-string licks inserted midverse often as an underpinning to a vocal line.

"Robert was the only guitar player with a little different style than all the other guys had," Edwards said. " 'Cause he had the turnaround to his blues. The turnaround is when you have a solo in betwixt the verses. You stoppin' to have a solo. But all the rest of the guys, like Tommy Johnson and them, they had a little short time. Wasn't enough for you to pay attention to. So Robert had a different style than the other blues players."

The third song recorded on that very first session is the one that listeners in Johnson's time would have known best. "Terraplane Blues" takes its name from the Hudson Terraplane, a popular automobile of the time. "Terraplane Blues" is an example of the risqué double entendre subgenre known as "hokum," or "party blues," that was extremely popular in those days. Examples range from "Baby Let Me Bang Your Box," ostensibly about a piano, to the ever-popular "Squeeze Your Orange."

One of several contributions to the genre by Johnson, "Terraplane Blues" runs the usual gamut of erotic innuendo, from fears of infidelity ("Who's been drivin' my Terraplane for you since I've been gone?") to boasts of lovemaking prowess ("When I mash down on your little starter, then your spark plug will give me fire").

Years later, the Rolling Stones would cop the song's central motif for their early B side "Who's Driving My Plane." Hokum comes down to the rock era through tracks like Led Zeppelin's "The Lemon Song" and just about every song AC/DC ever recorded. As with the blues shuffle bass figure, this isn't something Robert Johnson originated but a tradition he had a key role in passing down when he was rediscovered by the titans of Sixties rock.

By the time Johnson returned to Room 414 on November 26, three days after his first session, he'd spent a little time in the local jail and reportedly phoned Don Law to borrow a nickel to pay a prostitute who demanded the princely sum of 50 cents for her services. Johnson recorded just one track, "32-20 Blues," that Thursday but returned the following day to lay down more eternal classics, once again taking his place among the cowboys, mariachis and hillbilly acts scheduled to be recorded.

Perhaps the most significant song from that session was "Cross Road Blues." The track lies at the heart of the myth that Johnson sold his soul to the Devil at the crossroads one night in return for his formidable musical prowess. Tales of this nature are by no means unique to Johnson. Blues lore is rife with accounts of what would happen if you played your guitar in a graveyard at midnight, or placed a handful of graveyard soil in your guitar case or the body of your instrument.

Johnson certainly knew how to work this archetype. "Cross Road Blues" has one of the most chillingly effective final lines of all time: "Lord, I'm standing at the crossroads. I believe I'm sinking down." Johnson would return to this demonic leitmotiv repeatedly, with "Preachin' Blues (Up Jumped the Devil)," "Hellhound on My Trail" and "Me and the Devil Blues." His singing does indeed sound haunted on some of these. But did that stem from a genuine conviction or fear of damnation? Or was it just the artistry of a convincing singer who knew that nothing gets a rise out of folks like a good tale of Old Nick?

Johnson returned from San Antonio to his Mississippi home turf, having recorded enough material for a string of 78-rpm records that were released on the Vocalion label. They were minor hits on the race market, which meant they sold a fraction of what records by mainstream artists like Bing Crosby or Paul Whiteman were selling. Race records certainly weren't a "get rich" proposition for the artists. But, much as in our own post–record industry times, they could help build an artist's popularity and assist him in getting gigs, which is what happened for Johnson.

"The records was selling real good," Edwards said. "'Terraplane Blues,' 'Kind Hearted Woman Blues,' 'Come On in My Kitchen'...all that stuff was on the new jukebox playing all up and down the streets. And Robert was kind of famous back at that time. There wasn't much money to be made, but what was made, he was gettin' some."

The records sold well enough that Johnson was called back to do a second series of sessions in June 1937 in Dallas, where once again he lined up among cowboy and hillbilly acts to record his music in another makeshift studio. The location this time was in an office building, with Don Law once again in charge. To help quell the sweltering heat of a Texas summer, electric fans blew jets of air across blocks of ice in the recording room. Johnson laid down another 13 songs over two days, including "Stones in My Passway," "From Four Till Late," "I'm a Steady Rollin' Man," "Traveling Riverside Blues," "Stop Breakin' Down Blues" and "Love in Vain." The latter two songs of course, were recorded and made popular in our time by the Rolling Stones.

Blues purists have castigated the Stones for changing the rhythmic feel of Johnson's "Love in Vain" and adding a few more chords. But "Love in Vain" is itself Johnson's reworking of another Leroy Carr tune, "When the Sun Goes Down." Even the song's most poetic line, "the blue light was my blues, and the red light was my mind," was from Blind Lemon Jefferson's "Dry Southern Blues," released some 11 years prior to Johnson's recording.

While Johnson's records weren't big hits, the modest success and income they garnered made 1937 a banner year for him. Regrettably, he didn't live to enjoy the fruits

## BILLY GIBBONS

“ In my early teens, I actually heard about Robert Johnson through Eric Clapton. He mentioned Johnson's name in some teen magazine, and it opened a doorway. I thought King of the Delta Blues Singers was dark and smoky; you were really drawn into the meaningfulness of the Delta. His music is so enticing and it stands alone. His stuff was so finished. He created songs that were thematically consistent from opening line to the closing. Of all the rural bluesmen, his is the most listenable and the most compelling. ”

of his labor for very long. It was whiskey and a woman that brought his life to an end. In August 1938, Johnson and Edwards had a regular gig at a juke joint at a place called Three Forks, near Greenwood, Mississippi. "It was a club out on the Highway 82 and 47 betwixt Greenwood, going to Itta Bena," Edwards recalled. "And he was playing out there for this man. What happened was Robert started goin' with the man's wife. She had a sister living out in Greenwood, where Robert roomed at. And every Monday morning she get to go out to visit her sister, but she was visiting Robert. And people would see them out there and run to her husband and tell him. The husband didn't wanna kill Robert and go to penitentiary, Parchman Farm [*Mississippi's maximum security prison*]. So he just give the woman who was working for him a pint of poisoned whiskey and tell her to give it to Robert."

The fatal drink was administered at what would be Johnson's final performance, on August 13. That night, he was playing with another soon-to-be blues legend, the harmonica ace Sonny Boy Williamson II.

"It was a Saturday night," Edwards recounted. "He had been drinking. Robert loved whiskey and women; that's all he loved. 'Bout one o'clock, the people piled in there to have a good time, coming in off the street from little country towns back out there where he's playing then. He had got the whiskey then, sat in the corner."

Johnson began to feel ill, but carried on playing. "The people all thought he just needed another drink," Edwards said. "But he didn't need that 'nother drink, 'cause he had already got *the* drink. But the drink that he got was poisoned. The woman give it to him, but she didn't know what she's givin' him."

As the night wore on however, it became increasingly apparent that something was seriously wrong with Johnson. "People found out that he was really sick," Edwards said. "Take him back up to Greenwood, oh, about three o'clock, four o'clock Sunday morning. I went there Tuesday and he was still sick, crawlin' round. People give him soda water and different stuff, to try to heave that stuff up."

In Edwards' view, the substance that had been added to the whiskey given to Johnson "wasn't really deadly poison. If it was strychnine or something, it would have killed him right away. He would have died in a couple of hours. But it was something make him lie around for about three days before he died. Back around that time, it was the Depression. Black people couldn't get no doctor too much then. All the good doctors back in those days were for all the white people who had the money. 'Cause we didn't have the money to give away."

Had Johnson been able to receive a doctor's care, he might have lived into our own time to be celebrated by folkies and white intellectuals, and to jam with rock stars. As it was, he died on Tuesday, August 16, 1938, at the age of 26.

Given his relatively minor standing in the blues market of the Thirties, Johnson might well have been forgotten had it not been for the record industry pioneer John Hammond, who fostered the careers of artists including Count Basie, Billie Holiday, Aretha Franklin, Bob Dylan and Bruce Springsteen over the course of his career. Late in 1938, Hammond organized a concert at Manhattan's Carnegie Hall entitled *From Spirituals to Swing*, with the ambition of giving New York's elite a sweeping overview of the evolution and development of black music, from its origins in Africa through the days of slavery and right up to the sophisticated jazz sounds of the late Thirties.

And his first choice to represent the blues was none other than Robert Johnson. But when Hammond invited Johnson to perform at the New York concert, he was devastated to find out that the bluesman had died just months earlier. In the end, Big Bill Broonzy, another fine singer and guitarist, went on the Carnegie Hall stage to represent the blues on December 23, 1938. He was accompanied by the excellent blues harmonica player Sonny Terry. But two Robert Johnson records, "Walkin' Blues" and "Preachin' Blues," rang out in Carnegie that night. The only other nonlive music at the event were field recordings from Africa.

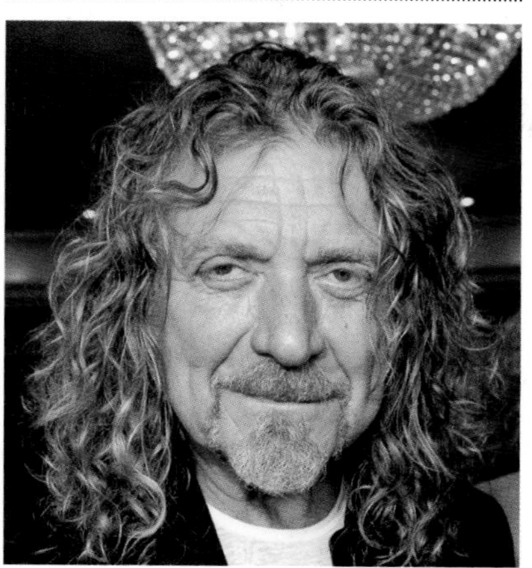

JON FURNISS/WIREIMAGE

## ROBERT PLANT

"I've never heard anything as seductive as Robert Johnson. It's the way his voice and the steel strings intertwine. They weave through so much pain and anticipated pleasure. I was really struck by the line, 'Goin' down to Friar's Point/If I be rockin' to my end,' from 'Traveling Riverside Blues.' The joy, the abandon with which Johnson looks forward to things! His music has followed me everywhere. The anguish and the desolation is beautiful."

It was through Hammond that the celebrated American folklorist Alan Lomax became interested in Robert Johnson. Lomax had sprung Leadbelly from prison and introduced Pete Seeger to Woody Guthrie, among other notable accomplishments relevant to the worlds of blues and folk. Inspired by the *Spirituals to Swing* concert, Lomax turned his attention to the Mississippi Delta, traveling there in 1941 and 1942 to record local musicians for the Library of Congress.

Edwards recalled Lomax pulling into Friars Point, Mississippi, in a big Hudson Super Six automobile. "He walked up, book under his arm. Young white boy. He said, 'I'm Alan Lomax; I'm with the Library of Congress. I'd like to record you.'"

On those fateful trips to the Delta, Lomax also recorded Son House and made the first-ever recordings of Muddy Waters. Lomax's work did much to fuel the folk music boom that peaked in the Fifties and early Sixties in America. Thanks to him, traditional Delta and acoustic blues performers like Son House, Mississippi John Hurt, Mississippi Fred McDowell, Bukka White, Mance Lipscomb, Sonny Terry, Brownie McGhee and many of their peers came into demand and began playing on college campuses and at prestigious folk festivals, like the annual event at Newport, Rhode Island.

Along with new recordings by these traditional artists, the folk boom sparked a vigorous trade in reissued recordings of folk and blues artists from the Twenties and Thirties. Among these was the 1961 Columbia release *Robert Johnson: King of the Delta Blues Singers*. The album collected 16 of Johnson's songs, including many of those best known today. In terms of influence and artistry, this disc ranks alongside groundbreaking albums like the Beatles' *Please Please Me* debut, Bob Dylan's *Highway 61 Revisited* and the Clash's *London Calling*.

Copies of this release made their way to England, where they fell into the hands of fledgling players like Eric Clapton and the Rolling Stones' Keith Richards and Brian Jones. Richards recalls, "Brian Jones had the first album, and that's where I first heard it. I'd just met Brian, and I went around to his apartment. All he had in it was a chair, a record player and a few records. One of which was Robert Johnson. He put it on, and it was just—you know, astounding stuff. I said to Brian, 'Who's that?' 'Robert Johnson.' I said, 'Yeah, but who's the other guy playing with him?' Because I heard two guitars and it took me a long time to realize he was actually doing it all by himself." ◆

Eric Wilson, Brad Nowell and Bud Gaugh with Lou Dog, Nowell's Dalmatian

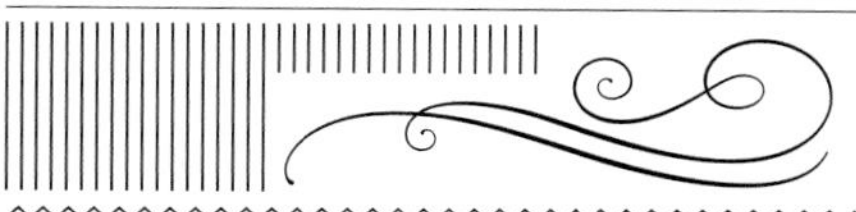
ROCK IN PEACE

# WRONG WAY

Sublime were headed for fame until Brad Nowell's drug abuse led him astray. In this oral history, bandmates, friends and associates recall the guitarist's inspired rise and tragic fall.

BY DAN EPSTEIN

BRAD NOWELL 1968–1996

## IT'S THE FALL OF 1996, AND SUBLIME'S

"What I Got" is all over the radio. Driven by an effortlessly funky groove and a sun-dappled acoustic guitar figure, the song is an instantly infectious alternative-rock anthem about looking for that silver lining in the greyest of skies. With its blunted SoCal beach vibe, artfully placed hip-hop samples and a chorus that echoes Jamaican dancehall heroes Half-Pint and Barrington Levy, "What I Got" is the freshest-sounding thing on the airwaves. And as the song shoots up the *Billboard* charts, carrying the band's new self-titled third album along with it, Sublime appear—to the casual observer, at least—to be on the verge of becoming one of the hottest acts in the music business.

There's just one problem: Bradley Nowell, Sublime's charismatic lead vocalist, guitarist and songwriter, has been dead for months. In the early hours of May 25, 1996, the man who sang, "But I got a Dalmatian and I can still get high," died of a heroin overdose in a San Francisco hotel room, with Lou Dog, his beloved Dalmatian, whimpering on his chest. He was 28 years old.

Without Nowell, there will be no tour for the album. Though they'd built up an enormous following in their native Southern California, and even coheadlined the inaugural Warped Tour the year before, Sublime have yet to break nationally. And with Nowell gone, the band has no way to reach a wider audience.

Yet, in the wake of Nowell's tragic death, Sublime's music miraculously takes on a life of its own. On the strength of "What I Got" and subsequent radio hits "Santeria," "Wrong Way," "Doin' Time" and "April 29, 1992 (Miami)," *Sublime* eventually grooves all the way to Number 13 on the *Billboard* 200, making the group arguably the most successful American rock act of 1997.

Seventeen years after the album's release, the spell of Sublime's visionary mixture of punk rock, reggae, ska, hip-hop and surf is no less potent. *Sublime* and its two DIY predecessors—1992's *40 Oz. to Freedom* and 1994's *Robbin' the Hood*—have found favor with a whole new generation of fans, many of whom were barely out of diapers when Nowell passed away.

In this exclusive *Guitar World* feature, Nowell's bandmates, colleagues and loved ones recount Sublime's unlikely rise to stardom and reflect upon the group's enduring legacy. They also share their memories of Nowell, a complex man who loved reading history books and lived for his music and family, but who ultimately succumbed to demons he couldn't control.

**TROY HOLMES (*Nowell's widow*)** Brad got his musical talent from both his parents. His dad played guitar and his mom taught piano and flute, and that contributed to Brad's perfect pitch. His upbringing was extremely sheltered; he had one sister, younger than him, and his parents split up when he was maybe 12 or 13. His mom got super-Christian, like scary fundamentalist Christian. She'd go into his room at night and make him pray the demons out of his room—and it freaked the fuck out of him. Then he moved to his dad's house, in the Naples part of Long Beach, and it was like the bachelor pad. And then his dad met his stepmom, and she had two daughters, and all of a sudden this perfect world that was shared between him and his dad was interrupted. So Brad was just lost.

**MARSHALL GOODMAN (*Sublime drummer/DJ*)** My first encounter with Brad was when I was around 14 years old. My sister was in high school and played saxophone, and she joined a band with Brad and Eric called Sloppy Seconds. They came over to the house to practice, and at the time I didn't have a drum set; I just had turntables, since I've been DJing since I was 13. Brad was like, "Wow, what is that you're doing?" He was all intrigued by the turntables.

**BUD GAUGH (*Sublime drummer*)** Eric [*Wilson*] and I grew up playing music together. His dad was a professional jazz musician, and he taught me how to read music and get handy with the kit. Eric had played with Brad, and he was like, "You've gotta meet this guy!" We came from more of a punk rock background; we didn't know as much about reggae as Brad did. Brad had gone down to the Caribbean and brought back a mix tape with a bunch of artists on it. We didn't know the names of all the artists on it, but Eric and I both dubbed it, and it was in all three of our cars at the same time.

*Calling themselves Sublime, Nowell, Wilson and Gaugh played their first show on July 4, 1988. An impromptu affair on the Long Beach peninsula, the gig's DIY nature and chaotic conclusion would pretty much set the tone for the band's future.*

**GAUGH** Fourth of July's a big party scene down on the Peninsula, so we just thought, Hey, let's grab our equipment and find a party and see if we can infiltrate. There was a guy who was having a party on the bay side, and we were like, "Hey, check us out—this is what we sound like!" I forget what tape we played him, but it wasn't us! He was like, "Oh yeah, right on! Plug in—you can use my power!" There was a little grass area at the end of the street, and we just set up there and ran an extension cord from his house. He was pouring us drinks, and the crowd kept getting bigger and bigger. And then the cops came and shut it down.

**GOODMAN** Brad was just a phenomenal intellect and a phenomenal writer, and he was a very good freestyler because of that. He was so well thought and well read. He could just go somewhere and not have it be contrived. Most people would have to think about it or plan it, but he would just go, "Oh, this song's in C—let me throw this hook in there!" A lot of that originated from the backyard parties—he would freestyle and see how people would respond to it. He was very bright. He was able to just compose these songs on the run and record them later. If you go back through a lot of early demos, Brad went through phases: he was sounding like Bauhaus for a while; he was sounding like Morrissey. But at the backyard parties, he really found where his voice was.

**GAUGH** Trying to get gigs in L.A. was nearly impossible. It was all hair-metal bands in Hollywood, and the promoters just didn't know what to do with us. So we just opted to play parties and stuff. We hooked up with some local party promoters, guys who would rent out warehouses, fraternities and sororities, playing parties at colleges.

*In 1990, Gaugh left the band. Goodman took over the drum throne and played on the bulk of 40 Oz. to Freedom, the band's first official*

LARRY BUSACCA/RETNA LTD.

*album. The record was tracked over a lengthy string of sessions at the 24-track recording studio at Cal State Dominguez Hills, where Sublime friend and sometime second guitarist Michael "Miguel" Happoldt was studying audio engineering.*

**GOODMAN** We didn't have a big budget. We didn't have a lot of two-inch tape, so instead of doing one song on 24 tracks, we'd do one song with the 12 tracks on the left and one song with 12 tracks on the right. That way we got twice the usage for our money on one two-inch reel. That was Miguel's genius move.

**MIGUEL HAPPOLDT *(Sublime second guitarist)*** 40 Oz. to Freedom is kind of a beautiful guitar record in the vision of it, but the tones are kind of strange. Rather than try to get tones like everybody else, we'd try to get tones that didn't sound like anybody else. When I met Brad, he had the classic metallic blue Ibanez that's in all the photos. And he had a Gallien-Krueger amp that had two 212 cabs and stereo effects, so he would split the 212s on either side of the stage. He thought that was the coolest shit ever. *40 Oz. to Freedom* was both me and Brad on guitar. He would do all the tracking, and then for the overdubs he'd either do them himself or he'd have me do 'em. He was the ringleader and the quarterback—but when he was stuck, it was my job to *not* be stuck. When we hit a wall, my job was to make sure we were going through or over that wall.

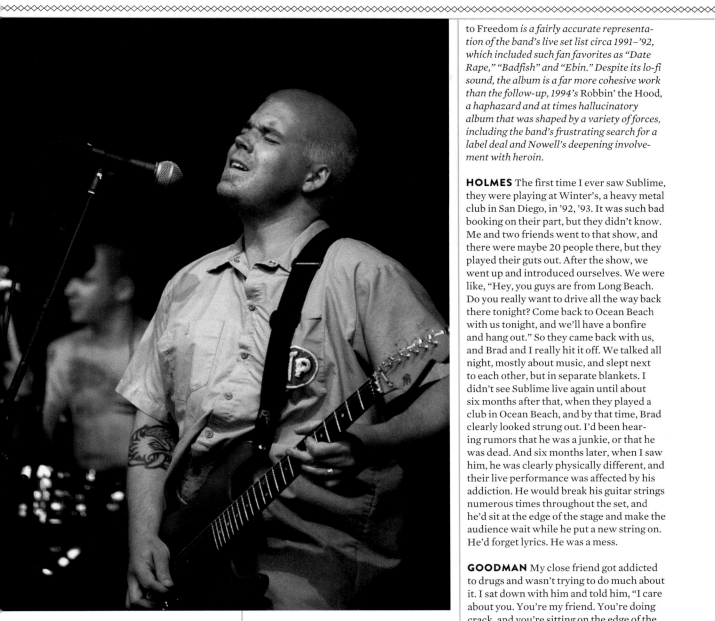

*Released in June 1992 on Happoldt and Nowell's Skunk Records imprint, and bearing Opie Ortiz' iconic "Sublime sun" cover art,* 40 Oz. to Freedom *is a fairly accurate representation of the band's live set list circa 1991–'92, which included such fan favorites as "Date Rape," "Badfish" and "Ebin." Despite its lo-fi sound, the album is a far more cohesive work than the follow-up, 1994's* Robbin' the Hood, *a haphazard and at times hallucinatory album that was shaped by a variety of forces, including the band's frustrating search for a label deal and Nowell's deepening involvement with heroin.*

**HOLMES** The first time I ever saw Sublime, they were playing at Winter's, a heavy metal club in San Diego, in '92, '93. It was such bad booking on their part, but they didn't know. Me and two friends went to that show, and there were maybe 20 people there, but they played their guts out. After the show, we went up and introduced ourselves. We were like, "Hey, you guys are from Long Beach. Do you really want to drive all the way back there tonight? Come back to Ocean Beach with us tonight, and we'll have a bonfire and hang out." So they came back with us, and Brad and I really hit it off. We talked all night, mostly about music, and slept next to each other, but in separate blankets. I didn't see Sublime live again until about six months after that, when they played a club in Ocean Beach, and by that time, Brad clearly looked strung out. I'd been hearing rumors that he was a junkie, or that he was dead. And six months later, when I saw him, he was clearly physically different, and their live performance was affected by his addiction. He would break his guitar strings numerous times throughout the set, and he'd sit at the edge of the stage and make the audience wait while he put a new string on. He'd forget lyrics. He was a mess.

**GOODMAN** My close friend got addicted to drugs and wasn't trying to do much about it. I sat down with him and told him, "I care about you. You're my friend. You're doing crack, and you're sitting on the edge of the stage, not even wearing your guitar, rapping Vanilla Ice and NWA lyrics when we're playing all these rhythms and great songs that people are coming to see us play." And he'd go, "Okay, okay, I see what you're saying"—and then the next show, NWA lyrics. That's when I finally quit.

**HOLMES** I'll never forget the first time Brad took me over to his mother's house. I was already forewarned that his mother was super-white, a fundamentalist Christian, and that everything that wasn't part of her church was "Satan." I was super-nervous, and at the time Brad was really strung out, super-skinny. His mom had no warning that we were coming over, but she pretended to be happy to see him and tried to hide her shock at his appearance. So she made herself busy, and he got on her piano and started playing "Mother" by Pink Floyd. And here I am, knowing that there's no fucking way she knows "Mother" by Pink Floyd, but I sure know why the fuck he's playing it. He was just belting it out, and she was just rambling around her house, trying to avoid being near him.

**JON PHILLIPS *(Sublime manager/A&R man)*** When I met them, between *40 Oz.* and *Robbin' the Hood*, there had been some industry interest. They had a small amount of demo money from Atlantic, which Brad used to record a lot of that album on a four-track with DJ Product [*of Hed PE*] in some abandoned house in Long Beach while he was all strung out. And then Brett Gurewitz from Epitaph had got word of the band, and they got studio time at Westbeach through him. The six band recordings, like "STP" and "All You Need," which have Bud and Eric playing with Brad, they did those tracks at Westbeach.

**GAUGH** I had just gotten back into the band, and Brad had a few songs written. We were talking with Mr. Brett [*Gurewitz*], and he was really interested in the project. A lot of our favorite bands were on that label, and it was punk rock like our attitude was, so we thought maybe it was a good fit. But once we finished recording the songs, Mr. Brett was busy negotiating a new deal for Bad Religion with Atlantic. He was in New York, and we were like, 'What's going on? Do you want this? Have you heard it?" And he was like, "Let me get back to you."

**PHILLIPS** Later, I got a chance to talk to Brett, and I asked him, "Why didn't you guys ever sign Sublime?" And he said, "Well, they had this chick in there that was singing with him, and we just didn't really get it." And that "chick" happened to be Gwen Stefani on [*the* Robbin' the Hood *track*] "Saw Red."

**GAUGH** We told Mr. Brett's engineer, "We don't have anything signed from you guys, so we're taking the tapes." We were flat broke, so we just decided to finish the album in various living rooms, just go low-budget, hoping that somebody would come around and say, "Hey, we really want this—let's go back into the studio and finish it!" But eventually we were like, "Hey, we've got all these recordings. Let's put 'em out, finished or not!"

**PHILLIPS** I think that album is a subversive masterpiece. Nobody ever accepted the demos, but it's sold over two million records now.

Robbin' the Hood, *which features the Sublime classics "Pool Shark," "Boss D.J." and "Greatest-Hits"—as well as a kaleidoscopic array of samples (including the Doors, Eazy-E, Steely Dan, Yellowman)—was released on Skunk Records in October 1994. Like its predecessor, it was hawked out of the band's van on endless tour jaunts up and down the California coast and sold by mail out of Happoldt's garage. Nowell, Wilson and Gaugh lived a hand-to-mouth existence while continuing their quest for a legitimate record deal.*

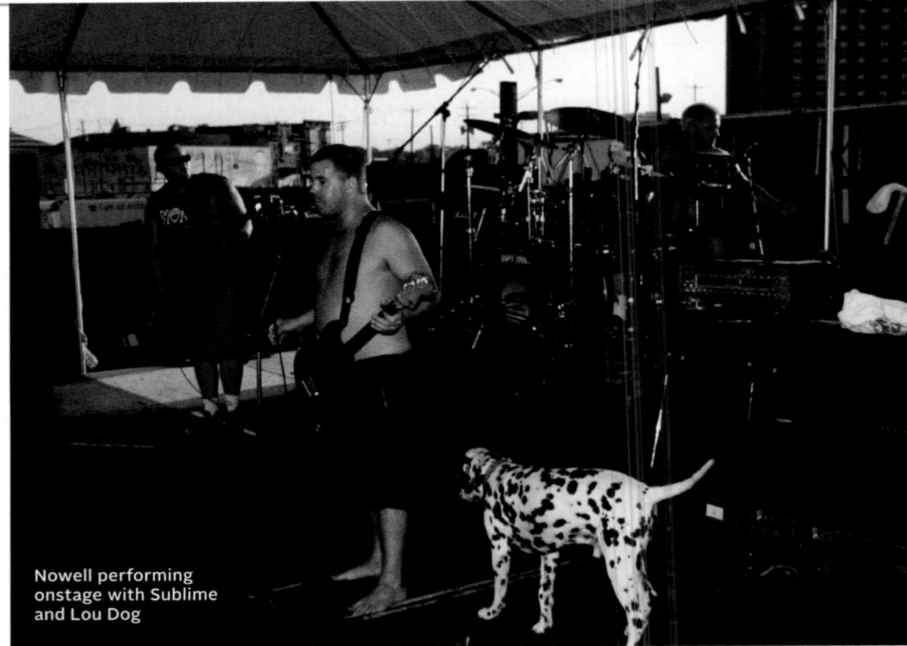
Nowell performing onstage with Sublime and Lou Dog

**PHILIPS** Nobody in the business at the time really knew anything about this band. They had this whole subculture unto itself that had formed down there in the Southern California beach cities. It was viral before the internet; there was this real energy and connection that was happening. And it didn't take long for me to realize that there was magic there.

**PHILLIPS** The first time they came in and met with [*record label*] Gasoline Alley, they stickered the car of the president of the label, Randy Phillips, who was also my uncle. They plastered a huge homemade Sublime sticker on the paint of his collector's BMW. The band left a little frustrated that they didn't sign a deal and walk away with a bunch of money in one day, and they put this sticker on Randy's car. It took a while to reconvince the label that this was a group to get into business with.

*Now onboard as their manager, Phillips unsuccessfully shopped the band to label after label before finally convincing Gasoline Alley—which was then part of a joint venture with MCA—to take a chance on his unruly charges. And then, in January 1995, something completely unexpected happened: KROQ, the influential L.A. radio station, started playing "Date Rape," a track released over two years earlier. The band's already sizeable SoCal following lit up the station's request lines, and the ensuing buzz helped the band land a coheadlining spot on the first-ever Warped Tour, and significantly boosted the sales of both* 40 Oz. *and* Robbin' the Hood. *Sessions for a third album, 1996's* Sublime, *began at Total Access studios in Redondo Beach with producer David Kahne at the helm. Nowell wanted Kahne because he'd produced the Fishbone records that the group loved. But things got off to a typically rocky start and would get even rockier when the band traveled to Pedernales Studios in Texas to finish the album with Paul Leary of the Butthole Surfers.*

**GOODMAN** I was working part-time at a Wells Fargo Bank, playing music part-time and going to school at Cal State Long Beach part-time; I had way too many hats on, but I was making it all work. Miguel came into the bank one day and said, "Man, you don't belong behind here—we've got a record deal going down, we've got a humongous budget, you've gotta come and write with us, man, you've gotta be involved with this." So I went over and hung out one night, and it was just easy, so I said, "Cool. Let's hunker down and let's do it. Let's make a mark!" Brad was all, "Let's get together and write," he was still messed up. So I flew out to Texas for the self-titled album sessions, and the rest is history, really.

**PHILLIPS** David gives me a call after the first day in the studio and says, "I think I should go home. I don't think the band is prepared. I don't know what's going on with these

STEVE EICHNER/WIREIMAGE/GETTY IMAGES

guys, but I don't want to waste your time and money." So I said to him, "Look, Sublime is like the kid who's gonna cram the night before the final and get at least an A minus the next day. You've gotta believe in the raw talent that's there. Let's keep the sessions intact and see what happens." So, he went back there the next day, and they ended up and having some amazing sessions at Total Access. I remember me and Brad listening to a reference cassette of the mixes and knowing that David took those songs to a whole new level. He turned them into a string of major radio hits, "What I Got" especially.

**GOODMAN** David did "What I Got," "Caress Me Down," "April 29, 1992 (Miami)" and "Doin' Time," and the rest were produced in Texas by Paul Leary. I'd done the loop for "What I Got" years back; in the *40 Oz. to Freedom* days, Brad and I recorded a bunch of drum loops with one microphone set up in this little room and a Tascam four-track cassette recorder. One of those loops made it to become the body of "What I Got," and then I came in behind it and played drums over the top of it. Everything was just kind of on the fly. They said, "We need a scratch break," so me and Miguel went through records, and he found the Barrington Levy "Lo-o-ove" bit, and I scratched it. It all just kind of fell into place; there wasn't much hold up. There was a little in Texas, because Brad was in and out. He was really fighting with his heroin usage at the time, and it was affecting his writing.

**PAUL LEARY (*Producer*)** It was a circus. The studio caught on fire one day, and the studio truck got wrecked the next day. Artifacts in the studio got damaged, and condos got wrecked. It was pretty hectic. They had a sauna downstairs, and somebody draped a towel over one of the light bulbs; we were in the control room, and we started smelling smoke. One day, one of the dogs got stuck in one of the studio rooms and chewed through the control room door. It was a new thing every day. At one point, they were thinking they were too drunk when they were working, so they asked if we could start earlier. I said, "We can start as early as you want." So we tried starting at 10 o'clock in the morning, and they would show up drunk, pitchers of margaritas in hand.

**HAPPOLDT** I remember when we were doing "Santeria," Leary brought out this beautiful Les Paul for Brad to use on the overdub. Brad was plunking away on it, and then he handed it to me like, "Yo, check it out." I started doing some Keith Richards–type three-string bends on it, because it looked like Keith Richards' Les Paul, and Brad got all mad. He was like, "What the fuck? Show *me* that shit!" So I showed it to him, and by the time they set up the amp and ran the track, Brad nailed that lead in, like, three takes.

> **"THEY WERE THE ONE BAND FROM OUR SCENE THAT I THOUGHT WERE THE MOST SPECIAL."**
> *—NO DOUBT'S TOM DUMONT*

**LEARY** I've still got that Les Paul. It's a 1981. It used to be a tobacco burst, but I had Mark Erlewine here in Austin paint it a pea-soup green. His main guitar was a custom-built guitar that [*Dan MacDonald*] made for him. He'd made a guitar for Brad and a bass for Eric. Those things didn't look very pretty, but they sounded great. The studio had a bunch of stuff, but they really liked their own amps. Brad had a Mesa/Boogie Dual Rectifier, a particularly sweet-sounding one. He had a clean "skank" setting and then an overdrive for the hard rock. He didn't need very many tricks.

**HOLMES** Every time Brad wrote a song, he'd be so fearful that the fans wouldn't like it. The self-titled album, that was the one he was most worried about, because he had only arranged and worked out those songs in the studio. He hadn't played them live yet.

**LEARY** Toward the end, when we were doing the overdubs and starting to mix in Arlyn Studios in Austin, I no longer felt like Brad was safe in the studio, so I sent him home. The band left, and all of a sudden the circus was gone, and I was left to piece the record together the best as I could. It was so devastating to have to send the band home before the record was finished. And I felt so bad for Brad. When I said goodbye to him, I had this feeling that I wouldn't see him again. I went to the airport to see him off, and he was wearing a short-sleeve shirt and had track marks all up and down his arm. I was telling Miguel, "You're not gonna get him on the airplane looking like that. You've gotta get him in long sleeves." And Miguel was like, "Well, Brad won't do it." When they got home, Miguel called me up, and I asked him what happened. He said they boarded the plane and the stewardess said, "What happened to your arms?" Miguel intervened and said, "He got stung by killer bees." And they let him on the airplane.

*While Nowell's worries about the acceptance of Sublime's third album would prove unfounded, Leary's fears for the Sublime singer's future would be borne out before the album even dropped. Just one week after his May 18, 1996, wedding to Troy, the mother of his 11-month old son Jakob, Nowell—who had gotten clean after leaving Texas—succumbed to heroin's fatal allure for the final time. Initially leery about even releasing* Sublime, *MCA put it out on July 30, then stood back and watched in wonder as the musical seeds that Nowell and his cohorts planted bloomed in Platinum. The reverberations of the harvest continue to be felt and heard to this day.*

**PHILLIPS** We wanted to put it out, and the family wanted to put it out. There was all this amazing music on it, and we knew "What I Got" was a hit. We had a sit-down meeting with the MCA people, and we said, "Look, you have to put this out." We sent "What I Got" out to radio, and in the first week we had, like, 50-plus adds at commercial alternative radio. And at that point, MCA's ears perked up—"We've got something!"

**DOUGHTY** What they did for music was like how Nirvana changed everything from hair metal. The Eighties was nothing but metal, and then Nirvana came in with grunge, and that kind of flipped the whole script. And then Sublime came along, and they flipped it again. It really revolutionized the sound, in the same way. You can never talk about this period of music without talking about Sublime, and it's still influencing new bands. If Brad hadn't passed, I really think they would have been the biggest band in the world.

**HAPPOLDT** We'd gone through such a rough period leading up to that album, and I felt that it was hard for Brad to find that real writing space. He was still kind of searching. Since nothing had really been successful yet, he didn't know where to stop. But if he had seen the feedback from the third record, he would have said, "Well, I'm there!" I don't think that much would have changed. He would have just kept writing better and better songs. It's heartbreaking to me, because I feel like the *Sublime* album put us where we needed to be. We were just right on track to make two or three records that were just as good, if not better.

**TOM DUMONT (No Doubt guitarist)** Great music just does stand the test of time. It gets passed from person to person and just keeps living. That's what Sublime were able to do: make something timeless. That's why we're still talking about it. I'm sad on so many levels that Brad isn't here anymore but so happy that at least Sublime's music lives on. ◆

# CLIFF BURTON

**BORN:** FEBRUARY 10, 1962, CASTRO VALLEY, CALIFORNIA
**DIED:** SEPTEMBER 27, 1986, LJUNGBY, SWEDEN

**LOCATION** Marshall Elementary School, 20111 Marshall Way, Castro Valley, California 94546; (510) 537-2331

**BASS** Guild electric bass, auctioned at Hard Rock Cafe, New York City, on November 9, 2004

**HIS SCRUFFY STONER** aesthetic notwithstanding, bassist Cliff Burton was a civilizing influence on his bandmates in Metallica, teaching them music theory and coaxing them to move from L.A. to the Bay area. Metallica were touring in Sweden when their driver lost control of the bus on an icy road. The vehicle plowed into a ditch and rolled over onto its side. Asleep in his bunk at the time of the accident, Burton was flung out a window and crushed to death when the bus landed on top of him. Back home, his body was cremated, with family and friends scattering his ashes into San Francisco Bay. Burton's grade school, Marshall Elementary School in Castro Valley, California, put up a memorial to him.

FIN COSTELLO/REDFERNS/GETTY IMAGES (BURTON); JAY BLACKESBERG (TOMBSTONE)

# WES MONTGOMERY

**BORN:** MARCH 6, 1923, INDIANAPOLIS, INDIANA
**DIED:** JUNE 15, 1968, INDIANAPOLIS, INDIANA

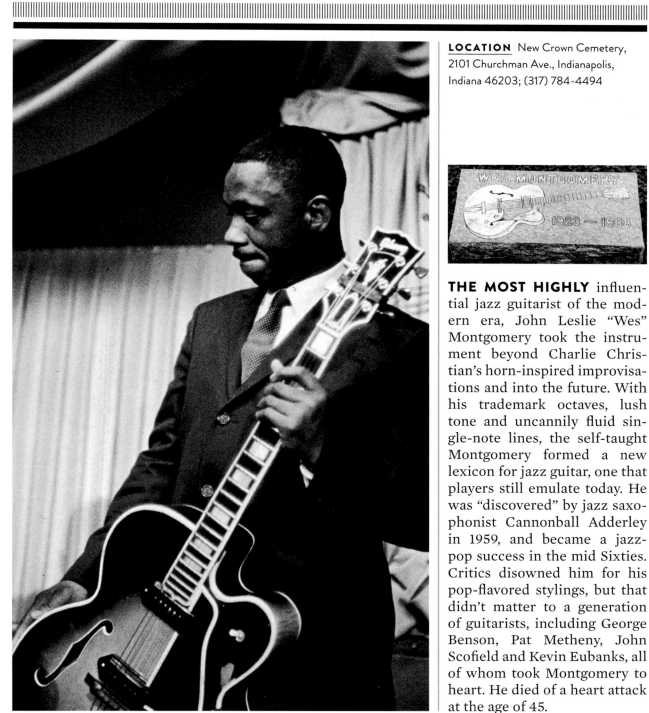

**LOCATION** New Crown Cemetery, 2101 Churchman Ave., Indianapolis, Indiana 46203; (317) 784-4494

**THE MOST HIGHLY** influential jazz guitarist of the modern era, John Leslie "Wes" Montgomery took the instrument beyond Charlie Christian's horn-inspired improvisations and into the future. With his trademark octaves, lush tone and uncannily fluid single-note lines, the self-taught Montgomery formed a new lexicon for jazz guitar, one that players still emulate today. He was "discovered" by jazz saxophonist Cannonball Adderley in 1959, and became a jazz-pop success in the mid Sixties. Critics disowned him for his pop-flavored stylings, but that didn't matter to a generation of guitarists, including George Benson, Pat Metheny, John Scofield and Kevin Eubanks, all of whom took Montgomery to heart. He died of a heart attack at the age of 45.

# DUANE ALLMAN

**BORN:** NOVEMBER 20, 1946, NASHVILLE, TENNESSEE
**DIED:** OCTOBER 29, 1971, MACON, GEORGIA

# BERRY OAKLEY

**BORN:** APRIL 4, 1948, CHICAGO, ILLINOIS
**DIED:** NOVEMBER 11, 1972, MACON, GEORGIA

MICHAEL OCHS ARCHIVES/GETTY IMAGES (ALLMAN, OAKLEY); DAVID REVERCHON (TOMBSTONE)

**AFTER DUANE ALLMAN** was killed in a motorcycle accident in his hometown of Macon, Georgia, his body lay in cold storage until family members could agree on burial arrangements. The occasion for his disposition came just over a year later, when Allman Brothers bandmate Berry Oakley missed a curve on his motorcycle, just blocks from where Duane was killed. The guitarist and bassist were buried side by side in Macon's old Rose Hill Cemetery, with matching tombstones. Their graves are near that of the woman celebrated in the Allman Brothers' "In Memory of Elizabeth Reed."

**LOCATION** Rose Hill Cemetery, Riverside Drive, Macon, Georgia 31201; (478) 751-9119
**GUITARS** Flametop Les Paul owned by his daughter Galadrielle Allman, on display at Rock and Roll Hall of Fame; Gibson SG used as primary slide guitar in his last year of life, owned by Graham Nash; Dobro used on "Little Martha," owned by former Allman Brother Dickey Betts
**BASS** "The Tractor," Oakley's main instrument, owned by Berry Oakley Jr., also a bassist

# DJANGO REINHARDT

**BORN:** JAN 23, 1910, LIBERCHIES, BELGIUM
**DIED:** MAY 16, 1953, FONTAINEBLEAU, FRANCE

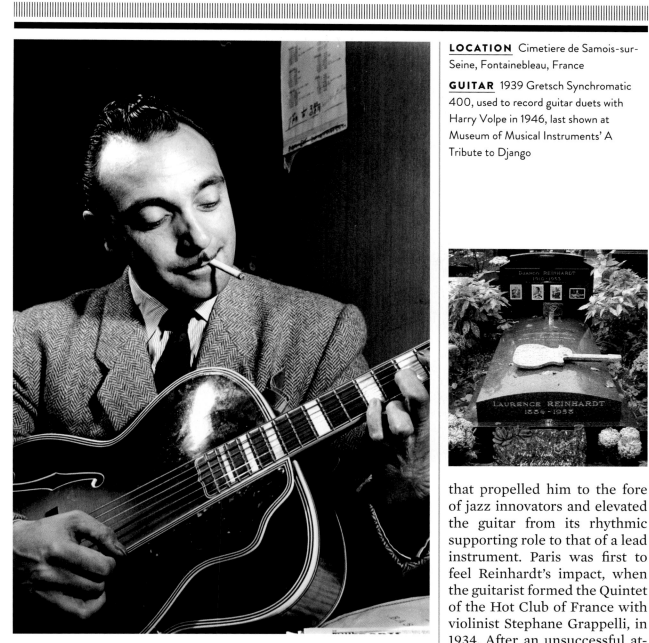

**LOCATION** Cimetiere de Samois-sur-Seine, Fontainebleau, France

**GUITAR** 1939 Gretsch Synchromatic 400, used to record guitar duets with Harry Volpe in 1946, last shown at Museum of Musical Instruments' A Tribute to Django

**AT THE AGE OF 18,** Gypsy guitarist Django Reinhardt lost the use of two fingers on his fretting hand when they were burned in a fire that broke out in his caravan. Forced to deal with his limitations, Reinhardt developed a dazzling, perfectly articulated soloing style that propelled him to the fore of jazz innovators and elevated the guitar from its rhythmic supporting role to that of a lead instrument. Paris was first to feel Reinhardt's impact, when the guitarist formed the Quintet of the Hot Club of France with violinist Stephane Grappelli, in 1934. After an unsuccessful attempt to play the newly emerging bebop, Reinhardt returned to swing. He died at age 43 following a stroke.

# JOHNNY THUNDERS

**BORN:** JULY 15, 1952, LEESBURG, FLORIDA
**DIED:** APRIL 23, 1991, NEW ORLEANS, LOUISIANA

**LOCATION** Section 9, Grave R78-82, Saint Mary's Cemetery, 17200 Booth Memorial Ave., Flushing, New York 11365; (718) 353-1560

**GUITAR** Les Paul Jr., Rock and Roll Hall of Fame

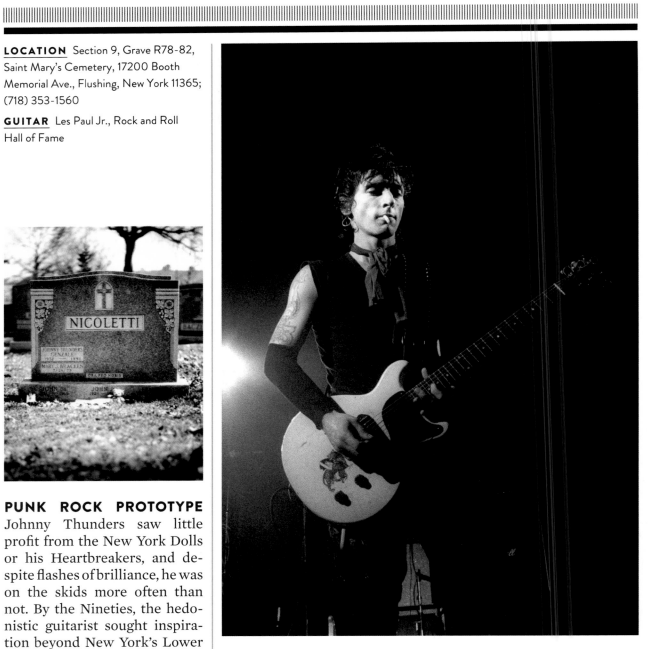

**PUNK ROCK PROTOTYPE** Johnny Thunders saw little profit from the New York Dolls or his Heartbreakers, and despite flashes of brilliance, he was on the skids more often than not. By the Nineties, the hedonistic guitarist sought inspiration beyond New York's Lower East Side, traveling down to New Orleans, where the ready availability of drugs ensured his downward slide continued unabated. Thunders died after a methadone/alcohol binge in a seedy hotel room off the French Quarter. John Anthony Genzale was buried in Mount St. Mary's Cemetery outside New York City, as is fellow Doll and Heartbreaker (and chronic drug abuser) Jerry Nolan.

ALASTAIR INDGE/PHOTOSHOT/GETTY IMAGES (THUNDERS); BRAD MILLER (TOMBSTONE)

# ALBERT KING

**BORN:** APRIL 25, 1923, INDIANOLA, MISSISSIPPI
**DIED:** DECEMBER 21, 1992, MEMPHIS, TENNESSEE

**LOCATION** Paradise Gardens, 212 N. 6th St., West Memphis, Arkansas 72301; (870) 735-2552

**GUITAR** 1958 Gibson V, owned by Danny Perkins of the Guitar Hall of Fame

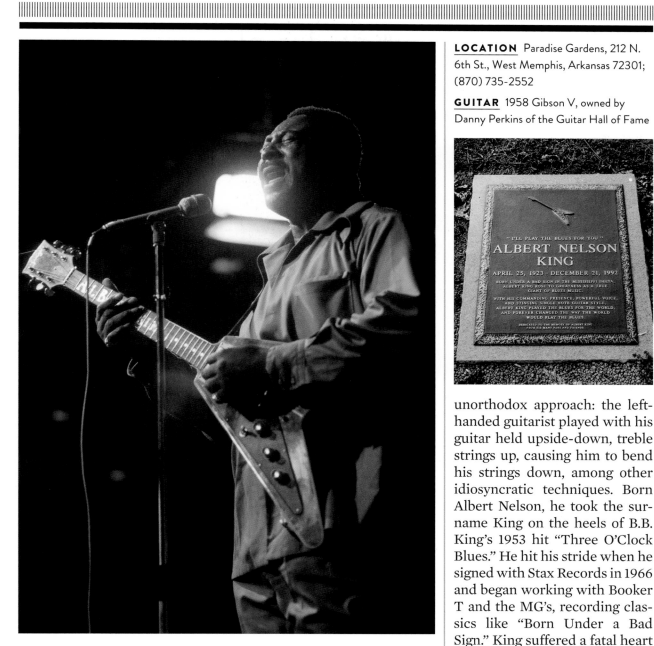

**MORE ROCK GUITARISTS** have copped from Albert than from any other bluesman. Standing six-foot-five, 250 pounds, the former bulldozer driver played his Gibson Flying V with frightening ferocity. King's lead playing was characterized by stinging, deep tone and an unorthodox approach: the left-handed guitarist played with his guitar held upside-down, treble strings up, causing him to bend his strings down, among other idiosyncratic techniques. Born Albert Nelson, he took the surname King on the heels of B.B. King's 1953 hit "Three O'Clock Blues." He hit his stride when he signed with Stax Records in 1966 and began working with Booker T and the MG's, recording classics like "Born Under a Bad Sign." King suffered a fatal heart attack in Memphis, Tennessee. His epitaph, the title of one of his finest albums, says it all: "I'll play the blues for you."

# STEVE GAINES

**BORN:** SEPTEMBER 14, 1949, MIAMI, OKLAHOMA
**DIED:** OCTOBER 20, 1977, GILLSBURG, MISSISSIPPI

**LOCATION** (markers only; remains at undisclosed locations) Jacksonville Memory Gardens, 111 Blanding Blvd., Orange Park, Florida 32073; (904) 272-2435

**GUITAR** Sunburst Fender Strat, Rock and Roll Hall of Fame

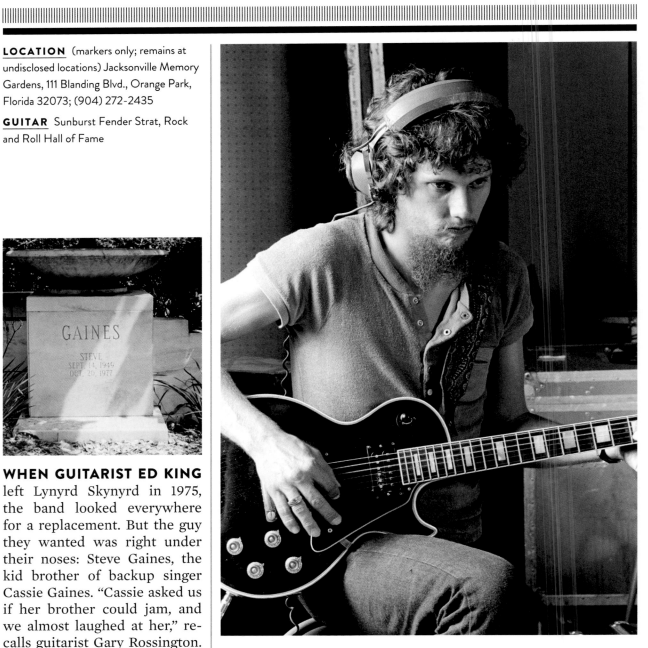

**WHEN GUITARIST ED KING** left Lynyrd Skynyrd in 1975, the band looked everywhere for a replacement. But the guy they wanted was right under their noses: Steve Gaines, the kid brother of backup singer Cassie Gaines. "Cassie asked us if her brother could jam, and we almost laughed at her," recalls guitarist Gary Rossington. As it happened, Gaines was an incendiary guitarist, and his playing put life back into the band, resulting in 1977's *Street Survivors*, Skynyrd's creative pinnacle. Just days after its release, their chartered plane ran out of gas and crashed into a Mississippi swamp. Steve and Cassie were killed, along with the group's singer and chief songwriter, Ronnie Van Zant.

TOM HILL/WIREIMAGE (GAINES); SCOTT STANTON (TOMBSTONE)

# SYD BARRETT

**BORN:** JANUARY 6, 1946, CAMBRIDGE, ENGLAND
**DIED:** JULY 7, 2006, CAMBRIDGE, ENGLAND

**THE LAST TIME** Syd Barrett was in a recording studio with Pink Floyd was in 1975. He showed up unannounced and watched as the band cut "Shine On You Crazy Diamond"—ironically, a song about him. When the group finally noticed the overweight man with the shaved head and eyebrows in the back of the studio, they were in shock. The sight of their once charismatic and photogenic leader was overwhelming. Bassist Roger Waters was, reportedly, in tears.

Syd was born Roger Keith Barrett on January 6, 1946, in Cambridge, England (he nicknamed himself "Syd" in honor of a local drummer, Sid Barrett). While still a teenager, he moved to London and, in 1965, formed a band with Waters, keyboardist Rick Wright and drummer Nick Mason. A naturally gifted musician, Barrett derived elements of his guitar playing from the bluesmen Pink Anderson and Floyd Council. Barrett combined the names and called his group Pink Floyd.

A free spirit and inveterate devotee of LSD, Barrett pushed Floyd to experiment musically as well as chemically. The 1967 single "See Emily Play" showcased Barrett's love of childlike lyrics and melodies along with his penchant for hallucinogens. Pink Floyd's first album, 1967's *The Piper at the Gates of Dawn*, was Barrett's unqualified triumph, but by the end of that year, while the group were recording their follow-up, *A Saucerful of Secrets*, Barrett's stewardship—expedited by signs suggestive of mental illness, and exasperated by drugs—had eroded. At times catatonic, he proved too unreliable to tour, and a friend, guitarist David Gilmour, took Barrett's place onstage. Eventually, Gilmour became a permanent member and Barrett went into semi-seclusion.

Barrett released two well-received solo albums, *The Madcap Laughs* and *Barrett*, in 1970, then disappeared from public view altogether. He lived out the rest of his days with his mother in Cambridge, where it is said he passed the time gardening and painting. The enigmatic guitarist, one of London's original "beautiful people" and an influence on millions, died there on July 7, 2006, at age 60, due to "complications arising from diabetes."

# JOHNNY RAMONE

**BORN:** OCTOBER 8, 1948, LONG ISLAND, NEW YORK
**DIED:** SEPTEMBER 15, 2004, LOS ANGELES, CALIFORNIA

**LOCATION** Hollywood Forever Cemetery, 6000 Santa Monica Blvd., Hollywood, California 90038

**GUITAR** Mosrite Ventures II

**AS THE RAMONES'** guitarist, the man born John Cummings created the template for punk rock guitar. The brutal precision of his muted, downpicked barre chords and ringing power chords energized Ramones classics like "Blitzkrieg Bop," "Rockaway Beach" and "Sheena Is a Punk Rocker," inspiring several generations of latter day punk bands. Drug free and politically conservative, Johnny was the drill sergeant who kept the Ramones on the road and in the studio for two explosive decades. And it was John who pulled the plug on the Ramones in 1996, putting into action his long-cherished scheme of retiring while he was still young enough to enjoy his well-deserved rest. He spent a few years of leisure at home in the Hollywood hills with his wife Linda and a circle of rock star friends before prostate cancer claimed his life at the age of 55. The memorial statue at his gravesite captures the image that Johnny Ramone emblazoned on rock history for all time: leather motorcycle jacket, pudding bowl haircut, Mosrite guitar cocked and loaded.

EBET ROBERTS/REDFERNS/GETTY IMAGES (RAMONE); SCOTT MICHAELS (TOMBSTONE)

# T-BONE WALKER

**BORN:** MAY 28, 1910, LINDEN, TEXAS
**DIED:** MARCH 16, 1975, LOS ANGELES, CALIFORNIA

**LOCATION** Inglewood Park Cemetery, 720 E. Florence Ave., Inglewood, CA 90301; (310) 412-6500

**GUITAR** Gibson ES-series electric, Rock and Roll Hall of Fame

**MUSIC'S FIRST TRUE** lead guitarist, T-Bone Walker was both an electric guitar pioneer and a style setter for blues and rock guitarists. As a player, Walker was a master of the smooth, urbane electric guitar style exemplified on his trademark tune, "Call It Stormy Monday." As a performer, he set the standard for flamboyance, holding his fat-bodied Gibson almost perpendicular to his body, playing behind his back and doing splits. Born Aaron Thibeaux Walker, he was a student of acoustic blues guitarist Blind Lemon Jefferson but switched to electric guitar by the Thirties, tearing up clubs in his adopted hometown of Los Angeles. A late-Sixties comeback led to his 1970 Grammy Award, but after years of drinking and health problems, Walker died following a stroke in 1974.

# STEVE CLARK

**BORN:** APRIL 23, 1960, SHEFFIELD, ENGLAND
**DIED:** JANUARY 8, 1991, LONDON, ENGLAND

**LOCATION** Wisewood Cemetery, Hillsborough, England

**GUITARS** With Clark's family in Sheffield, England

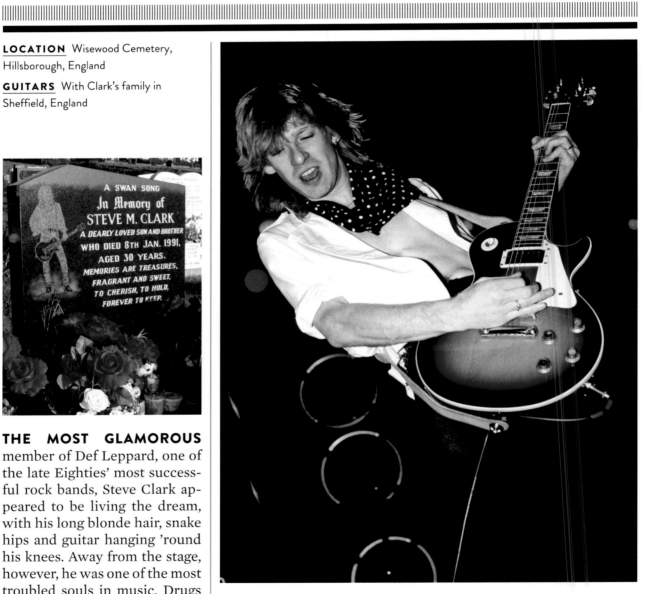

**THE MOST GLAMOROUS** member of Def Leppard, one of the late Eighties' most successful rock bands, Steve Clark appeared to be living the dream, with his long blonde hair, snake hips and guitar hanging 'round his knees. Away from the stage, however, he was one of the most troubled souls in music. Drugs and alcohol were the symptom, not the cause. The real issue was one of self-esteem, of which he appeared to have none. And yet, it was Clark who first forced Leppard out of the garage and onto a stage. The one the fans called Steamin' Steve Clark came up with the killer riffs to early Leppard crowd pleasers like "Another Hit and Run," "Rock! Rock! Till You Drop" and "Photograph." He died in his sleep from a fatal combo of alcohol and prescription painkillers. As Leppard singer Joe Elliot later observed, "He was our Steve, but there was fuck all we could do to help him, short of tying his hands behind his back. He was a lost cause, no matter what anyone tried to do."

EBET ROBERTS/REDFERNS/GETTY IMAGES (CLARK); TONY WOOLLISCROFT (TOMBSTONE)

# TOMMY BOLIN

**BORN:** AUGUST 1, 1951, SIOUX CITY, IOWA
**DIED:** DECEMBER 4, 1976, MIAMI, FLORIDA

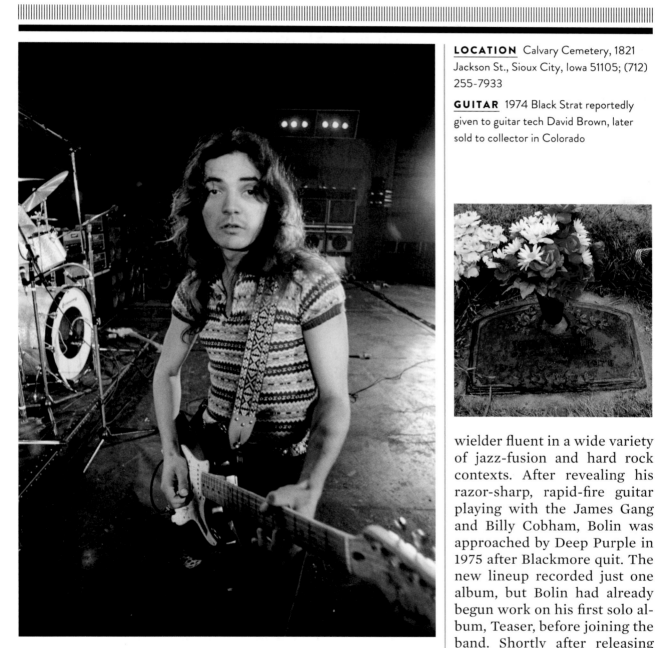

**LOCATION** Calvary Cemetery, 1821 Jackson St., Sioux City, Iowa 51105; (712) 255-7933

**GUITAR** 1974 Black Strat reportedly given to guitar tech David Brown, later sold to collector in Colorado

**TOMMY BOLIN MAY** be best remembered as the guitarist who replaced Ritchie Blackmore in Deep Purple during the Seventies, but to many he was nothing less than America's answer to Jeff Beck, John McLaughlin, Jimmy Page and Blackmore—a Strat wielder fluent in a wide variety of jazz-fusion and hard rock contexts. After revealing his razor-sharp, rapid-fire guitar playing with the James Gang and Billy Cobham, Bolin was approached by Deep Purple in 1975 after Blackmore quit. The new lineup recorded just one album, but Bolin had already begun work on his first solo album, Teaser, before joining the band. Shortly after releasing his second album, *Private Eyes*, Bolin overdosed from a drug binge the day after he opened for Jeff Beck in Miami.

# JOE STRUMMER

**BORN:** AUGUST 21, 1952, ANKARA, TURKEY
**DIED:** DECEMBER 22, 2002, BROOMFIELD, SOMERSET, ENGLAND

LARRY HULST/MICHAEL OCHS ARCHIVES/GETTY IMAGES

**JOE STRUMMER,** the gravel-voiced frontman of punk rock pioneers the Clash, died of sudden cardiac arrest on Sunday, December 22, 2002. The 50-year-old singer and guitarist collapsed in his Somerset, England, farmhouse after returning from walking the family dog. He is survived by his wife, Lucinda, two daughters and one stepdaughter.

Born John Graham Mellor in 1952 in Ankara, Turkey, to a British diplomat, Strummer attended school in London but spent his holidays traveling to whatever exotic locales his father's work took the family. Presumably, this globetrotting helped him develop the broad worldview that informed much of his music with the Clash.

As a teen, Strummer began playing music on London street corners and later served as singer for the pub-rock act the 101ers. In 1975, inspired by the sound and fury of the Sex Pistols, he joined forces with lead guitarist/vocalist Mick Jones and bassist Paul Simonon to form the Clash.

While the Sex Pistols established punk's parameters with politicized lyrics and raw fury, the Clash gave the genre dimension with their great melodies and sense of dynamics. Their 1979 double album *London Calling*, which combined punk, reggae and rock and roll with R&B and rockabilly, proved the group was a creative force for the ages. Moreover, it established Strummer as a classic frontman, one whose inimitable voice could start a riot or break a heart with just one note.

After disbanding the Clash in 1986, Strummer laid low for the better part of a decade, but he resumed his music career in 1999 with his new band, the Mescaleros. At the time of his death, Strummer was working on a third album with the Mescaleros and was reportedly planning to reunite with the original members of the Clash—something he had resisted for years—in March 2002 for the group's induction into the Rock and Roll Hall of Fame.

# SHAWN LANE

**BORN:** MARCH 21, 1963, MEMPHIS, TENNESSEE
**DIED:** SEPTEMBER 26, 2003, MEMPHIS, TENNESSEE

**LOCATION** Memorial Park Funeral Home and Cemetery, 5668 Poplar Ave., Memphis, Tennessee 38119; (901) 767-8930

**GUITAR** Vigier Excalibur Supra, location unknown

**LEGEND HAS IT** Billy Gibbons fell off his barstool when he heard Shawn Lane's warp-speed, high-precision guitar work. But Lane was far from a flash guitarist. His diverse range of styles was the product of his fascination with everything from classical composers and painters to electronic and pop artists. Lane showed promise as a guitarist well before he reached his teens. At the age of 15, he was hired by country rockers Black Oak Arkansas. But Lane's most enduring legacies are the eight largely improvised albums he cut from 1995 forward, records that highlight his world music fusion fluency in everything from blues to Indian ragas. Recurring health problems sidelined Lane in the last years of his life. He died from complications associated with lung disease.

# NOEL REDDING

**BORN:** DECEMBER 25, 1945, FOLKESTONE, KENT, ENGLAND
**DIED:** MAY 11, 2003, CLONAKILTY, COUNTY CORK, IRELAND

K & K ULF KRUGER OHG/REDFERNS/GETTY IMAGES

**IT'S HARD TO THINK** of Noel Redding—bassist for the Jimi Hendrix Experience, who passed away May 11, 2003, at 57—without remembering the story of how he and Hendrix were ejected from a pub in rural England because the barman was convinced they were with the circus. "He said they wouldn't serve clowns," Redding said in one of his last interviews. "We tried to convince him that we were musicians, but because of the way we were dressed, and our hair, he wouldn't believe us."

Redding may have been a social outcast, but his place in rock and roll history was assured in September 1966, when he auditioned in London with a then-unknown Seattle-born guitarist. "I was a guitar player," Redding recalled, "but Jimi asked if I could play bass, so I picked one up and played."

Although Redding was usually humble about his technical skills—Hendrix was, after all, a deft studio bassist—his distinctive but clean style became a cornerstone of the Experience's sound, both on record and in concert. He left the Experience in 1969 and went on to play with Fat Mattress, Road and 3:05 A.M.

"Neither he nor the rest of the Experience ever got the credit they deserved," the Who's Roger Daltry said of Redding. "He was a truly great bass player." Paul McCartney, Tom Petty and numerous other musicians made similar statements upon hearing of Redding's death. His funeral in Clonakilty, Ireland, drew more than 1,000 mourners, including folk-rock singer Donovan, who sang his mid-Sixties song "Catch the Wind."

Guitarist Keith Dion toured with Redding extensively in the Nineties and remembers him as someone "who was very proud of his past. He wasn't one of those guys who said, 'I'm not going to play that or talk about that.' He was proud that he was in one of the biggest bands of all time."

## CLARENCE "GATEMOUTH" BROWN

**BORN:** APRIL 18, 1924
**DIED:** SEPTEMBER 20, 2005

## LITTLE MILTON

**BORN:** SEPTEMBER 7, 1934
**DIED:** AUGUST 4, 2005

## R.L. BURNSIDE

**BORN:** NOVEMBER 23, 1926
**DIED:** SEPTEMBER 1, 2005

GILLES PETARD/REDFERNS/GETTY IMAGES (GATEMOUTH AND MILTON); JON SIEVERT/MICHAEL OCHS ARCHIVES/GETTY IMAGES

**THE BLUES WORLD LOST** three of its leading old-school figures when Clarence "Gatemouth" Brown, Little Milton and R.L. Burnside died in August and September 2005. Though vastly different from one another, the three bluesmen were linked by their lifetime of dedication to guitar.

Brown, who played fiddle as well as guitar, hated being called a blues player, and indeed, he played swing, jazz, Cajun and country as well. "Folks call me a bluesman because I'm black and...play guitar," Brown once said. "But my music is American music—Texas style." He had a 1954 hit with the hard-charging, fleet-fingered instrumental "Okie Dokie Stomp," which helped launch a 50-plus-year career. Brown was diagnosed with lung cancer, heart disease and emphysema last year, but he refused treatment and continued to perform. He died in Orange, Texas, two weeks after evacuating his home in Slidell, Louisiana, to escape the path of Hurricane Katrina. He was 81.

A pioneer in mixing R&B and blues, James "Little Milton" Campbell Jr. was a strong-voiced singer and a pungent guitarist in the B.B. King mold. He had several Sixties hits for Chess Records and recorded the latter-day staple "The Blues Is Alright" in '84. He was a five-decade staple of blues clubs and festivals and occasionally appeared with the Allman Brothers Band. "Little Milton" died following a massive stroke. He was 70 years old.

Burnside's droning, hard-edged songs were the very definition of "Mississippi hill country blues." For decades he was a noted juke joint performer near his home in Holly Springs, Mississippi, and made his living primarily as a farmer. Burnside gained popularity after he was featured in the 1991 documentary *Deep Blues* and began recording for Fat Possum Records. His numerous albums earned him an alt-rock audience and made him one of the blues' most popular performers in his final years. Burnside's health had been declining following a heart operation in 1999. He died in Memphis, Tennessee, while in the hospital. He was 76.

# CHET ATKINS

**BORN:** JUNE 20, 1924, LUTTRELL, TENNESSEE
**DIED:** JUNE 30, 2001, NASHVILLE, TENNESSEE

MICHAEL OCHS ARCHIVES/GETTY IMAGES

**CHET ATKINS—KNOWN** variously as Mr. Guitar, the Country Gentleman and Certified Guitar Player—died on June 30, 2001, after a long battle with cancer. He was 77. During his career, Atkins revolutionized guitar technique in particular and country music in general. The genre BC—Before Chet—was still close to its rural origins, rough-edged music that was gradually being left behind on the farm as young people moved to the city and suburb. Country AC—After Chet—was "countrypolitan," a smooth and sophisticated blend of traditional country and pop that opened up a huge, new audience for whom rock was too loud and R&B too black.

Atkins the guitarist made it all look easy, his virtuoso technique as smooth and comfortable as a well-oiled saddle. Confined to his room by childhood asthma, young Chet invested untold hours of sweat and strain into shaping the down-home, thumb-and-finger guitar technique of his Tennessee boyhood, until he could play like a multi-fingered orchestra. Graduating to the studio, he backed Elvis Presley, Hank Williams and the Everly Brothers, while ultimately turning out 75 records of his own, for which he was occasionally joined by such stellar—and starstruck—company as George Benson, Mark Knopfler and George Harrison. As VP of RCA Nashville, Chet demonstrated an unerring ear for talent, signing such country superstars as Jerry Reed, Waylon Jennings and Charlie Pride. As a producer, he was essentially responsible for creating the "Nashville Sound," an amalgam of lushly arranged strings, horns and backup singers that directly presaged the profoundly pop country of Garth Brooks and Shania Twain.

Despite the acclaim of his fans and peers, including 14 Grammy Awards, membership in the Country Music Hall of Fame and guitar awards beyond number, Atkins was eternally self-effacing. "I'm constantly fighting mediocrity with all my energy, afraid that it might catch up with me," he remarked.

# BRIAN JONES

**BORN:** FEBRUARY 28, 1942, CHELTENHAM, GLOUCESTERSHIRE, ENGLAND
**DIED:** JULY 3, 1969, HARTFIELD, SUSSEX, ENGLAND

**LOCATION** Priory Road Cemetery, Prestbury, Gloucestershire, England

**GUITAR** Vox "Teardrop," Hard Rock Cafe London Vault

**THE ODD MAN OUT** in the Rolling Stones' rock and roll circus, Lewis Brian Hopkins-Jones met a famously mysterious end not long after being dismissed from the band (for excessive substance abuse, ironically enough). Jones' drowning was labeled "death by misadventure," but the circumstances remain murky more than three decades later. One commonly held theory has him being held underwater—by the hands of resentful construction workers—during an impromptu party at his Cotchfield Farm estate. The Stones played Hyde Park a few days after his death, releasing thousands of butterflies as a memorial gesture.

# LINK WRAY

**BORN:** MAY 2, 1929, DUNN, NORTH CAROLINA
**DIED:** NOVEMBER 5, 2005, COPENHAGEN, DENMARK

**FREDERICK LINCOLN WRAY JR.,** a key architect of rock and roll's primal, distorted, power chord aesthetic, first came to prominence via the 1958 instrumental "Rumble," a smoldering gangbang bolero that became his signature tune. Legend has it that Wray jabbed holes in his speaker with a pencil to achieve the raunchy guitar tone heard on this. Whatever the case, the tune's lewdly suggestive melody got the record banned by some radio stations. The song was nonetheless a huge influence on a rising generation of rockers, including the Who's Pete Townshend, who eagerly embraced Wray's slashing power chords, paving the way for both heavy metal and punk.

Wray cut numerous sides throughout the Sixties, most of them family affairs on which he was backed by his brothers Vernon and Doug plus bassist Shorty Horton (collectively known as Link Wray and His Ray Men). Too dark and dangerous ever to achieve mainstream success, Wray nonetheless became an underground legend by the Seventies. Director John Waters chose Wray's "The Swag" as the signature song for his deviant debut film tour de force, 1972's *Pink Flamingos*.

In 1977, he teamed up with Robert Gordon, former vocalist for the New York punk group Tuff Darts, and their album, *Robert Gordon with Link Wray*, endeared Wray to the first generation of punk rockers. The Cramps took a major cue from Wray on their 1978 debut, *Gravest Hits*, thus making Link a major icon of the neorockabilly and psychobilly movements. Wray's flaming guitar raveups have become a universal signifier of untamed outsider defiance, and have graced influential films, including *Pulp Fiction*. In 2002 *Guitar World* named Wray one of the 100 Greatest Guitarists of All Time.

MICHAEL OCHS ARCHIVES/GETTY IMAGES (WRAY); SADDHIYAMA (TOMBSTONE)

# MUDDY WATERS

**BORN:** APRIL 4, 1915, ROLLING FORK, MISSISSIPPI
**DIED:** APRIL 30, 1983, WESTMONT, ILLINOIS

**LOCATION** Restvale Cemetery, 11700 S. Laramie Ave., Alsip, Illinois 60803; (312) 236-4077

**GUITAR** 1958 Red Fender Telecaster, the Collection of the Estate of McKinley Morganfield

**MCKINLEY MORGANFIELD GREW UP** on Stovall's Plantation in Clarksdale, Mississippi, yet he would rise far from his cotton-picking roots. Nicknamed Muddy Waters as a little boy, he came to his first recording session in 1941 without shoes, sitting down to play country blues for musicologist Alan Lomax; years later, Muddy would fill South Side Chicago jukeboxes with his electric Chess sides. He fell on hard times when rock and roll swept the boards, but a generation of British rockers recognized his sound as the very essence of their music and helped revitalize his career. The Grim Reaper stole Muddy's mojo while the guitarist was at home recuperating from a busy schedule of touring and making records. As his gravestone says, "The Master has won..."

# PHIL LYNOTT

**BORN:** AUGUST 20, 1949, WEST BROMWICH, STAFFORDSHIRE, ENGLAND
**DIED:** JANUARY 4, 1986, SALISBURY, WILTSHIRE, ENGLAND

**PHIL LYNOTT WAS** 21 years old and had only just learned to play bass when he formed Thin Lizzy in 1970. Yet, the Dublin, Ireland–based band recorded its self-titled debut album within a year. Over the next five years, Thin Lizzy would record six more albums, an ambitious undertaking that brought the band moderate success in Ireland and England. The effort helped Lynott hone his songwriting, however, and in 1976 the band released *Jailbreak*, the album that brought them fame in the U.K. as well as America. Chief among *Jailbreak*'s songs was the breakthrough hit, "The Boys Are Back in Town," a hard-rocking ode to blue-collar buds.

Thin Lizzy furthered their reputation with strong live performances and a host of hot guitarists—among them Gary Moore, Snowy White and John Sykes—who teamed up with Scott Gorham to engage in melodic dual leads. But as hot as their playing was, Lynott remained the band's heart and soul.

The son of a working-class Irish mother and a black South American father, Lynott wrote songs about blue-collar heroes, describing their tales and feats over music that packed a hard-hitting yet melodic crunch. Lynott was also an early and loud supporter of punk rock, and in 1978 he formed a side group, the Greedy Bastards, with Rat Scabies of the Damned.

IAN DICKSON/REDFERNS/GETTY IMAGES

Plagued by infighting and Lynott's worsening drug problems, Thin Lizzy disbanded in 1983. Lynott released several solo records and published a book of poetry while continuing to struggle with his demons. Following a drug overdose, he was found unconscious in his London house and died of heart failure and pneumonia on January 4, 1986. Lynott is buried in Saint Fintan's Cemetery, in Dublin. The Gaelic inscription on his stone reads: "May God give peace to his soul."

# RITCHIE VALENS

**BORN:** MAY 13, 1941, PACOIMA, CALIFORNIA
**DIED:** FEBRUARY 3, 1959, GRANT TOWNSHIP, CERRO GORDO COUNTY, IOWA

**LOS ANGELES TEENAGER** Richard Valenzuela built his first electric guitar by himself and learned how to play it. He combined rock and roll with his own Mexican-American musical heritage to create the 1958 hits "La Bamba," "Come On Let's Go" and "Donna." Rock and roll was a brand-new form of music back then, and Valenzuela was the first artist to put a Latin spin on this exciting new sound. The world knew him—all too briefly—as Ritchie Valens.

On the evening of February 2, 1959, Valens played a gig in Clear Lake, Iowa, with rock legend Buddy Holly. After the show, he climbed onboard a small airplane that Holly had chartered. Holly's guitarist Tommy Alsup had given up his seat on the plane to Valens, who wasn't feeling too well and wasn't up to a long ride to the next venue on an unheated bus. The third passenger seat on the tiny plane was supposed to go to Holly's bass player (future country great Waylon Jennings, ironically enough). But Jennings got on the bus instead, surrendering his place in the airplane to another artist on the bill that night, the Big Bopper, who'd scored a major hit with "Chantilly Lace."

Just minutes after taking off, the plane crashed in a frozen cornfield, killing all onboard. Valens was just 17. Although his career was brief, he had a long-lasting impact on rock. In 1987, Valens became the subject of director Taylor Hackford's popular bio-pic *La Bamba*. Los Lobos' soundtrack recording of "La Bamba" became a substantial hit.

Valens is buried at the San Fernando Mission Cemetery in Mission Hills, California.

## EDITORIAL
**EDITOR-IN-CHIEF**
Brad Tolinski

**MANAGING EDITOR**
Jeff Kitts

**EXECUTIVE EDITOR**
Christopher Scapelliti

**SENIOR EDITOR**
Brad Angle

## ART
**DESIGN DIRECTOR**
Alexis Cook

**ART DIRECTOR**
Patrick Crowley

**PHOTOGRAPHY DIRECTOR**
Jimmy Hubbard

## PRODUCTION
**PRODUCTION COORDINATOR**
Nicole Schilling

## CONSUMER MARKETING
**CONSUMER MARKETING DIRECTOR**
Crystal Hudson

**CIRCULATION BUSINESS MANAGER**
Chris Dyson

**FULFILLMENT COORDINATOR**
Ulises Cabrera

**MARKETING COORDINATOR**
Dominique Rennell

## NEWBAY MEDIA CORPORATE
**PRESIDENT & CEO** Steve Palm
**CHIEF FINANCIAL OFFICER** Paul Mastronardi
**CONTROLLER** Jack Liedke
**VICE PRESIDENT OF PRODUCTION & MANUFACTURING** Bill Amstutz
**VICE PRESIDENT OF DIGITAL MEDIA** Joe Ferrick
**VICE PRESIDENT OF AUDIENCE DEVELOPMENT** Denise Robbins
**VICE PRESIDENT OF CONTENT & MARKETING** Anthony Savona
**VICE PRESIDENT OF INFORMATION TECHNOLOGY** Anthony Verbanac
**VICE PRESIDENT OF HUMAN RESOURCES** Ray Vollmer

## TIME HOME ENTERTAINMENT
**PUBLISHER**
Jim Childs

**VICE PRESIDENT, BRAND & DIGITAL STRATEGY**
Steven Sandonato

**EXECUTIVE DIRECTOR, MARKETING SERVICES**
Carol Pittard

**EXECUTIVE DIRECTOR, RETAIL & SPECIAL SALES**
Tom Mifsud

**EXECUTIVE PUBLISHING DIRECTOR**
Joy Butts

**EDITORIAL DIRECTOR**
Stephen Koepp

**DIRECTOR, BOOKAZINE DEVELOPMENT & MARKETING**
Laura Adam

**FINANCE DIRECTOR**
Glenn Buonocore

**ASSOCIATE PUBLISHING DIRECTOR**
Megan Pearlman

**ASSISTANT GENERAL COUNSEL**
Helen Wan

**ASSISTANT DIRECTOR, SPECIAL SALES**
Ilene Schreider

**SENIOR BOOK PRODUCTION MANAGER**
Susan Chodakiewicz

**DESIGN & PREPRESS MANAGER**
Anne-Michelle Gallero

**BRAND MANAGER**
Katie McHugh

**ASSOCIATE PREPRESS MANAGER**
Alex Voznesenskiy

## SPECIAL THANKS
Katherine Barnet, Jeremy Biloon, Rose Cirrincione, Jacqueline Fitzgerald, Christine Font, Jenna Goldberg, Hillary Hirsch, David Kahn, Mona Li, Amy Mangus, Kimberly Marshall, Amy Migliaccio, Nina Mistry, Dave Rozzelle, Ricardo Santiago, Adriana Tierno, Vanessa Wu

**SUBSCRIBER CUSTOMER SERVICE:** Guitar World Magazine Customer Care, P.O. Box 6305, Harlan, IA 51593-1805
**ONLINE:** www.guitarworld.com/customerservice **PHONE:** 1-800-456-6441 **EMAIL:** GWOcustserv@cdsfulfillment.com

**BACK ISSUES:** Please visit our store: www.guitarworld.com/store

**REPRINTS:** NewBay Media, LLC, 28 East 28th Street,
12 Floor, New York, NY 10016. Attn: Linda Waldman. **PHONE:** (212) 378-0414

**EDITORIAL AND ADVERTISING OFFICES**
149 5th Ave., 9th Floor, New York, NY 10010 (212) 768-2966; FAX: (212) 944-9279

**NEWBAY MEDIA, LLC**
28 East 28th Street, 12th Floor, New York, NY 10016 www.nbmedia.com

**COVER PHOTOS:**
**John Lennon:** K & K Ulf Kruger OHG/Redferns/Getty Images; **Jimi Hendrix:** Marc Sharratt/Rex USA; **Kurt Cobain:** Charles Hoselton/Retna Ltd.
**Randy Rhoads:** John Livzey/AtlasIcons.com; **Dimebag Darrell:** James Cumpsty/Redferns/Getty Images
**Stevie Ray Vaughan:** Robert Knight Archive/Redferns/Getty Images

**BACK COVER:**
**Bob Marley:** Gijsbert Hanekroot/Redferns/Getty Images; **Jerry Garcia:** Michael Ochs Archives/Getty Images;
**George Harrison:** K & K Ulf Kruger OHG/Redferns/Getty Images; **Frank Zappa:** Chris Walter/Getty Images